ISLAM AND SOCIAL WORK
Culturally sensitive p
in a diverse worl

2nd edition

Sara Ashencaen Crabtree, Fatima Husain and Basia Spalek

First published in Great Britain in 2017 by

Policy Press
University of Bristol
1-9 Old Park Hill
Bristol BS2 8BB
UK
t: +44 (0)117 954 5940
e: pp-info@bristol.ac.uk
www.policypress.co.uk

North American office:
Policy Press
c/o The University of Chicago Press
1427 East 60th Street
Chicago, IL 60637, USA
t: +1 773 702 7700
f: +1 773-702-9756
e:sales@press.uchicago.edu
www.press.uchicago.edu

British Library Cataloguing in Publication Data
A catalogue record for this book is available from the British Library.

Library of Congress Cataloging-in-Publication Data
A catalog record for this book has been requested.

ISBN 978-1-4473-3010-3 paperback
ISBN 978-1-4473-3009-7 hardcover
ISBN 978-1-4473-3011-0 ePub
ISBN 978-1-4473-3012-7 Mobi
ISBN 978-1-4473-3013-4 ePdf

Cover design by Policy Press
Front cover: image kindly supplied by istock
Printed and bound in Great Britain by CPI Group (UK) Ltd, Croydon, CR0 4YY
The Policy Press uses environmentally responsible print partners

Dedicated to Jonathan and in loving memory of Jack and my mother, Elvira Ranz y Diez de Artázcoz. **SAC**

To my children, Sakina and Zakary and my parents, with immense gratitude. **FH**

Dedicated to the memory of Jo Campling. **BS**

Sara Ashencaen Crabtree is Professor of Social & Cultural Diversity at Bournemouth University, UK.

Fatima Husain is Research Director for the Children, Families and Work Team, NatCen Social Research, UK.

Basia Spalek is Professor in Conflict Transformation at the University of Derby and Director of Research for Assist Trauma.

Contents

Contents

List of case studies, figures and tables

Case studies

Figures

Tables

Acknowledgements

A number of people assisted in the development of this book, some of whom cannot be named. Nonetheless I would like to thank all the anonymous individuals in the UK, the Far East and the Middle East who contributed their stories. To those who happily can be named, I owe a real debt of gratitude to Furqan Taher of Muslim Youth Helpline, my former social work student, Ahmed Jama, as well as Farzana Beg and Liz Gould of ROSHNI, David Pitcher of CAFCASS and Julie Siddiqi of the Siddiqi Charitable Foundation. I would also like to acknowledge colleagues with whom I have worked over the years, who helped me to develop my understanding of Islam further: Professor Ismail Baba, Dr Belkeis Altareb, Dr Abdullahi Barise and Professor Alean Al-Krenawi are four names that come to mind in this respect.

My loving thanks are due to my husband and comrade, Professor Jonathan Parker, for his endless faith, help and devotion. A harassed mother's gratitude is owed to my young daughters, Isabel and Miranda, who have been so good-natured and encouraging about the long hours spent labouring over this new edition, with the occasional much needed reminder about how there is more to life than publishing deadlines. Here, too, I also wish to commemorate two important people without whom the first edition of this book would certainly never have been written: Jo Campling, who helped to bring the original book to fruition and second, the great help and encouragement given by my late husband, Professor Jack Crabtree. Both Jo and Jack went beyond the call of duty to assist me in the publication of this book right up to the final days of their lives. Additionally, of course, this book would certainly have been greatly impoverished, and almost certainly impossible to complete in its current form, without the invaluable help of my two colleagues, Dr Fatima Husain and Professor Basia Spalek. Last but not least I would like to thank the editorial staff at Policy Press for offering such an efficient but friendly service that always felt totally person-centred.

Sara Ashencaen Crabtree

ONE

Introduction

Paradoxically both little and much has changed since the first edition of *Islam and Social Work: Debating Values, Transforming Practice.* The first volume sought to draw attention to the marginal status of Muslims in the Global North, together with the wealth and depth of Islamic heritage and how these could serve to enrich social work. Today, marginal status remains a continued feature of Muslim minority groups along with concentrated levels of social scrutiny – and, arguably, disproportionately so in respect to their population size or influence. What then has changed in terms of both perceived needs and risks? How do and should social workers view and seek to work constructively with Muslim service users and client groups? These are some of the questions that this, the second edition, seeks to answer.

Aims and scope

On the bookshelves of those with a genuine interest in social work, the chances are that there will be at least one well-thumbed text on the issue of 'race' and ethnicity and how this relates to, and the impact it has on, social work practice. So complex is this area that it continues to provide a rich source of academic inquiry, resulting in impassioned debate. The best known of these polemics rightly continue to feature on every social work student's reading list, and therefore we shall not spend too much time in revision here.

Under these circumstances, it may seem rather unlikely therefore that there can be anything new to add to this topic, especially where social work could well be viewed by other professions as being extremely well supported by the volume of information available on the market. However, at the same time, never before in living memory has there been so much focus devoted to a proliferation of articulated concerns from the media, politicians and the general public regarding the question of the social integration of Muslim minority ethnic (ME) groups in the west (Solomos, 2003).

This is normally framed in relation to the perceived irreconcilable conflict between the cultural values and practices of European nations and those of migrants from other cultures. In the early 2000s two murders took place in the Netherlands, a country well known for its liberal social policy, which appeared to underline the difficulties of multiculturalism in Europe. The first murder was that of outspoken politician, Pim Fortuyn, who espoused xenophobic and Islamophobic rhetoric on the grounds of the threat to Dutch liberal values posed by migration (Marranci, 2004). Theo van Gogh, the controversial film director, was later murdered by a perpetrator embracing extremist interpretations of Islam after training as a social worker, a rich irony that will not be lost on readers (Ahmed, 2005). Since then the threat of religious extremism has taken a more gory and sinister path in the form of the so-called 'Islamic State of Syria and Levant' (variously known as ISIS, ISIL, IS or Daesh), in Iraq and Syria and the targeting of 'soft targets' in the Middle East and in Europe. The flow of refugees escaping war and seeking safety within the EU has been a consequence of this. Images of desperate journeys and huddled masses walking miles with children, the elderly and the infirm, has led to a huge humanitarian response, one which has been countered by political responses embedded in the fear of Muslims as well as of migration by those identified as 'other'. This is particularly the case for the UK, where a bid by the House of Lords to allow entry to 3,000 unaccompanied children residing in camps in France was rejected by the House of Commons.

In addition to the concerns of the 'radicalisation' of disaffected youth, the problem of the 'immigrant other' is played out at many levels, including immigration itself, detention, security, the variables of socio-economic status and those structural barriers restricting access to often inadequate public services. In respect of the UK's Muslim communities, recent debates have centred on issues of security.

Consequently, analysts, policy makers and politicians have seriously questioned the UK's multicultural model as supposedly resulting in segregated communities with little or no interaction across communities and ethnicities. Pervasive general suspicion, heightened by media headlines and an increase in Islamophobic attacks, has been supplemented by the questioning of some Muslim women wearing the *niqab* – a topic that we discuss in further detail in Chapter Two.

The UK government continues its policy focus on family and parenting, emphasising the 'problem' of young people and of families via the Troubled Families programme. Young Muslim men are scrutinised for their allegiances together with the perceived inappropriateness of some young Muslim women's personal choices and the sphere of 'Muslim' family life, relationships and transmission of values is being additionally questioned. Arising from the idea that Muslim parents needed to keep a closer eye on their sons, the UK's contested anti-radicalisation policy, PREVENT, increases the emphasis of the Muslim family as the first level of a tightening, national security buffer (Ashencaen Crabtree, forthcoming).

Poynting and Mason (2006) explore legislation evoked by the European nations in response to the terror attacks of 11 September 2001 (9/11), where it was the UK that reacted in the most extreme way, through, for example, the invoking of a state of emergency in order to pass the 2001 Anti-Terrorism, Crime and Security Act.

Furthermore, following the 7 July 2005 (7/7) bombings in London, there has been considerable discussion within the media and political arenas about the extent to which second- or third-generation Muslim men, particularly South Asian men, have been assimilated into British culture. More recently, this has been exacerbated by incidents of Muslim young people, both male and female, who have left Britain to cross the border into Syria to join Daesh in order to fulfil a desire, however misguided, of living under an 'Islamic caliphate' (Crampton, 2005; Taseer, 2005).

Debates around assimilation appear to miss out key issues that arise when considering British Muslim identities and Muslim youth subcultures. Since the first edition of this book describing Muslims as then constituting the most socially and economically deprived faith group in the UK, little appears to have changed. At that time statistics showed that Muslims were the most likely faith group to experience poor housing conditions, and that 42 per cent of Muslim children lived in overcrowded accommodation, compared with an overall figure of 12 per cent for the general population. Commensurately, a further 12 per cent lived in households with no central heating, compared with 6 per cent for all dependent children, and that 35 per cent were growing up in households where there were no adults in employment, compared with 17 per cent for all dependent children (Choudhury, 2005, p 14). A Joseph Rowntree Foundation research report by Heath and Li (2014) notes that British Muslims standing at 50 per cent, irrespective of ethnicity, are much more likely to experience poverty than others, with Sikhs standing at 27 per cent and Hindus at 25 per cent following behind. Christians across denominations offer a variable picture but with lower levels of poverty, although the Jewish community are the least likely faith group to experience poverty at 13 per cent.

Again, the first edition stated that almost one third of Muslims of working age had no qualifications, the highest proportion for any faith group, and 17.5 per cent of young people between the ages of 16 and 24 are unemployed compared with 7.9 per cent of Christians and 7.4 per cent of Hindus (Choudhury, 2005, p 16). Today, the useful demographic report produced by the Muslim Council of Britain (MCB, 2015), reports a somewhat more positive picture in terms of education, where a quarter of young Muslims are educated to degree level, marginally below the national average, although in terms of overall qualifications lagging behind the comparator groups of Sikhs and Hindus.

The economic and social deprivation experienced by a significant number of young Muslim men means that they, like other socially and economically deprived male youth, are likely to form subcultures, which are also likely to have strong masculinist ideals underpinning them (Young, 1999). Indeed, Archer (2003) argues that such men may construct a 'strong' Islamic identity for themselves as a way of resisting the 'weakness' that they perceived to be associated with the category 'Asian'. Similarly, Saeed et al (1999) argue that the concept of *ummah* (the universal community of the 'Faithful') means that a global Islamic community supersedes national or ethnic identities. Young people may be claiming an Islamic identity for themselves, because this places them within a global community, thereby reducing their sense of marginalisation.

Islamist extremists who are intent on recruiting young British Muslim men have combined masculine imagery with religion in order to try to connect with potential recruits (along with turgid propaganda peppered with pictures of either sensationalised violence or romanticised warrior imagery but, notably, via increasingly sophisticated social media). For example, Mohammed Siddique Khan, the eldest London bomber, recorded a video message to explain his reasons for the attack, and within this message it is clear that he was 'doing masculinity' saying:

> Jihad is an obligation on every single one of us, men and women; (whereas) our so-called scholars of today are content with their Toyotas and semi-detached houses...they are useless. *They should stay at home and leave the job to real men – the true inheritors of the* Prophet. (BBC News, 2005a; Spalek, 2007, p 204; emphasis added)

The rise of extreme views within Muslim communities is matched by 'far-right' groups such as Britain First, whose hate-filled messages resonate among some. On the other hand, with the May 2016 election of London's first Muslim mayor, Sadiq Khan, there is much to celebrate concerning inclusion and how Londoners have rejected a negative, racist campaign by the opposing party.

The general background of under-privilege suggests, however, that multiple strands of oppression bearing down on the lives of Muslim individuals and families give rise to a formulation of resistance among sectors of society, which in turn are regarded as an increasing threat to social stability. If social work is to work effectively with the communities they serve, the complex and interwoven factors of ethnicity, religion, gender, identity and class need to be more fully disentangled, analysed and addressed within the profession.

It has often been pointed out that Islam is the fastest growing religion in the west (Barise, 2005; Hodge, 2005). Al-Krenawi (2012) states that approximately 1.57 billion people follow Islam, making it the second largest global religion next to Christianity. At the same time there is scant social work literature that is specific to Muslim individuals and families. Accessible information that does pertain to Islamic worldviews is often of a highly generalised nature or tends to offer descriptive rather than in-depth analysis of social situations and issues with Muslim communities – thereby reducing the chances of applicability for effective intervention.

The premise of our book, therefore, is based on the firm conviction that practitioners require not only a foundational understanding of Islamic belief systems and perspectives for cultural competent and sensitive intervention, but that this needs to be considered from the dual understanding of both religious mandates and cultural interpretation, which it is vital to tease apart.

We also argue, however, that of equal importance, is a preliminary, academically critical approach towards the problematisation of issues and implications pertaining to Muslim individuals, families and communities. Without this expansive depth of understanding and analysis social work practitioners will lack the basic background knowledge and critical thinking skills they need to be able to work more confidently with Muslim communities, particularly given a socio-political, multicultural arena of competing tensions. To this end, we have offered a number of case studies throughout the book to facilitate the process of reflective learning, some of which are taken from our own social work practice and some of which are drawn from anonymous practising contributors and social welfare agencies.

Furthermore, in writing this book we have consciously tried to avoid subsuming the lives, experiences and perspectives of Muslims under the broader umbrella category of black perspectives (Graham, 2007). Since significant segments of the British black and minority ethnic population (BME) identify themselves as Muslim in the 2001 Census (ONS, 2002), these multiple standpoints may well overlap. However, we feel that it would be a mistake to fail to identify what is specific to Islam and to Muslim families, as this would only serve to prevent social workers from being able to identify the particular issues that are relevant to Muslims alone. We therefore overtly focus only on the needs of Muslim clients who may come from a wide variety of socioeconomic, cultural, national and regional backgrounds. For many, the fundamental tenets of Islam serve as a unifying force, regardless of 'race', ethnicity and localised or cultural differences, although these of course are in turn highly influential.

Definition of terms

Here we define the terms we commonly employ throughout the text, as well as to establish the parameters of the book and how we intend to address emerging topics in relation to social work with Muslim clients. Just as there is no such thing as value-free research, or indeed politically unmediated social work practice, so too are the terms that authors adopt subject to politically loaded meanings, all of which represent potentially hazardous, contentious areas for further debate. Although we have consciously not fenced the text in with a barrage of terminology to perplex readers, nonetheless we have been at some pains to find nomenclature that is both accurate and non-oppressive, and which we attempt to use consistently throughout the text.

Accordingly, in discussing the divide between certain racial and ethnic groups primarily in the UK, we have preferred to adopt the term 'minority ethnic' (ME). In addition to this, the simple and factual term 'Muslims' seems to be preferable to the long-winded term 'Muslim families and individuals', in general, except where families are specifically referred to. Such terms are not necessarily politically loaded; however, this is not necessarily the case in relation to some terms, such as 'orthodox', which implies a universal norm. For this reason we prefer to substitute this for the more neutral but descriptive term 'conservative'.

Such changes of terminology have, however, been necessary. In the first edition, we deliberately avoided using the term 'Muslim extremism' as one loaded with emotive and stereotypical images, substituting that for 'extreme interpretations of Islamic principles' or 'concepts'. However, given the global, geo-political landscape of violence, attrition and national defence, we have found it necessary to use the term 'Islamist extremism' as and when appropriate, without in any sense wanting to convey an inherent relationship between Muslims and aggression – a notion we completely reject. We therefore use the term 'Islamist extremism' to refer to those notorious groups who promote and commit acts of violence and aggression in the name of Islam, thereby serving to bring the faith into disrepute.

In respect of social work terminology, we note that in the UK the term 'client' has largely been replaced by the term 'service user'. However, we believe in using each as occasion requires, for these carry distinctive connotations that need some recognition. The term 'service user' implies a focus that is much more resource-based and more impersonal than that of 'client', where resourcing is semantically decentred in favour of the personalised, professional relationship.

Organisation of the book

Here we orientate the reader by offering a short description of the book's content. Accordingly, Chapter Two takes a broad perspective in order to discuss the diversity of the Muslim *ummah*. In so doing, we borrow lenses from sociological and anthropological disciplines through which to view the current position of migrant and settled ME communities in western Europe, in which we include the UK. We also consider issues of relevance that are emerging from Muslim communities in the wider international area. These all serve to contextualise some of the more crucial contemporary debates revolving around multiculturalism and social inclusion, as well as that of nationalism and conservative interpretations of Islam.

Education is the topic of Chapter Three, particularly in relation to the training of social workers, and what can be done to enhance educational effectiveness in this area. Social work values and practice are considered in relation to Islamic principles and epistemology. Once again, concepts and cases are drawn from the international Muslim community, as well as closer to home.

Chapter Four focuses on the centrality of the family in Islam, as the main unit of socialisation of individuals in the Islamic worldview. The wide-ranging morphology of Muslim families is considered. So too are gender norms, especially in terms of child-rearing, and the demarcation of the roles between the sexes. The prevailing stereotypes in the west of Muslim women and men are also discussed in relation to perceived dilemmas for social workers in relation to the professional value-base.

Having set the general scene, subsequent chapters are devoted to specific practice issues. Chapter Five examines issues implicating Muslim families, in terms of addressing problematic sexuality and domestic violence, including so-called misnomer 'honour-based violence'. The sexual exploitation of underage children is also examined in detail.

Chapter Six considers health issues in the Muslim family. Controversial practices such as female genital mutilation (FGM) are reviewed according to different cultural interpretations. More conventionally, needs associated with disability and mental abuse together with the religiously problematic issue of substance abuse are also considered.

Chapter Seven focuses on ageing as both a demographic and social construction in relation to ME service users. Accordingly, ageing is discussed within a religio-cultural framework, which provides a context to analyse and comprehend Muslim experiences of ageing.

The penultimate chapter by Basia Spalek with Tracey Devanna, considers penology, crime and Islamophobia. This is of especial relevance following the aftermath of terror attacks in Paris, the UK, US, Spain, Turkey and Bali. This issue of religious conversion and regenerated identity in the penal system is also explored here.

Chapter Nine, offers some concluding remarks drawing together the separate strands of debate with some final thoughts on 'where next...?'

Addressing ethnicity in social work

In this section we briefly introduce ethnic and faith identities, a topic that is considered in more detail in Chapter Three. This area has commonly focused on the concepts of 'race' and culture with the aim of enlightening white practitioners to the cultural practices and lifestyles of clients from BME groups. Although social work education and practice in the UK has for some time hinged on anti-oppressive practice (AOP) (Ashencaen Crabtree et al, 2014; Bartoli, 2013), writing from the US Robin Sakina Mama (2001) identifies two main approaches derived from social science qualitative research methodologies, used to gather and decipher knowledge of other cultures: the 'ethic' and the 'emic' approaches.

To summarise, 'emic' approaches deliver specific knowledge of a particular culture, in addition to here offering a set of strategies and guidelines for practitioners (Mama, 2001, p 376). Yet this has led to the critique that clichéd stereotypes of cultures are thereby perpetuated through the essentialising of individuals down to a set of properties regarded as typical of that culture (Mama, 2001). This is only a short step away from pathologising such clients in terms of perceived 'cultural deficits' (Ely and Denney, 1987, p 70). Clients who do not come from a dominant cultural or ethnic group are often then viewed as coming from a context that is problematic in terms of family functioning, general lifestyles and cultural values. These real or assumed differences are then regarded as liable to make social work intervention more likely (Ahmad, 1990; Ely and Denney, 1987). It also serves to underline how racist overtones in social work practice become embedded, such as in relation to the patronising, colour-blind attitudes that overlook institutional and structural inequalities that have an impact on the lives of BME communities in the west (Dominelli, 1994, p 36).

The 'etic' approach by contrast adopts a more universal perspective in attempting to develop broad concepts that are regarded as germane to the particular culture under study. However, this too is problematic in failing to address the issue of diversity within the cultural context, as is the case of Muslim communities, where homogeneity is assumed.

Tsang (2001) in turn argues that the 'cultural literacy model', as embodied in anti-discriminatory practice, and which, to an extent, straddles both the emic and etic points of view, has become the dominant approach in cross-cultural social work education. Unfortunately, here too, the general features and properties are assumed to belong to all individuals of that particular culture in question.

Apart from the fallacies of over-generalisation, this also fails to take into account the ethnicity, socio-economic background, ethical and value perspectives of white authors and practitioners through an ethnocentric perspective that assumes 'that ethnicity belongs only to the client' (Tsang, 2001, p 234).

The notion of culturally competent social work, however, as developed in the US, is gaining recognition in the UK as a viable framework that is easily transferable into effective practice (Becher and Husain, 2003). Cultural competence along with Critical Race Theory are therefore explored in more detail in Chapter Three.

In this book we have considered both the emic and etic approaches, and have attempted to draw out the most useful aspects of each, while trying to avoid the pitfalls. Following Tsang's point, we take into account our own cultural heritage as highly influential in informing our perspectives and our analyses, as will be explained further. The result, we hope, is a text that is consciously broad in scope, international in perspective, detailed in specifics and, we hope, thereby useful to a wide audience of readers wishing to enhance their knowledge and stimulate their critical understanding in a reflective exercise, while hopefully sharpening their practice skills.

Social work, ethnocentrism and the influence of postmodernism

Social work developed from the roots of social reform in the nineteenth century, led by a small but energetic number of philanthropic enterprises, such as those connected with the Quakers and the Fabians (Payne, 2005). The appetite for massive industrialisation and the profit motive was belatedly reflected in some quarters of society by a concern for a more humanitarian regard for the children, women and men who made the manufacturing might of Great Britain possible. The modernist assumption of universal social progress would be an idea with which postmodernism would later take issue, where a proliferation of critiques would emerge from the humanities, the social sciences and, later, popular culture against modernist and ethnocentric perspectives. Later in the twentieth century the dominant white, masculine and single-voiced viewpoint and authority of modernity would be challenged and fractured. This fragmentation enables multiple experiences from the margins of ethnicity, gender, culture and now faith, to be heard. This multiplicity stands effectively as the hallmark of postmodernist trends.

In this guise postmodernism, in relation to the celebration of diversity, appears as a benevolent and empowering force. Indeed, one to be openly embraced by the social work profession as being more egalitarian and therefore more in keeping with social work values of equality and advocacy. Yet postmodernism has taught us that such apparent bedrocks of certainty offer an unreliable foundation on which to build. Writing of the apparent crisis in social work in the US, David Stoesz has accused the profession of failing to keep faith with its social contract to tackle mainstream social problems, such as poverty, child welfare and disability. This failure, he argues, is rooted in a pseudo-academic haze of 'postmodernist relativism' (Stoesz, 2002, p 22). Furthermore, Webb (2009) offers an excoriating critique of social work's postmodernist fetishisation of the 'right to difference' in its celebration of diversity and difference, thereby validating crude, hierarchical binary differences – a position not normally endorsed within the profession.

Stoez's argument is that social work has flirted too closely with postmodernism and has therefore abandoned the profession to strategic irrelevance in meeting the needs of individuals, families and communities. In turn Webb (2009, p. 309) argues that social work should be 'indifferent to difference, transcending the politics of power driving such positionings'.

The language of market-driven productivity is taken up by Lena Dominelli. Here anti-racist social work, feminist social work and consumer perspectives stand in radical opposition to social work characterised by bureaucracy, managerialism and the 'fragmented service provision' in the postmodernist era (Dominelli, 1996, p 157). In a similar vein, Preston-Shoot describes a grim scenario where social work in the postmodernist climate becomes 'chaotic, fragmented and alienated and alienating' (Preston-Shoot, 2000, p 88). In such a climate, social workers are tied to the purchase of care packages rather than building core therapeutic relationships with clients – a move described as the 'dehumanisation of individuals', both clients and social workers (2000, p 90).

Separate from the issue of postmodernism however, but nonetheless commensurate with critiques of social work, is how the criminal justice system is changing its focus. The rise of the 'actuarial regime' in criminal justice refers to the governance of populations through statistical analyses of risk (Simon, 1988; Ewald 1991; O'Malley, 1992). The fragmentation of human identity, which forms a primary example of depersonalisation, is manifestly evident in the actuarial approach, viewing people as statistical risk-based distributions rather than in terms of their personal properties. This is a pronounced departure from understanding the individual in an ecosystems orientation, seeking to identify actors and the variables of situations within the context of their environment (DuBois and Miley, 2005).

To return to postmodernism, however, critiques levied here emphasise the essential inability of postmodernism to enable clients and social workers to form effective coalitions that can challenge existing hierarchies of power in order to create social change. By rejecting generalisations and the politics of solidarity this undermines the aims of collectivisation, for postmodernist perspectives regard political power as dispersed rather than having a central locus. In such a diffused and ambiguous atmosphere, all are implicated in power plays, both those who are apparently disempowered, as well as those who attempt to unmask power differentials (Hartsock, 1990). Racism, sexism and other forms of discrimination cease to become potent and structural forces in people's lives, but instead collapse into being merely competing discourses and perceptions.

Postmodernism focuses on the fluidity and diversity of identities losing sight of those discriminatory norms that help to produce and perpetuate oppression. By stressing the locally produced and contingent nature of any knowledge claims, regimes of power in relation to whiteness, patriarchy, heterosexism, secularism, disablism and ageism remain unchallenged and therefore largely intact.

If postmodernism cannot provide impetus towards action that overtly alters the relations of power in client–worker interactions, it can instead create space in which the processes of social work are analysed, and this may lead to change. Accordingly, Fook suggests that a 'critical' reflective approach is essential for *praxis* in enabling practitioners and educators to explore the extent to which theory fits with action (Fook, 1996, p 4; Preston-Shoot, 2000, p 89). Thompson concurs, saying that reflectivity steers a prudent middle path between the rejection of theory, and a rigid over-reliance on theory (Thompson, 2005, p 147).

Reflectivity and reflexivity

Critical reflectivity enables an exploration of social work practice (including at times our own) in the context of Islam, through analysing one's own personal and professional points of view. In addition to reflectivity, we have found the postmodernist strategy of reflexivity to be a useful device (Alcott, 1991; Lyons, 1999). Reflexivity means the self-identification of speaker location and is used to good effect in ethnographic work, typical of anthropology and sociology, in determining how the author's perspective influences the research process and outcome. In this text we have additionally adopted reflexivity, bringing in the interplay of our authorial voices, in which individual perspectives and personal histories have added to our critical analyses.

To clarify our intentions, we are not attempting to reach a uniform consensus with each other at all costs in this book. The topics discussed are too complex and multi-layered for that to be easily achieved. In addition, our own particular backgrounds are sufficiently diverse to make such an endeavour an impractical one, even if consensus were considered to be the ultimately desirable outcome.

Having embarked on our own continuous learning curve, we believe that our approach offers a multifaceted way of looking at and approaching social work practice with Muslims. In keeping with our dialogic aims therefore, readers are encouraged to think critically for themselves, through the issues raised, and in relation to formulating their own professional responses. Consequently, we do not offer a 'cookbook' set of instructions to be unthinkingly adopted by readers. We argue, we advise, we suggest, but we do not rigidly prescribe.

Thus by identifying our speaker locations through reflexivity, our experiences and assumptions are made more explicit to the reader in understanding how these may have coloured our perspectives on issues.

To this end, we would like to clarify our own speaker locations and to explain how these have informed our views of social work and social welfare with Muslims.

Sara's story

I am a white British woman of mixed European family living in London. My first stirrings of interest in Islamic traditions are owed to my aristocratic Spanish mother, who throughout my childhood enjoyed recounting stories of the glories of the Moorish civilisation (and their encounters with the Catholic sovereigns) in historic Andalucía. Years later I was intrigued to find that in the Arabian Gulf this historical period continued to be immortalised in the name 'Al Andalus'. Nowadays this title is liberally bestowed on primarily educational establishments seeking to bask in the ideal of an elite borrowed from a lost and noble culture – one, furthermore, that had been shaped by the harmonious contribution of Muslims, Christians and Jews living for centuries under a particularly enlightened Islamic governance.

Returning, however, to the less romantic and more prosaic, my professional interest in the topic of this book has developed from two main, but complementary, areas emerging from practice and academia, respectively. Prior to and after qualifying as a professional social worker in the early 1990s, I worked in a number of social work settings in London and the nearby commuter county of Hertfordshire. Here I worked with a wide range of clients, including Muslims. I found that with the latter I was often hampered in not having the basic cultural knowledge I needed to work with them effectively. This was primarily because detailed and targeted information was rarely available on the needs of Muslims in the social work curricula.

Several years later, in between academic posts and completing my doctorate, a relocation to the town of Luton[1] as a locum social worker brought me into close contact with Muslim clients, who now formed the bulk of my caseload. Due to my previous experiences my Asian team manager regarded me, maybe somewhat unwisely, as something of a minor expert on social work with Muslim minority groups. In the opinion of the management, since there was no other person better qualified in the immediate vicinity, most cases involving Muslim clients ended up on my desk.

In fairness, however, I found that most Muslim families in Luton were deeply relieved to have someone to work with, who at least had a basic familiarity with their customs and points of view, and almost invariably I was warmly welcomed once these informal credentials were accepted.

My academic experiences, on the other hand, were instrumental in exposing me to some of the rich diversity that exists in the Islamic world. For over a decade from 1995 I took up lectureships in local universities in Malaysia and the United Arab Emirates, both being predominantly Muslim nations, albeit that Malaysia boasts a thriving multicultural, multi-faith population as well.

This provided key lessons in terms of personal and professional adaptation to two very different Muslim societies. Each had a distinctive social context and different population needs, together with dissimilar social welfare services, informed by alternative underlying assumptions of service provision. Furthermore, social work education differs widely in offering contrasting educational environments, curricula and general educational targets.

What I learned primarily from these experiences was a due appreciation of indigenous social work based on differing client beliefs and needs. Moreover, I discovered that there is a distinct gap between Islamic principles, as found primarily in the Holy Qur'an, and those beliefs and customs that were not basically Islamic, but instead were embedded in localised, traditional responses. In some cases, the latter pre-dated Islam or ran parallel with it, an area that is considered in more detail in this book.

I realised, with concern, that although many of the issues I covered in classroom situations seemed relevant according to an international social work curriculum, there was sometimes a cultural dissonance between theory and my Muslim students' perceptions and perspectives. This provided me with some serious food for thought and in due course generated further research (Ashencaen Crabtree, 1999, 2008; Ashencaen Crabtree and Baba, 2001).

Another career relocation took place, this time to the rigorous, academic hothouse of Hong Kong, where my research agenda focused on ME groups. Once more I gravitated towards work with Muslims, specifically impoverished families. Preliminary findings from my Hong Kong research indicated that although some families had gained a firm foothold in Hong Kong, many others led highly marginalised lives. Muslim families in Hong Kong are variously hampered by poor educational opportunities, unemployment problems, poverty and language barriers. These findings therefore appeared to hold some interesting resonance with the situation in the UK. Another move back to the UK brought fresh academic challenges and now as Professor of Social and Cultural Diversity at Bournemouth University I continue to excavate faith, marginalisation and social work with zeal.

So although my professional and personal journey from the west to the east and back again has been a fascinating one, it has not always been an easy road to travel. However, fundamentally it has also represented a dialogue and one that is essential to engage with, *if* the dichotomies and dilemmas of differing and diffused national, cultural and religious identities are to be addressed successfully within an accountable and contemporary social work discipline.

Based on all these important experiences I believe increasingly that the locus of truly innovative and effective social work is shifting away from its historical countries of origin. Social work is in the process of being re-interpreted and re-cast into powerful new forms of social engagement, practice and civic responsibility, serving to renew and re-invigorate this vital pan-international profession, where those who were the past learners will become the new and welcomed teachers.

Fatima's story

I was born in Karachi, Pakistan, into a practising and rather devout Dawoodi Bohra Muslim family. Both my parents were born under the British Raj in what is now India, from among a privileged minority – educated and financially well-off, with a family tradition of producing lawyers.

My mother and her family fled India soon after partition, as did my father, and arrived in Pakistan as 'Muhajir' or refugees. I left Pakistan at the age of six and from then until my final arrival in Britain in 1997 my life has been marked by dislocation and external identifiers such as 'foreigner', immigrant, woman of colour, 'brown' and so forth in a number of countries on three different continents. Even today, questions about belonging, about citizenship and which box on ethnic monitoring forms best defines me are ever present; and in Pakistan, my country of birth, my ethnic label is still that of 'Muhajir' – the child of a refugee is still labelled a refugee. Further complexity in my subjective position is added by my identity as a Muslim. I am a member of a minority denomination (the Bohras) within another minority (Shi'as) within a larger Muslim minority that, currently, is often and consistently vilified in the west.

With family members residing in Bangladesh, India, Pakistan, Scotland, New York, Texas and Canada, and expressing different levels of allegiance to being Bohra, mainstream Shi'a and orthodox Sunni, as well as agnostic and atheist, family gatherings have often been characterised by heated discussions about nationalism, the politics of belonging, faith allegiances and the importance of belief in one God. At the same time, acknowledging and appreciating – as well as confronting – my family background of privilege in a society ridden by class divisions, poverty and illiteracy has been a constant challenge.

Living in western countries, I have had to respond from a very early age to questions such as 'Do you have trees in Pakistan?', 'Why does Islam treat women so badly?', 'Why is polygamy allowed?' and 'Why is it that it's always the children of "foreigners" who have problems?' And have suffered comments such as 'You aren't really like them, you don't smell', 'Paki go home' and 'You know what we do with people like that' – this a response by a US immigration officer to my family name, Husain, after the first Gulf war. Not to mention the raised eyebrows, stares and questions from fellow Muslims (male and female) and devout family members who sometimes struggle to comprehend my positioning as a Muslim. It is precisely my position as a Muslim woman in the west that led me to study gender and Islam for my PhD, having been inspired by North African fiction, as well as writers and thinkers such as the late Fatima Mernissi and Mohammed Arkoun. I have also been deeply influenced by post-colonial and feminist theoretical perspectives, in particular Albert Memmi, Franz Fanon and Trinh T. Minh-ha.

Today I am a researcher working principally on issues related to the lived experiences of marginalised and disadvantaged in the UK and Europe. I am also a single mother bringing up two mixed-race and inter-faith children in a society that is increasingly becoming fractured along class, ethnicity and community divides.

Reflexivity is a guiding principle through which I approach research and communicate with people. Critical to my understanding of the communities I research is an understanding of self and my own subjective position in society, as well as an awareness of how others might perceive me, both as a researcher and a person.

Each and every position I take or identifier I use is subjective, situational and fluid, and each is significant to who I am and what I do. However, the dichotomous position that has been consistent in my life, both professionally and personally, is that of outsider/insider, a positioning that has served me well in researching communities, families, children, women, young people and men who are marginalised and disadvantaged.

Basia's story

I am a British-born, white female whose parents are Second World War refugees, who as children were forced to flee Poland when the Soviet army invaded eastern Poland. As a child I attended Polish school every Saturday, where I learned to read and write in Polish, where I learned about Polish history and culture, and where I sang the Polish national anthem.

I am currently a Professor of Conflict Transformation in the Department of Therapeutic Practice at the University of Derby, UK. I have undertaken international, national and local research exploring community-based approaches to conflict and violence, alongisde understanding trauma and victimisation. I also act as a consultant to the Crown Prosecution Service, the Institute for Strategic Dialogue, the Royal United Services Institute, West Midlands Police, the London Metropolitan Service, HM Prison Service, the Department for Communities and Local Government in the UK, the Australian Government Families and Communities Taskforce, the North Sea Working group on Proactive Policing in the Global Neighbourhood, the Open Society Institute, and the Organization for Security and Co-operation in Europe (OSCE).

I am an integrative psychotherapist, working with wide-ranging clients in relation to trauma, anxiety, depression, bereavement, traumatic grief, addiction, violence and other issues. I run a private counselling practice: connect-and-reflect.org.uk and I lead the 'walk and talk' and 'run and reflect' sessions close to my home at Rutland Water.

Previously I held a post as a criminologist based at Birmingham University and my research interests include Muslim communities in relation to criminal justice issues. Birmingham is a multi-ethnic, multicultural city, and having a significant number of Muslim students on the criminology courses that I ran, made me think about the extent to which criminology as a subject discipline reflects Muslim identities. It has been claimed that criminology 'was born with the death of God'

(Morrison, 1995, p 5), and so part of my research has involved a focus on faith communities and criminological knowledge production.

Reflexivity is a key part of my approach to research, drawing very much on feminist research principles, whereby the values and characteristics of the researcher are made visible. Reflexivity is viewed as being a key way of ensuring rigorousness and reliability when carrying out research, as it might be argued that the beliefs and behaviours of social scientists influence the perception and documentation of social experience.

My subject positions are multitudinous, including being white, a woman and a western researcher, as well as a wife, friend, daughter and sister. All of these positions are significant, as these constitute the sites at which the social world is experienced and acted on, and so will have an impact in different ways on the research process. Moreover, while some aspects of my subjectivity might be linked to marginalised, outsider positions, which help to produce oppositional knowledge, other aspects of my self-identity might serve to maintain and reproduce dominant racial and cultural discourses and power relations. Reflection for me is part of a personal ethic, particularly as in the present political climate we are asking Muslim communities to reflect on their faith and citizenship, and yet it seems this reflection is largely lacking on the part of western governments, public officials and extensive parts of the media.

Tracey's story

I was born in South-East London to an English mother and Scottish father. My background always seemed to me rather dull, although I longed for a surname that didn't generate interest from teachers at school.

My Scottish grandparents died young so I never had a chance of meeting them and my father's life now centred round policing in London. He was one of many who, leaving school early for a life in the pits, decided that it wasn't for him and left for London, rarely looking back home. It was only as I grew older that my interest in my Scottish roots developed, later finding out that my grandfather was both a Labour and a Union man. I regret the missed opportunities for getting to know him and hearing his stories, as well as my lack of early curiosity towards my family background. It is so often the case that only when we start to ask others about their identities and backgrounds that we reflect and recognise knowledge gaps in our own biographies.

Growing up in the 1970s and 1980s meant a construction of fear towards the Irish as a result of the Troubles. For me, there was minimum interest in what was occurring across the Irish Sea, other than bemusement towards Gerry Adams when he was seen, but not heard, on our television screens due to a media ban. With my father's role as a policeman, Ireland as a holiday destination was discouraged. And yet it would become such an important place in my life. At that time, though, it appeared to me a place of violence and as such to be avoided.

When living in Canada during the early 1990s, I became fascinated by Irish politics, one minute showing limited interest, the next unable to fill the craving for understanding what had been happening so near to me all of my life. It was the 1994 IRA ceasefire and an interview I conducted with a member of the Front de liberation du Québec that stirred my curiosity and led to what would become one of the most enjoyable stages of my life. Putting distance between places of familiarity can often inspire us to view them differently and it was only then, in Canada, that I appreciated what had been so close to me. This also inspired me to ask more questions of my father about my Scottish roots leading to my identity as English being challenged as a result. Important to my research is recognition that not only are identities fluid and relationships changeable; it is the *process* of positioning ourselves that is vital. In studying young male Muslim ex-prisoners, their history, just like mine, must be understood and that emanates from understanding the important role of agency within identity construction. In centralising this, one can better listen to their voices and hear what it is they are saying about life in Britain today for young male Muslims.

Note

[1] Luton in South England, once a town famous only for its hat industry in the historical county of Bedfordshire, has these days an unfortunately ghettoised ethnic profile and is known as the hometown of the infamous London Bombers of 7/7.

TWO

The Muslim *ummah:*
context and concepts

Introduction

In providing an overview of Islam and diversity within Islam, this chapter acts as a basic introduction to a highly complex subject area that has been extensively discussed. The contextual nature of Islam is emphasised and particular references are made to the historical migration and settlement of Muslim communities in Europe and the UK. The authors are aware that any discussion of Islam and Muslims can be contentious and loaded, and therefore we attempt to open a window to the complexity of discussions referring to what it means to be 'Muslim'.

First published in 1997, Huntington's description of the clash of civilisations might today be perceived as a prediction come true, with global power struggles increasingly defined by homogeneous categories of 'us' versus 'the other'. In this sense 'us' constitutes the 'civilised west', while 'the other' may be perceived as an 'orthodox, hate-filled Islamic' mass. Dichotomised discourses, such as Huntington's, have been reinforced by both radical Muslims and those who have rejected Islam.

These divisions form the background of dangerously heightened global conflict, political expediencies and how 'Islamic' terrorism is played out and reported and interpreted by the media. It is this context that plays consistently in the background as people (Muslims and non-Muslims alike) try to live their daily lives in contemporary, multicultural western societies.

The establishment of an Islamic community

Islam, the third of the monotheistic religions, followed closely in the ideological steps of Judaism and Christianity with Abraham as the grand patriarch. Mohammed (570–632 BCE), the Prophet of Islam, brought to the Arabian peninsula a new social order that had its base in the revealed divine word. In defying the social order of the time, and the polytheistic Hijazi society, Mohammed (pbuh[1]) created a new community of believers: the *ummah*. If the divine revelation could be considered a strategic intervention (Arkoun, 1994), then it can be stated that Mohammed through the symbolism of Islam created a social and political framework that challenged the order and power of the day, moving away from tribal allegiances towards allegiance to a divine entity: God or Allah. Mohammed's articulation of the divine word was fundamental in establishing a society distinct from, yet embedded in, existing cultural traditions (for example by incorporating a pagan ritual, the *hajj*, into the new Islamic symbolism).

While the Islamic calendar may divide historical time into 'before' and 'after', Islam as a religion has roots that lie deep in a monotheistic past; however, the historical framework is rooted in localised cultural and political factors (Arkoun, 1994). It is often the conflation of the two that leads to references to a monolithic Islam, and this conflation, sometimes difficult to separate, is increasingly used in current political discourses and policy formulations.

The Qur'an, the *hadith* and the *shari'a*

The Muslim *ummah* was formed based on the divine discourse as revealed to Mohammed. These revelations were recounted by Mohammed to his followers and disciples who later wrote them down, creating the written text of the Qur'an: the *al kitab*. The sacred word of the Qur'an is the foundation of Islam and is considered by the majority of Muslims to be the word of Allah, the divine word par excellence (Shimmel, 1992).

During the life of Mohammed, the *ummah* directly addressed him with questions, problems and issues to be clarified. However, when revelation stopped with the death of Mohammed, the community strove to fill this gap by remembering and writing down the Prophet's own words and actions. These texts form the *sunna* or the prophetic tradition. The *sunna* comprises *hadith*, or sayings of the Prophet, and authenticated *hadith* are considered infallible examples of how believers should conduct themselves. The *hadith* therefore are read by Muslims in close connection with the Qur'an.

Similarly, in a desire to establish and implement a way of life guided by the Divine, the *shari'a* was written as a Muslim law guide. The *shari'a* or 'the Way' is not the word of God but is a divinely inspired guide that extends and elaborates on the teachings of the Qur'an and *hadith*. The *shari'a* was formulated in the seventh century, seeking to inspire legal practice with Islamic principles, and is also referred to as 'Islamic family law'. The *shari'a* has been incorporated to some extent in most Muslim societies or nations. Although, as discussed further in Chapter Four, women's groups in some countries are campaigning against versions of the *shari'a* that are part of national legislation but which are considered to undermine women's quest for justice and equality (Mehdi, 1997; Anwar, 2006). Conservative fringe groups in the UK have also called unsuccessfully for the establishment of *shari'a* law. In 2005, the premier of the province of Ontario, Canada, rejected a call for the establishment of Islamic tribunals to arbitrate in civil and marriage disputes after lobbying by Muslim women's groups. The former Archbishop of Canterbury, Dr Rowan Williams raised a storm of controversy in the media when he suggested the idea of adopting aspects of *shari'a* law in the UK (BBC News, 2008).

The Qur'an, the *hadith* and the *shari'a* form the foundation of 'Islamic' thought and practice. The Qur'an is considered the divine text and thus closed and unchangeable, but the *shari'a* has been open to interpretation and elaboration, leading to some level of transformation within specific socio-cultural contexts. While some have argued that the Qur'an should be viewed as a strategic intervention within a particular historic context, it, the *hadith*, *shari'a* and Mohammed, as a true follower of Islam, are held in high reverential regard by most Muslims. This veneration is understood with great difficulty by many non-Muslims in the western world and has led to mischievous provocation, such as the Danish cartoon affair, or the DKNY jeans with Qur'anic verses on the back pocket, Nike shoes with a symbol resembling Allah in Arabic, together with the designer dress produced in 1994 with embroidered Qur'anic verses on it.

Islam and Muslims

The word 'islam', as derived from the Arabic root 'SLM', is defined as 'submission, resignation to the will of God', whereas the verbal forms of 'SLM' mean 'to submit, surrender, resign', as well as 'to be secure' and 'to be protected from harm'. Additionally, the word for peace, 'salam', is derived from the same root.

In the context of the religion, *islam* can be defined as 'giving one's whole self over to God', and other connotations associated with the word include transcendence: a move towards God and to a higher level of existence. A derivative of SLM, 'muslim' is defined as someone who submits to the will of God, or acts in loving obedience to God, and not necessarily a follower of Islam. This distinction is explained in some detail by Arkoun (1994) with respect to Qur'anic references to Abraham as not Jewish or Christian but as a 'muslim'. In the Qur'anic context then, *muslim* indicates an 'ideal religious attitude' towards God, a complete obedience exemplified by Abraham's willingness to sacrifice his son. Therefore, it is possible to talk about *islam* and *muslims* at two different levels. The first is the *Abrahamic islam*: a religious experience, a purity of communication with God that pre-dates rituals and legislation, and that is reaffirmed in the experiences of Mohammed. The second are the notions of *Islam* and *Muslim* as defined and written within the historical, social and political framework of the revelation. Again we find these words, which are steeped in significance and connotation, existing at two different levels that are often intertwined as meanings become conflated and the *din* and *dunya* (sacred and profane) are woven together.

These definitions are relevant in contemporary discourses as these words are used freely to define social, political and national movements, and often synonymously. What is an Islamic Republic, for example as in the Islamic Republic of Pakistan? What shades of meaning are there when one refers to 'Muslim communities' as opposed to 'Islamic communities'? 'Islamic terrorists' or 'Muslim terrorists'?

These terminologies are constantly being debated, and although these discussions might not appear to be directly relevant in the context of a social work intervention, it is worth noting that how we identify and refer to others, and how others self-identify, is constantly shifting and changing. Ethnic monitoring in the UK has been transformed with the faith question, with many Muslims preferring to self-identify as 'Muslim' rather than use an ethnic identifier (for example, British Muslim versus Asian of Pakistani origin). Additionally, at the margins there are voices questioning the notion of a Muslim identity that is British – a troubling topic that we shall consider later in the chapter. Consequently, a discussion of identifiers and their significance is critical in developing an understanding of the complex nature of what is happening in contemporary society, both nationally and globally, as our consciousness continues to be pervaded by references to 'Islam' and 'Muslims'.

Fundamental principles of the *ummah*

The debate about the historical context versus the unchanging divine word forms another backdrop in understanding the complexity of what it means to be Muslim. This, however, should not overlook the issue of national, cultural and ethnic heterogeneity among self-identifying Muslims, as these aspects are likely to influence daily practices, values and attitudes to a large degree. It is important to bear in the mind the anomalies of homogenising diverse peoples on the basis of religion alone. An easy parallel of this discrepancy may be grasped by the hypothetical assumption that all self-identifying Christians share the same social and cultural norms – clearly this is untrue.

Yet grasping the basic nuances underpinning issues arising from the concept of the *ummah* enables the reader to consider the multiplicity of factors that interact in creating a Muslim consciousness. Although there are many competing voices attempting to articulate the meaning of being Muslim, it is still legitimate to attempt to extract factors that contribute to the creation of a unifying *ummah* and a common Islamic discourse. At its most simple, this leads to a consideration of the five fundamental duties, the so-called 'pillars of Islam' that are obligatory for all believers.

The first principle is of the *shahadah* or bearing witness to the monotheistic nature of Islam and the prophecy of Mohammed. The *shahadah* sums up the central points of Islam, that there is only one God and that Mohammed is His prophet. The recitation of the *shahadah* is usually considered sufficient to confirm conversion to Islam.

The second fundamental duty is that of prayer or *salat*. This is the most important duty and structures daily life for Muslims. While the Qur'an does not mention the number of daily prayers that should be undertaken, so far as is known the ritual prayer was practised five times a day by the Prophet Mohammed. The times of these prayers are fixed according to the daily movement of the sun, whereby Muslims are required to stop whatever activity they are engaged in and pray at the designated times: before sunrise, midday, late afternoon, at sunset and after nightfall. The ritual prayers are performed facing the holy site in Mecca and while all denominations of Islam accept the five daily prayers, some have reduced the five ritual prayers to three designated time slots (before sunrise, midday and after sunset).

The third principle is that of *zakat*, an alms tax aimed at benefiting the poor and needy in society, which is discussed in greater detail in Chapter Three. This obligation is clearly delineated in the Qur'an, which indicates the amount payable together with how the collected money should be disbursed.

The fourth pillar, which seems to be increasingly observed with greater strictness, is that of fasting or *saum*. Ramadan, the ninth month in the Muslim lunar calendar, is the month of fasting when practising Muslims refrain from eating, drinking and smoking from sunrise to sunset. It is quite common that Muslims who might not follow any other rituals during the year will fast for the entire month. While the basic premise of fasting is consistent across all Muslim communities, there are some who interpret the fast with exacting rigour. It is therefore important to develop an understanding and awareness of the basic principles and have access to a source of knowledge to follow up on issues that may consequently be raised.

Case study 1: The importance of contextual knowledge

In a recent consultation with British secondary school teachers about their teaching experiences, one teacher mentioned how some of her Muslim pupils wanted to constantly spit in class during Ramadan, stating that while fasting they were not permitted to swallow their own saliva (Husain, 2007). When the teacher contested their actions, these pupils from the British Somali community became aggressive and accused the teacher of 'dissing' their religion. At first the teacher tried to explain that spitting was not allowed in the classroom irrespective of who was doing it.

Unsure of how to adequately resolve the situation and understanding that additional information was needed, the teacher discussed the situation with her colleagues. A Muslim colleague of South Asian origin then explained some of the different interpretations and practices that take place during Ramadan. In the presence of the Muslim colleague the teacher then spoke to the pupils who were involved and explained that swallowing saliva did not invalidate the fast. The understanding reached was that in the classroom there were rules that all pupils had to abide by and that while she respected the pupils' fasting practices, she knew that this particular practice varied across communities and cultures. Because of this variability in practice, they agreed that spitting would be suspended during class. The presence of or knowledge that can be gleaned from a 'cultural expert' is often useful for professionals who may be unfamiliar with the details of cultural and religious practices within families and communities, even if only to highlight differences in practices.

Another example emerges from a national Arab university where the first author taught. A white American convert to Islam took up cudgels with the predominantly foreign faculty staff for continuing classes during Ramadan, instead of suspending them during the Holy month. She was duly informed by an Arab student that her interpretation was wrong and that abstention from normal daytime activities, despite the extra fatigue, was not religiously condoned as a condition to fasting. Unfortunately, however, matters can deteriorate quickly where misunderstandings and miscommunications abound in relation to issues of rigid interpretations of faith, as the following case exemplifies.

Case study 2: The 'anti-Islamic' academic

A non-Muslim academic visited a Muslim social work student on placement for a routine supervisory session. During this visit the academic enthusiastically commented on population demographics, moving on to expand on the topic of increasing longevity in most developed countries. The student retorted that according to her understanding of the Qur'an the lifespan of individuals could not exceed a certain age (70 years old). Perplexed by this anachronistic point of view, the academic pointed out that the demographics of their particular society showed that this was far from the case, but on the contrary proved a generally accepted point. She went on to offer the explanation that of course when the Qur'an was written 70 years would probably have seemed the maximum age any human could reach. The Bible held the same opinion, but clearly this was no longer true for people living in the modern age.

The student angrily retorted that the Qur'an was written 'for all time' and its words were not just relevant to one historical period. The academic, realising she had inadvertently put a foot wrong, apologised for any offence caused but suggested that perhaps the student would care to check the demographic figures for herself.

Assuming that all was now peacefully resolved, the academic was later very bewildered to discover that the student had decided to publicly denounce her to numerous other Muslim students as 'anti-Islamic'. This allegation served to escalate classroom tensions to the point of achieving severe disruption for the rest of the semester, to the detriment of the students and the academic alike.

The last pillar of Islam is the pilgrimage to the *Ka'aba* in Mecca, Saudi Arabia. Taking place at a particular time of the year, millions of Muslims will travel, at least once in their lifetime, to perform the rituals of the *hajj*. Ancient Arab rites have thus been transformed and sacralised into the ultimate spiritual experience for Muslims. The *hajj* is not only a purification ritual but also unifying ritual: a coming together of Muslims from all over the world and thus affirming the existence of the *ummah*. Such unity, for instance, profoundly affected the black activist, Malcolm X, on his pilgrimage in 1964, where he experienced 'the equality of all believers regardless of race, tribe, or nation' (Esposito, 2002, p 54).

While the *hajj* remains the ultimate pilgrimage for all Muslims, there are other pilgrimages that are of relevance to different denominations. Certain local and cultural variants of Islam incorporate visits to the shrines of saints, and in particular the visitation of the holy sites in Iraq is strongly associated with Shi'a Muslims. Such differences are not generally known about beyond the Muslim world, although invasion and sectarian violence has revealed both the diversity and tensions that exist between denominations within the monolithic concept of Islam.

Although differences in the practice of fundamental duties do exist, the five pillars of Islam, *shahadah*, *salat*, *zakat*, *saum* and *hajj* are the unifying threads that bind the *ummah* together. In so doing they provide a set of core rituals and practices that enable consistency and continuity to exist on both spiritual and historical levels.

Sacred spaces

In every social grouping there is a specific ideology or frame of reference that is used to form and structure society and to establish the boundaries of that social structure. This is also true for the groupings of Muslim societies within the overarching notion of the *ummah*, where to 'be' and 'live' as a Muslim entails defining clear boundaries governing social activities. One basic division, not unique to Muslim societies, is that of 'public and private space'. The public space is male dominated, and the private space, being dominated by family life, is comprised in general of the 'world of women' (Mernissi, 1983); this is a topic we revisit in more detail in Chapters Four and Five in drawing out the implications for women and children.

Furthermore, public spaces within Muslim communities can be further divided into two distinct spaces: the socio-economic and the socio-sacral. The latter space within Muslim communities is the mosque, which serves not only as a religious space for performing the rituals of prayers but is also a social space (Al-Krenawi, 2016). As a religious space, the mosque facilitates and strengthens the spiritual bond between an individual and the divine entity. As a social space the mosque provides a space where people can gather to discuss religious, social and political issues. As discussed in Chapter Three, this is the supreme space of social reconciliation where believers seek empowerment and reconciliation as a collective.

Mosque attendance is largely a mandatory male activity; although most purpose-built mosques have a separate section for women, many carry out their devotions at home owing to gendered domestic commitments. This is a possible consequence of the ideological division of public and private spaces into male and female domains, although this too carries cultural implications. In some countries, such as Senegal, women are forbidden entry into mosques altogether, although in others, mosques are open to both sexes equally. Certainly, some mosques in Britain will not allow women into the male sections of mosques even outside of prayer times, as this scathing observation from a Muslim woman makes clear:

'When I converted to Islam 20 years ago I was refused entry into a Mosque purely for being a woman. It happened to me last year and several times in between. "No space" is the comment that usually comes back coldly and without emotion. It's become the norm for some, men and women. The status quo continues, few people seem to be taking on the issue and championing women's right to worship in the House of God.' (Julie Siddiqi, personal correspondence with main author)

Culturally accepted by some, this division remains a contentious issue with Muslim women's groups, who argue against this practice by using the example of the *Ka'aba* in Mecca, where men and women pray side by side as equals before Allah.

In the contemporary era with purpose-built mosques in every major British city, the nature and function of the mosque has not changed but instead has been expanded, with some mosques providing a range of social support as well as religious education for children. As elsewhere mosque attendance remains largely a male activity with some mosques in Britain not providing any space for women to worship. This issue was sensationally highlighted in the media when a women's group vocally campaigned to be permitted into such mosques and was followed avidly by camera crews. Predictably it was also raised in a speech on multiculturalism by former Prime Minister Tony Blair in terms of British values (Blair, 2006).

It should also be noted, however, that the wider development of mosques on the British landscape has altered over time. The first real mosques pre-dated the initial wave of Muslim migrants in the twentieth century. Proper mosques, however, had already been established in the cosmopolitan cities of London and Liverpool in the late nineteenth century under the energetic patronage of a Dr Leitner, a Hungarian academic and Orientalist, and 'Shaykh Abdulla' Quilliam, an English convert to Islam, appointed by the Shah of Persia as his consul for Liverpool (Nielsen, 1999, p 4). Nonetheless, in general, mosques evolved in Britain from the more common arrangement of creating a place of worship in houses, following the need for a sacred space by male migrant workers from Muslim countries (Peach, 2006).

Sex segregation nevertheless carries further ramifications in relation to worship and gender differentials. Muslims are required to pray at the designated time, wherever they are. To enable this, the mosque's sacred space is easily transferred to the prayer rug which functions as a transportable sacred space permitting believers to recreate the link with the divine anywhere. For women who do not go or are not allowed into mosques, the prayer rug is their only way to create the sacred space needed to perform the prayer ritual. However, as Nielsen notes, given this gender segregation it has not been uncommon for the content of prayers to be quite different between men and women, in which those of women are considered far less authentic and more superstitiously grounded than the more profound piety of men (Nielsen, 1999, p 23). Thus we can see that equal entry to mosques by females along with males carries implications in terms of physical access and access to sacred content, which accordingly affects the status of pious Muslim women in relation to the dominant male elite in the *ummah*.

Gender and Islam

Debating the status of women in Muslim societies has inspired volumes of speech and script, often descending into endless and all-consuming preoccupation of comparison and contrast – and usually focused on women' dress, particularly the veiling of Muslim women, as the *main* signifier of difference in gender politics. The topic of women's status invites the utterance of banalities in creating caricatures to attack rather than a more analytical unpicking of the nuances of gender as normative social performance.

Some Muslim feminists have analysed the concept of veiling in great detail, noting how the intersection of class, status and denominational affiliation play significant roles. Indeed, it should also be noted that the politicisation and 'Arabisation' of Muslim communities in the west have also had an impact on women's clothing. Suffice to say, at this point that the appropriation of women and, in particular, their bodies as symbolic spaces to be elevated, debased or to be fought over is not a uniquely Muslim concept but one that is as old as patriarchy itself (Lerner, 1986; Minh-ha, 1989; Jeffery, 1998).

The underlying fact is that the Qur'anic revelations did not modify the prevailing social conditions governing elementary kinship structures, the control of sexuality and the distribution of wealth and power in a society (Levi-Strauss, 1967). This is certainly not unique to Muslim societies and Lerner states that patriarchy, or the gendered distribution of power in societies, is a historical phenomenon that 'arose out of a biological determined given and became a culturally created and enforced structure over time' (Lerner, 1986, p 42).

Within the Muslim world polemics on this issue range widely. These extend from the conservative discourses, such as *Wahabism*, which is supported by political structures in countries such as Saudi Arabia. Conservative scholars, like Maududi, from South Asia, declare that a woman's 'natural' place is in the home as mother and nurturer. In contrast feminist discourses challenge this orthodoxy, as well as western feminist discourses of female oppression (Mernissi, 1983; Ait Sabbah, 1986; Maududi, 1986). Many of these issues are developed in more detail in Chapter Four. However, in the brief discussion permitted here, we argue that the situation of 'women in Islam' should be examined in the context of each society and every ethno-cultural group. In the battle for female emancipation, whether in the 'west' or in 'Islam', the biological, anthropological, historical and socio-cultural condition of women has yet to be completely mastered (Arkoun, 1994).

Culture, faith and tradition

The different levels and layers of history, ethnicity, culture, tradition, ideology and denomination all contribute to creating what can be viewed as an unvarying, unified Islam and *ummah*. As one slowly peels away the onion-skin layers, it becomes apparent that, although marginal voices call for some kind of return to a pure Islam and *ummah* that existed during the time of the Prophet, the original framework was strictly coloured by the local context that existed at the time the revelations were received by Mohammed. Therefore, in discussing Islam or Muslims it is imperative to establish the precise contextual references. In the Muslim world, the notion of a monolithic Islam, devoid of cultural nuance and traditional texture, conflates diversity, as does the stereotype of a single essentialising characteristic defining the so-called 'west'. Consequently, it would be obvious to most that when speaking of the notorious cartoons of Mohammed, it is nonsensical to refer to them as 'the European cartoon affair' when it initially involved the Danish media. However, the sensationalisation of this issue by others, such as the *Charlie Hebdo* magazine in France and the bombings in Paris and Brussels is leading to an entrenchment of the divisive view which pits two monoliths – the 'west' and 'Islam' – against each other.

Moreover, the dichotomy inherent in the idea of 'us' versus 'them', or 'the west' versus 'Islam', is one that is exploited by extreme voices on both sides of the divide. Consequently, for 'Islamic' extremists and conservative clerics, as well as the political neo-conservatives and extreme nationalist movements (such as Britain First), the notion of static and closed social communities is used as a convenient untruth that serves both sides equally well in promoting self-serving agendas.

Denominational diversity

Denominationally, Islam is as rich and diverse as the variety of branches of Christianity. The first split in the *ummah* took place soon after the death of the Prophet. The conservative branch of Sunni Islam accepted the leadership of the three orthodox Caliphs, while the Shi'a rejected these three Caliphs and recognised the Prophet's son-in-law, Ali (appointed as the fourth Caliph), as the first *Imam* and the legitimate spiritual heir to Mohammed. This divide is significant and resonates deeply within the global *ummah* with some *Sunni* sects claiming that *Shi'a* are 'non-Muslims'. Certain Muslim countries have been marked by sectarian Sunni–Shi'a violence, with the majority Shi'a countries being Iran, Iraq and Yemen. These sectarian differences have been played out on the global stage in Iraq; in Pakistan armed groups on both sides have been involved in Sunni–Shi'a violence for decades. In recent years, on the political and military stages, this divide has become more pronounced, exemplified by Bahrain's suppression of its Shi'a population with impunity, the civil war in Syria and the rise of Daesh, together with the Saudi bombing of Yemen against the Shi'a Houthis and the escalating stand-off between Wahabi Sunni Saudi Arabia (along with its satellite Gulf nations) and Iran, with its Shi'a majority.

Within the Sunni tradition there are four main schools of thought and jurisprudence; however, the differences between these groups are minor. The majority of Muslims in Britain are Sunni, and it is worth noting that Sunni and Shi'a mosques are distinct, with worshippers frequenting their denominational mosques, similar to the ways that Catholics and Anglicans frequent their own churches. The Shi'a tradition comprises the majority Twelve Imam Shi'as and the Ismailis. There are further distinct groups of Ismailis, such as the *Alevis* who are Twelve Imam Shi'as and reside mainly in Turkey and Syria. Apart from these main Shi'a groups there are other smaller, related sects that are localised minorities within larger Muslim societies.

Away from the dogmatic definitions and the conservative ritualisation of religious practice, there arose another current in Islam, that of ascetic mysticism known as *Sufism*, which today continues to attract many converts in the west (Esposito, 2002). Marked by a pure devotion to God and love for humanity, Sufism is practised by both sexes and is characterised by the influence of poetry and devotional music. David Waines (2003) sets out the often tortuous but profoundly spiritual 'inner' path of Sufism by drawing on the legendary tale of Hayy b Yazqan, an allegory written by the multi-talented Abu Bakh Ibn Tufayl, a philosopher, teacher and physician born near Granada, al-Andalus, in the year 581 BCE. In the story, the hero Yazqan starts life as a feral child reared by a doe, yet through innate human ingenuity, aided by sense data, finally attains a state of enlightened and ecstatic metaphysical wisdom (Waines, 2003, pp 133–4).

Sufi sects exist in most Muslim countries and in some instances their influence permeates into localised socio-cultural practices. Equally, however, Sufism is open to adopting new, local practices, and consequently has been criticised for this and for their devotional focus that considers emphases on 'laws, rules, duties, and rights to be spiritually lacking' (Esposito, 2002, p 57).

As mentioned, a contrasting denomination that has become highly influential in recent decades is Wahabism, the majority Sunni sect in Saudi Arabia. It is characterised by orthodox purity and, in the view of many, conspicuously tribal traditions regarding gender rights. Nonetheless, its message is increasingly promoted via proselytising initiatives, generous endowments to educational institutions, and the building of mosques, not forgetting the high regard the *ummah* has for Saudi Arabia as the guardian of the holiest shrines (the *Ka'aba* in Mecca and the Prophet's mosque in Medina) in Islam. It has, however, also achieved some notoriety in relation to the association with Osama bin Laden (Esposito, 2002). Historically the iconoclastic Wahabism has known a bloody past in its puritanical quest for purity, waging war on Muslim dissenters and unforgettably destroying many sacred Islamic sites, including 'the sacred tombs of Muhammad and his Companions in Mecca and Medina' (Esposito, 2002, pp 51–2). John Esposito goes on to add that this legacy inspired the Taliban's deplorable, philistine destruction of the superb, ancient Buddhist sites that Afghanistan once boasted of, and which was duly condemned by Muslim leaders worldwide. This vandalism has been followed by another atrocious act, this time by Daesh of the destruction of significant parts of Palmyra, the ancient Syrian World Heritage site accompanied by the ritualistic murder of the Palmyran scholar, Khaled al-Asaad, the octogenarian archaeologist and long-time protector of the site (BBC News, 2015a).

Nationalism and fundamentalism

Radical Islamic movements are a recent development in the history of Islam, which can be traced back to the colonial era in the creation of nations with majority Muslim societies and the secularisation of political discourses. The notion of Islamic 'fundamentalism' includes many groups, which combine religious revivalism with political ideology together with social welfare, offering an alternative to secularised ideologies.

Up until the 1970s these revivalist movements were localised and existed within the context of nation states where groups, such as the Muslim Brotherhood in Egypt, filled a vacuum created by secular regimes that had failed to provide a sense of identity or educational and social welfare structures that would benefit the poor and needy. Therefore, underlying the creation of these movements was a class struggle and a sense of social justice that sought to follow Islamic principles to improve the social condition of the impoverished and illiterate majorities. Certainly, these movements also viewed historical developments as part of a greater cosmic struggle between good and evil, between the righteous who followed Islam 'properly' and those who corrupted or rejected it.

Three major factors have contributed to the expansion of these movements from contextualised local politico-religious movements to international players with an increasingly strong grip on the consciousness of a global *ummah*. The first factor was increasing levels of repression in their home nations, which led many leaders into exile and settlement in the west where they were able to express their ideologies with more freedom. The second factor was the broader struggle between western democracy and communism. This led to the funding and creation of the *Mujhadeen* (Holy Warriors) in the 1970s, to fight the invading forces of the Soviet Union in Afghanistan in support of the repressive but capsizing Afghan government. The third and final factor was the post-colonial migration of large segments of the *ummah* to western European countries where the consequences of migration, settlement and minority status have strengthened the voice for a unified global *ummah*.

The extraordinarily misconceived and tragic modern history of Afghanistan is one worth reviewing in relation to its complexity and the later ramifications that continue to throw a malignant pall over world events today. From 1979 to 1989 the Soviet occupiers of Afghanistan, being both communist and atheist, were strongly opposed by Afghan resistance leaders preaching *jihad* (the meaning of which indicates the struggle to follow a virtuous, moral life and one free from injustice and oppression, which may or may not include armed opposition)

(Esposito, 2002, p 117). Their followers, the *Mujhadeen* were trained, armed and funded through western assistance, channelled via Pakistan's military intelligence agency, specifically under the direction of the US President, Ronald Reagan, and aided by the more modest assistance from then British Prime Minister, Margaret Thatcher – both viewed as 'enthusiastic' supporters of the Afghan *jihad* (Waines, 2003, p 270).

Thus was created the most unholy alliance of competing and lethal intervention from the Soviet and opposing western alliance, synergised with Muslim zeal, in the form of a rising, international cadre of Muslim resistance fighters ready to sacrifice their lives in the *jihad* and to free part of their *ummah* from oppression and occupation. Elements of the *Mujhadeen* would eventually mutate into the infamous Taliban, but in the meantime the fallout in terms of the death toll and social upheaval of the Afghan conflict was enormous (Waines, 2003, p 273).

The Taliban imposed their own conservative interpretation of Islam upon the hostage Afghan nation through strict *shari'a* law and forcing women out of the public[2] sphere (Raqib and Barreto, 2014). However, the notion of returning Afghanistan to its purer, uncontaminated religious roots was a convenient Taliban myth, which overlooked the complex, cultural forms of indigenous Afghan *Pashtunwali*, which for instance, promoted strong notions of hospitality, as well as restorative forms of justice regarded as reconciliatory rather than solely retributive (Raqib and Barreto, 2014).

Afghanistan was embroiled in an even bloodier conflict following the al-Qaeda attack on the World Trade Center Building in New York on 11 September 2001 (9/11), when the Bush administration pronounced an ultimatum that the Taliban were to hand bin Laden and his cronies over to the US or face military action (Waldman, 2014). Although the Taliban were thought to be consequently defeated in 2001, violent Taliban insurgence continued in Afghanistan, leading to a high presence of NATO and US peacekeeping forces with significant losses of troops.[3] Given entrenched resistance by the Taliban, and no doubt having learned hard lessons from the bloody Troubles in Northern Ireland, British policy altered in 2008 towards recognising that reconciliation with the Taliban was required for peace: a dramatic *volte face* that was not accepted by the US for some time owing to its sensitivity (Waldman, 2014). Now with the returning vigour of the Taliban, along with the increasingly worrying developments in the region, the importance of such talks is being reemphasised.

Yet since then the power and territory held by al-Qaeda has been greatly eclipsed by the unexpected success and psychopathic aggression of Daesh, whose proclaimed jihadist mission is to establish by force a global caliphate based on fundamental notions of law (Cockburn, 2014). To clarify, Daesh emerged as an off-shoot of al-Qaeda (the latter later disassociating itself from the former) in the ferment of destabilisation in the Middle East against a backdrop of despotic regimes. The tyrannical corruption of these regimes generated the Arab Spring resistance and critically, the inflammable interference of the US and its allies on their crusade against terrorism. The now notorious issue of 'weapons of mass destruction', allegedly held by Saddam Hussein, provided the excuse to depose a tyrant but left a dangerous power vacuum in Iraq with an exponential rise in insurgent terrorist attacks (Stern and Berger, 2015). The long awaited Chilcot Report (2016) on Britain's involvement in the Iraq war confirmed what critics had long asserted, that there was insufficient justification for invasion and resulting anarchy leading to the deaths of a minimum number of 150,000 Iraqi civilians and the displacement of over a million people (Chilcot, 2016). The west cherished a fruitless wish to depose the Syrian military dictator, General Assad, suspected of supporting al-Qaeda jihadists in Iraq (Weiss and Hassan, 2015). However, the widespread torture and bloodshed inflicted on his people created divided loyalties regarding whether Assad or the Daesh caliphate form the worse fate for many Syrians (Stern and Berger, 2015). In the meantime the United Nations (UN) has warned of the fate of the ethnically diverse Iraqi population in the continuing conflict and the staggering number of civilian deaths, capture or displacement suffered there (UN, 2016).

It is important to note that a murderously stark dichotomy is drawn by Daesh between the followers of fundamentalist Wahhabian Sunni Muslims and everyone else, including non-Wahhabian Sunnis, Shi'a and Sufi Muslims, condemned as *Takfir* (unbelievers and apostates) and all non-Muslims (Cockburn, 2014). Interestingly personal letters found following bin Laden's death expressed his deep concern at Jihadist groups attacking fellow Muslims (Stern and Berger, 2015). Accordingly, although the media devote considerable space to Daesh, the real threat may not be to the west but to the pan-Muslim world and freedom from sectarian persecution. In this vein, Stern and Berger (2015, p 256) quote King Abdullah of Jordan who describes this as a 'Muslim problem' to be 'owned' and solved by Muslims.

The jihadist mission is fuelled in large part by perceived injustices to the Muslim *ummah* as enacted in social and civil conflict globally. A prominent issue for many people, whether Muslim or not, is the continuing and intolerable Israeli–Palestinian conflict, which has seen the Palestinian territories shrink dramatically over the years owing to Israeli incursions, as easily accessible maps show. The plight of those living in occupied Palestinian territories (oPt) has generated much media coverage, human rights critique and general outrage from a concerned public regarding what appear to be disproportionate levels of Israeli retaliation on civilian areas in the wake of *Intifadas* (Palestinian uprisings). Trauma and severe post-traumatic stress disorder affect the Palestinian population with the greatest brunt shouldered by children, women and elders (Shalhoub-Kervokian and Khsheiboun, 2009). Some Israeli apologists have in turn argued that anti-Semitism lies at the heart of much international critique of Israel, irrespective of whether critics are *goyim*[4] or Jews themselves (Gardener, 2007). Such accusations make the unfortunate conflation of anti-Zionism with anti-Semitism, which is not at all the same thing, the latter being clearly racist and would include all Semite groups, of which Arabs are of course members.

Jerusalem, the holy city for all the Abrahamic religions – Jews, Christians and Muslims – provides a good example of local hardships borne. Here Palestinian areas are ghettoised (with all that that implies) by very high walls, often topped by barbed wire, snaking throughout the city, cutting off neighbourhoods and families from each other. Armed checkpoints slowly funnel the Palestinian public through, including children trying to reach their schools and adults their workplace or families. Checkpoints are actively unpleasant, being long and wearying as well as uncertain (people can be and are turned back) and seem to constitute more than anything an exercise in daily ritual humiliation (Ashencaen Crabtree, 2015).

In terms of human services Lindsay (2012) comments that the Palestinian Authorities have responsibility for offering education and health services together with social services in the oPt, although as might be expected these operate under extremely arduous and troubling professional and civic conditions. The highly deleterious impact on the very fragile, local Palestinian economy by Israeli control of Palestinian imports and exports in addition to restricted access of movement on the grounds of 'security first' has also been critiqued (Agnew, 2012, p 121; Sherwood, 2013). A wider examination of this tragic situation is unfortunately beyond the scope of this book; however, a professional network entitled 'Palestinian–UK Social Work' offers an opportunity for British social workers to meet their Palestinian counterparts and learn more about the situation (see 'Useful websites and resources') at the end of the book.

Finally, we consider the less known but highly desperate plight of the Rohingya Muslim minority ethnic group in Myanmar. This internationally recognised and long established minority population was subject to severe persecution in Myanmar for decades by Buddhist nationalists – a religious philosophy not normally associated with violently racist oppression. The Rohingya were stripped of their citizenship status by the Myanmar government in 1982 thereby becoming 'Stateless' (Southwick, 2015) and consequently disenfranchised from the vote. Since then they have been subjected to violence and assaults on their persons, their identity and culture. In 2012 140,000 Rohingya people were displaced and detained in enforced camps where severe malnutrition and medical neglect causes high mortality rates (Amnesty International, 2015; Zarni and Cowley, 2014). The Myanmar government have recently banned the humanitarian service, Médecins Sans Frontières, from continuing their work providing healthcare to the Rohingya, and where additionally UN and Red Cross workers have been forced to leave as well (Southwick, 2015). Many thousands of other Rohingya refugees have made desperate attempts to flee the country for refuge in Malaysia, Indonesia and Thailand, under extremely hazardous trafficking conditions (Human Rights Watch, 2015). Taken altogether these State organised or condoned oppressions are clearly suggestive of genocide, leaving the international press to question why Myanmar's famous cause célèbre, Nobel Prize winner and pillar of rectitude, Aung San Suu Kyi, has remained so ominously silent to-date on the issue (Hume, 2014; Hasan, 2015; Perria, 2015). In the meantime, the Organization of Islamic Cooperation ('OIC') representing numerous Muslim countries have appealed strongly to the Myanmar government to observe the human rights of the Rohingya and restore their citizenship status.

Migration and Muslim communities in Europe

The migration of Muslims to continental Europe has followed a similar pattern in which, according to Nielsen (1999), four main waves of migration have occurred. The first founded historical Andalucía under the Moors. The second was that of the Mongol armies, which overran much of the Balkan states in the thirteenth century, destroyed Baghdad, a famous seat of Islamic intellectualism, along with other Islamic cities (Masood, 2009), and whose permanent residents in the former USSR (Union of Soviet Socialist Republics) would be known as the Tatars. The great Ottoman Empire was the next in line and would leave a residual Turkish population, mostly around Eastern Europe and Greece. Modern Europe is now experiencing the fourth and latest wave, and in this section we will primarily concentrate on the post-colonial migration to the UK, before a brief review of the situation in Continental Europe.

The majority of Muslims in the UK are of South Asian origin and arrived in the UK to fill acute labour shortages in British industry, particularly in the textile towns in the North of England. Another surge of migration took place in the 1970s when East African Asians arrived in the UK after expulsion from Uganda under the dictatorship of Idi Amin, as well as from other countries such as Kenya, Tanzania, Zimbabwe and Malawi. The last major migration of Muslims occurred in the 1980s and was from particular areas of Bangladesh. Most of the early migrants from South Asia were young men and family reunification took place at a later date. Nielsen notes that a study of the Pakistani community in Oxford showed that the women were keen to join their menfolk to '"save" them from moral corruption', some of whom were establishing relations with local Englishwomen and on occasion contracting marriage as well (Nielsen, 1999, p 27).

Muslims of South Asian origin are mostly Sunni Muslims from Pakistan, comprising a significant population from the Mirpur district of Kashmir. The large Bangladeshi community is primarily from the Syleth region and have settled mostly in the East End of London. This has long been a traditional settlement area for migrants, such as the seventeenth-century Huguenot refugees, as well as Jewish migrants, and now Bangladeshis followed by Somalis. Other Muslim groups have arrived from multiple locations, such as the Turkish, Kurdish, Iranian, Iraqi and Moroccan communities, as well as those from different African countries including Somalia, Sudan and Nigeria, not forgetting the former Balkan states: Bosnians and Albanians, in addition to white Anglo-Saxon converts to Islam.

Thus, practitioners should consider the different countries of origin, and the cultural-specific as well as regional-specific factors that have an impact in different ways on the way faith is manifested. Even within the same groups, such as Muslims of Pakistani origin, linguistic and denominational differences as well as levels of education have a significant influence on how Islam is promoted and practised.

To reiterate, the majority of the Muslim population of the UK is concentrated in large urban areas, although until the last census in 2001, there were only estimates given of the overall number of Muslims in the general population. According to new census information, the demographics show an increase in Muslims from 2.7 per cent of the general population in 2001, with at least 68 per cent of the Muslim population being of South Asian origin (Indian, Pakistani and Bangladeshi) to the 2011 National Census where now, 'Muslims form 4.8 per cent of the population in England and Wales. The population has increased from 1.55 million in 2001 to 2.71 million in 2011. There are 77,000 Muslims in Scotland and 3,800 in Northern Ireland…and where 47 per cent are UK-born' (MCB, 2015, p 6).

The latest Census data also indicates that in the Muslim ethnic categories 'black African, black other' and 'Asian other' are growing, while the Pakistani and Bangladeshi figures are falling (MCB, 2015).

The majority of the Muslim population in the UK has to-date been Sunni, but there are no clear estimates of the numbers of different denominations. According to Peach (2006), based on the vernacular languages used in mosques, the majority are defined not just by denomination but by the use of a South Asian language or dialect; whether that remains the case is unclear.

The diversity of Muslim communities in the UK is reflected in the range of practices and the development of mosques, where there are a wide range of Sunni mosques that are affiliated with different denominations. In the recent past plans to build a mosque by the Tabligh-i-Jamaat in the East End of London were rejected, as the local Bangladeshi Muslim population, along with other local communities, felt that it was a radical movement. Mosques in Britain have been divided by linguistic and regional differences, for example sermons in mosques in the East End of London might be delivered in Bengali or Sylethi (a regional dialect) as the majority of the congregation is of Bangladeshi origin.

Within the Shi'a community, which traditionally establish *Imambargahs*, a place of worship but also where the martyrdom of Imam Husain[5] is commemorated, the language in which sermons are delivered will depend on the linguistic background of the congregation. Certainly Sunni and Shi'a will, if the option is available, worship in their own religious spaces, much as Anglicans, Roman Catholics and Baptists, for example, tend to do.

For Shi'a Muslims there is always the fear of marginalisation and reprisal, based on historic events together with current perceptions of the faith. Those who listen regularly to the news will have heard of the Shi'a–Sunni conflicts in Iraq as well as Pakistan, but there is also a tendency for these tensions to be played out within the wider Muslim community. While these differences are often hidden and sometimes marginal, contextualising the wide range of Muslim communities as a monolithic whole may lead to great insensitivities, not only for social care practice, but also in the overall understanding of how Islam is interpreted and practised by different groups.

When they came to power in 1997 the Labour government attempted to create a unified voice for all Muslims in the UK, assisting in the establishment of the Muslim Council of Britain. For the government this eased their ability to communicate with 'the Muslim community', but many Muslims, and in particular those from minority denominations, felt that they could not identify with such an organisation and regarded its establishment as a matter of political expediency rather than as a sincere effort to engage in genuine dialogue.

The Muslim population in Britain suffers from significant socio-economic and educational disadvantages. In particular, the asylum seeker and refugee communities, such as the Somali community, remain the most vulnerable in society. The profile of the British Muslim population has remained consistent for over a decade at least, being characterised by a strong family formation, high rates of marriage and a larger household. In 2005 it was estimated that 33 per cent of the population were under the age of 16 with a variation of 38 per cent for Bangladeshi Muslims (TUC, 2005). A more recent survey reported very similar findings where 33 per cent of British Muslims are aged 15 or under (MCB, 2015).

According to the Muslim Council of Britain's (MCB, 2015) useful statistical data mining sets of Census information, the British Muslim population is regarded as generally less well qualified than other comparator groups, where 26 per cent of Muslims have no qualifications compared to Sikhs (standing at 13.2 per cent) and Hindus (standing at 19.4 per cent). This forms an interesting contrast to the US picture where it is estimated from a 2009 Gallup report that of 1.4 million Muslim adults (Graham et al, 2010), Muslims have the second highest rate of education among major religions (Council on Foreign Relations, 2011). In Britain the Muslim population is hampered by higher rates of unemployment and economic inactivity compared to the general population, where only 19.2 per cent are in full-time employment. However, employment rates for Muslim women have improved over the years, with 29 per cent of younger women (16–24 years) compared to over 50 per cent in the general population. During the important career-track years of 25–49, nearly 56 per cent of British Muslim women are employed compared to 80 per cent in the general population (MCB, 2015). The overall picture of the number of British Muslim children living in workless households remains a prominent issue (Children and Young People Now, 2003). Of the minority ethnic (ME) populations in the UK (distinct from refugee and asylum seeker communities), the Bangladeshi community is the most disadvantaged in terms of housing, education and income (Platt, 2002).

Other parts of Europe show some similarities with this depressing picture, as well as some significant differences; nonetheless increasingly mass immigration is being framed as a threat to both European infrastructure and civil harmony.

The Muslim population in France reflects its colonial past (as is true of Britain), in that the majority of Muslim migrants settling in France came originally from existing and former areas of influence in North-West Africa, particularly Morocco, Algeria and Tunisia. Apart from these Maghreb Muslims, other Muslims would follow in the 1970s, such as Turks and black African Muslims from Mali, Mauritania and Senegal (Wihtol de Wenden, 1996, p 53).

The challenge for the *ummah* in France has related to the underprivileged position of French Muslims in general, where education levels have been low and unemployment figures high. The secular values underpinning the Republic may constitute an additional ideological obstacle to overcome. Interestingly, while the French government notes the 'problematic' of Muslims residing in France, no official statistics are collected on religious affiliation or ethnicity. In a survey of French Muslims and the general French population it was found that there were high levels of agreement (72 per cent and 74 per cent respectively) that there was no conflict between being a devout Muslim and modernity (Ajala, 2014). This is compared with the far lower rates of agreement between British Muslims (47 per cent) and the general British public (35 per cent).

In this vein, a poll conducted in the US reveals that American Muslims appear to be more assimilated into society than those in Britain and Europe (McAskill, 2007). The role of social class and education are often overlooked in these discussions. Unskilled Muslims migrated from rural and poor areas to Europe primarily to fill labour market gaps in industry and manufacturing following the Second World War. The US visa system prioritised access for those who were educated and this is a factor in the attribution of the better living standards experienced by the *ummah* in the US, in addition to the higher levels of religion in American society. While religiosity in American society is more accepted, since the attacks on the World Trade Center there has been a steady increase in anti-Muslim sentiment. More recently, with the rise of Donald Trump as the Republican candidate for the 2016 elections, the animosity against Muslims has found a fervent voice that appeals to particular sections of US society.

Spain continues to have a poignant passion for its Islamic past, which, it is argued, is one that is both idealised and ahistorical in the minds of most people of Spanish descent, who are proud to claim their stake in such a romantic, ethnically diverse and richly cultured past (Abumalham, 1996). Yet, apparently this is sharply delineated by a very different and pervasive attitude towards deprived Muslim minority groups in contemporary Spain. Unlike the educated, discreet and assimilated Muslim professionals in Spanish society, labouring Muslim Maghrebian migrants are in danger of being seen as an underclass of social undesirables, living in shanty towns, 'ignorant of the Spanish language and social norms', who, due to 'labour marginalization' problems, tend towards criminal activities in relation to smuggling and drug trafficking (Abumalham, 1996, p 29). However, encouragingly in Andalusia, the gateway into Southern Spain for North African migrants (Paloma et al, 2014), new co-existence initiatives are being put forward by the local government and Spanish social workers to facilitate integration between established residents and migrants, which appears to be showing some success in easing community segregation and tensions (Calvo et al, 2014).

In Eastern Europe the multicultural, intellectual harmony that existed in Sarajevo, Bosnia, has been compared to that of the glories of medieval, Islamic

Spain prior to the ferocious, ethnic-cleansing Serbian attacks stridently encouraged by the nationalist Serbian President, Slobodan Milošević, on their Muslim neighbours: 'Our hauntingly beautiful, beloved Bosnia became a symbol of intractable ethnic hatred and hyper-intolerance, of all that is worst in the human community' (Shenk, 2006, p 8).

As David Waines recalls, barbarity and cruelty laid to waste this peaceful and productive society culminating in the worst massacre since the Second World War when 7,000 Muslim men and boys were slaughtered in Sreberenica (2003, p 207).

Germany hosts the second largest number of Muslims in Europe, although unlike France and Britain this is not owed to its former imperialist influences, but rather to the modern labour market. In the 1960s Muslim immigrants, mostly from Turkey, arrived in the capacity of cheap *Gastarbeiter* (guest-workers) (Waines, 2003, p 258). Although the assumption of many migrants was that they would eventually return to their homeland, the second generation who were born in Germany are now taking up German citizenship and establishing themselves in society more firmly than their parents did. One irony for Turkish migrants specifically, is that they may have felt more able to practise their religion freely in Germany than they were able to do in Turkey, which was strongly influenced by the sweeping secular reforms of Kemal Ataturk in the early twentieth century (Henkel, 2004). Viewed ambivalently by many Muslims globally, Ataturk established the modern Turkish state, abolished the spiritual leadership of Sunni Muslims (the Caliphate), and replaced *shari'a* with European laws (Fuller and Lesser, 1995, p 39; Waines, 2003, p 221).

German immigration policies have promoted a friendly 'open door', 'Willkommenskultur' towards mass migration under Chancellor Angela Merkel, where a million refugees of various nationalities and faiths entered Germany in 2015 alone (Elliott and Treanor, 2016). This policy has stood in marked contrast to those of other European countries, like the UK (Asch, 2015), and even otherwise liberal Denmark (Bendixen, 2016). However, Merkel's policy has been seriously questioned by the German media and public following the widely reported attacks on scores of German women and girls out celebrating New Year's Eve 2015, by aggressive gangs of apparently North African immigrants, fanning both anti-immigration and right-wing nationalist flames in the country (Connolly, 2016; *Der Spiegel*, 2016).

In terms of Muslim immigration to the Netherlands, initially the Dutch assumed that past strategies of maintaining a policy of *equal but different*, in which specific social, political, religious and cultural groups lived and worked in separate 'social compartments', would also work in the case of Muslim migrants (Gowricharn and Mungra, 1996, p 116). This tactic employed the concept of 'pillarisation', in which minority groups could achieve an upwardly mobile, vertical thrust through the influence and help of peers further up the hierarchy (Gowricharn and Mungra, 1996; Spruyt, 2007).

Such a strategy worked for other religious groups such as the Catholics in Dutch society, but pillarisation has yet to succeed in the case of Muslim migrants.

A partial explanation is that groups are far less internally homogenised than the Dutch Catholics. In addition, they do not have a sufficient vertical infrastructure to create an effective pillar in the first place due to on-going educational and economic problems, despite the rise of some Muslim politicians and the increase of second- and third-generation Moroccan and Turkish Dutch social workers entering the professions (Gowricharn and Mungra, 1996; Spruyt, 2007; Hendriks et al, 2015). However, the generous welfare system in the Netherlands supporting many Muslim migrant families has not successfully ameliorated the yawning divisions between their condition and perspectives of life compared with those of indigenised Dutch citizens, on whose consciousness was being imposed the deeply unpleasant idea that 'second- and third-generation Muslims were less integrated than the first generation' (Spruyt, 2007, p 320), and where some individuals have rallied to the Daesh cause. Citing two recent surveys, Wirz et al (2015) note that 64 per cent of Dutch Muslims surveyed had experienced personal discrimination and that 41 per cent of Dutch majority population surveyed felt that Islam and a 'westernised' way of life were incompatible.

Finally, Britain, like many other European countries, experiences the tension between embracing liberal, multicultural values and the pull towards right-wing nationalist politics, as exemplified by the rhetoric of the English Defence League and the UK Independence Party (Mason, 2016). This serves to crudely demarcate citizens into those that inherently 'belong' and are thereby legitimised, from those that are perceived to be alien outsiders and thereby delegitimised. Such rhetoric deliberately sets up a xenophobic discourse, appealing to some, exploiting pejorative stereotypes that can justify resentment and hostility. However, it is not only the extreme right wing groups that convey such divisive messages. Former Prime Minister, David Cameron, targeted Muslim women migrants on a spousal visa with threats of deportation if they failed to pass a language test two-and-a-half years after arriving in the country as a controversial means of tackling extremism (Mason and Sherwood, 2016; BBC News, 2016).

Politicisation and the quest for identity

In the UK, the Salman Rushdie affair in 1989 marked a turning point in the politicisation of Britain's Muslim communities. As Waines comments, 'It has been observed that had Salman Rushdie's *The Satanic Verses* been written, say, by a Moroccan Muslim and published in France, there would have been no controversy' (Waines, 2003, p 259).

In addition to the Rushdie episode, socio-economic disadvantage, structural racism and the quest for a unifying empowering identity exposed a gaping hole in Britain's multicultural model. This gap in recent years has been quickly filled by marginal and extreme voices that promise strength in a collective voice that is pure and distinct from a local context, in which many Muslims, particularly the young, feel increasingly marginalised. A case in point relates to the alienated response of the Pakistani community in Manchester towards the first Gulf conflict, following Iraq's invasion of Kuwait. Saddam Hussein was duly elevated to a symbolic Muslim hero battling in a righteous *jihad* against the Manichean and crusader force of George Bush and his British allies (Werbner, 1994).

At the time the image of Saddam Hussein taking on the might of the west was apparently an appealing one for much of the Muslim diaspora, however corrupt, brutal and flawed his regime evidently was. This serves to illustrate just how alluring the promise of a *just* society based on Islamic principles is, in being cleansed of 'localised contamination' from a majority non–Muslim social and political structure. Harking back to a 'golden age' of Islam is compelling for those seeking to understand their marginalisation and socio-economic oppression. This powerful image resonates intensely for Muslim populations, who are painfully conscious that hundreds of years of cultural, intellectual and military superiority in preserving and adding to the knowledge of the ancient civilisations came to an end during the period of the Renaissance (Fuller and Lesser, 1995). Europe, having absorbed and been nurtured by these extraordinary examples, was coming of age and would no longer look back for inspiration to the foster parent of eclectic Islamic culture.

Today in Britain, politico–religious, ideological movements have grounded themselves in the localised experiences of Muslim communities and seek the creation of a collective through the individual compliance to rituals and practices. Where secular models have failed these movements have become the voice of political and social change, and to some extent have succeeded in providing a sense of identity, belonging and continuity, as well as an agenda for radical change (Esposito, 2002).

It is argued that these radical movements are in a symbiotic relationship with western nations where a Eurocentric interpretation of Islamic history and of Muslim–Christian history prevails. This history, characterised by fear and disdain, is still present in the consciousness of European Christian nations and is expressed socially and culturally at many levels (Hourani, 1991). Indeed, it is the combination of this fear and the loudness of extreme, opposing voices that provide the headlines for the media in speaking to millions, thereby providing a space where marginal voices become normative but where the majority of 'average' voices are silenced.

It is also asserted, however, that the demise of historical supremacy has left behind a sense of profound loss and trauma in the Muslim collective consciousness (Fuller and Lesser, 1995). The stunning past success in the spread of Islam, which travelled so far from its original birthplace, was regarded by Muslims as an incontrovertible sign of God's favour. Although much of the evangelical rewards were retained, in that so many of the world's population are practising Muslims, Islam's place as a dominant global power decayed, as did over time its great seats of learning through the forces of modernisation, as well as through the impact of colonialism.

Muslim migrants living in the contemporary west are faced with both the general problems of all immigrants in finding their niche in a new society where they may be discriminated against, but additionally have a unique set of obstacles to overcome as well, argues Jørgen Nielsen (1999). First, *shari'a* was never originally visualised as applying to minority Muslim groups living in non-Muslim societies – where the attempt to realise this is clearly problematic (Nielsen, 1999; Waines, 2003). Additionally, the *ummah*, in comprising a wide diversity of people from Asia (including the Middle East), Africa and Europe, inherently creates uncertainties when unravelling which practices are pivotal to Islam, and therefore to be retained and strengthened, over which are traditional, localised customs that may or may not be incompatible with the competing rights and needs of others in a multicultural society (Nielsen, 1999).

Islamophobia

While this is a commonly heard concept it is by no means unambiguous or uncontested (Ashencaen Crabtree, 2014). The term 'Islamophobia' was originally coined in the ground-breaking UK Runnymede Report *Islamophobia: A Challenge for Us All* published in 1977, which went on to outline the main characteristics of this form of prejudice as deeming Islam and its adherents to be,

1. monolithic and static
2. separate and 'other' – not sharing other values
3. inferior to the west
4. an aggressive enemy
5. manipulative
6. critical of the west
7. patriarchal and sexist. (Runnymede Trust, 1997)

In addition to these Taras (2013) has added other prejudicial attributes including the blanket assumption of Muslims as irrational and aggressive, and that Islamic ideology is used for political and military agendas (generally rather than specifically, is the inference here), in addition to an assumption of Muslim intolerance towards western critique – which taken altogether leads to a perception that Muslims deserve to be excluded in society and that anti-Muslim hostility is thereby a natural and normal reaction (Ashencaen Crabtree, 2015).

Islamophobia is a problematic concept in not conforming to the more easily recognised determinants of discrimination (Hussain and Bagguley, 2012), being neither solely prejudice against religious affiliations nor ethnicity (Lorente, 2010). Taras (2013), following Tariq Modood, argues that such discrimination could more accurately be described as 'Muslimophobia', a position that Frost (2012, p 547) might concur with in reference to attitudes of 'hate' towards Muslims as a form of racist ideology and practice carried out along a continuum of harassment and hostility to outright violence. At the less extreme end a range of practices have been described as Islamophobic, including objection to headscarves in educational settings to failure to produce Halal diets in institutional settings (Ashencaen

Crabtree, 2014), while the self-appointed forum for British Muslims, the so-called Muslim Parliament of Great Britain, apparently describes Islamophobia as 'hatred of the truth' – of which the sacred source is Allah (Hopkins and Kahani-Hopkins, 2006, p 254). In short, as Lorente (2010, p 117) comments, Islamophobia as a concept appears to act as a 'universal container' of all and any perceived discrimination of Muslims or offence thereto.

The dangers of this stance are argued by Malik (2005) who poses a serious concern that an accusation of 'Islamophobia' is sufficient to stifle debate, which most people would regard as a fundamental principle of democracy. Nevertheless, it seems indisputable that prejudice towards and fear of constructed notions of Islam and Muslims (resonant with the idea of 'imagined communities') is on the increase across the global north (Bangstad and Bunzi, 2010; Kreamelmeyer, 2011; Fleischman et al, 2011; Hopkins and Kahani-Hopkins, 2006). This is exemplified by the well-publicised demands in December 2015 by US Republican, Donald Trump, for a 'total and complete shutdown' of Muslim immigration to the US (Brazile, 2015). In the wake of the furore of indignation this statement has excited, British Labour Leader, Jeremy Corbyn, somewhat tongue-in-cheek, offered to take Mr Trump on an educational visit to a London mosque (Mason, 2016). Finally, Wirz et al (2015) distinguish between intergroup conflict posed by 'realistic threat' (actual, physical) and 'symbolic threat' (cultural attacks, for example), strengthened by negative stereotypes of the behaviour of the perceived other. Islamophobia would thus appear to clearly fall into the latter category.

Human dignity and *insan al-kamil*

In this comparatively short discussion about Islam, it is apparent that 'Islam' and 'Muslim' are not static, ahistorical notions fixed in time and space, but are dynamic and in a continuous state of flux. History, nationality, locality and language all colour individual lives and create a rich tapestry of the *ummah*. Although areas of ambiguity, paradox and contradiction do exist, the tapestry would have little meaning if separated into its component threads.

This dynamic vision of Muslims and Islam is underpinned by unifying characteristics and values, which act as guiding principles in leading an Islamic way of life. Accordingly, although so far we have reviewed many problems and conflicts, as well as historical legacy and Islamic precepts, the diverse and the unified aspects of Islam remain key elements in comprehending Islamic perspectives. Consequently, apart from the fundamental five pillars there are other important concepts to consider, such as that of *ashan*, mutual care and respect, an idea that is clearly compatible with social work values. In addition there is also *izzat*, meaning respect or honour, an idea that resonates strongly among most Muslims, and although open to adverse interpretations is of value in understanding Muslim attitudes and consciousness.

Above all, at an individual level, Islam in its purest form seeks, like social work, to promote human dignity, with the additional mandate of raising consciousness to a higher spiritual level. Despite contention and localised variations of custom, the accepted principles and rituals act as a guide for individuals to follow the 'straight' path. This is one that promotes the aspiration of the ideal and complete human, *insan al-kamil*, and in conformity with the other monotheistic religions aspires to lead believers to eternal life.

Notes

[1] 'Peace be upon him' is normally added to Prophet Mohammed's name in its abbreviated form of 'pbuh', as a mark of respect. In this book we would like to signify that this is meant at every reference to his name.

[2] The story of Malala, the young Pakistani girl shot in the head on a school bus by the Taliban for the crime of publicly asserting her right to schooling exemplified to an appalled world the extent of ruthless sexist oppression by extreme Islamist forces.

[3] A total of 456 British members of the Armed Forces have been killed in the Afghanistan conflict since 2001 (BBC, 2015b). The number of casualties among other combatants is unclear.

[4] Somewhat derogatory, colloquial Yiddish term for anyone who is not a Jew.

[5] Husain was the grandson of the Prophet Mohammed. He is considered to be the third 'Imam' by Shi'ite Muslims. Imam Husain, his immediate family and a small group of followers were killed by the Ummayid Caliph, Yazid, in what is now Karbala, Iraq.

THREE

Social work education and Islam

Addressing discrimination in social work education

Social work education and practice in the UK has been subject to continuous transitions and radical changes over a number of decades, owing primarily to government interference under the purported, clichéd rationale of 'improving standards'. Demands by social work academics for clear evidence of such a need has generated some questionable justifications, leading to the suspicion that policy changes merely feed into a prevailing, cynical neoliberal political agenda for the fragmentation of public (and therefore publicly funded) services in social care and health. The tightening of the social work curriculum to focus primarily on 'safeguarding' issues with a heavy focus on practice learning (practicums), compresses a formerly comprehensive academic education in social work that was once traditionally grounded in the social sciences and psychology. If this were not bad enough, the government promotion of fast-track social work qualifications in children and families work is exemplified by two initiatives in England: 'Step Up to Social Work' and 'Frontline' (Ixer, 2013). The former is premised on the idea of partnerships between local authorities and institutions of higher education (HEI) and is now beginning to be adopted by a number of HEIs as inevitable, although Frontline remains highly controversial and has only been taken up by one English HEI. Fast tracking serves to undermine social work education further and to replace this with an instrumental, training protocol that may serve the interests of local authorities (the main employer of social workers in the UK) in producing a specifically trained workforce but with limited remits which are unlikely to serve service user/client groups equally well. Parker and Doel (2013) note that the demise or reallocation in Britain of former social work specialisms, such as family work, casework, group work and community work, not forgetting counselling, once social work provinces, are now replaced by a restricted focus on undertaking social work assessments. These trends in British social work form a glaring anomaly in relation to the global context of increasing appreciation of the diverse and complex range of professional expertise across international social work. A varied but overarching remit is one particularly recognised in the 'Global definition of social work' by the International Federation of Social Work (IFSW).

Social work is a practice-based profession and an academic discipline that promotes social change and development, social cohesion, and the empowerment and liberation of people. Principles of social justice, human rights, collective responsibility and respect for diversities are central to social work. Underpinned by theories of social work, social sciences, humanities and indigenous knowledge, social work engages people and structures to address life challenges and enhance wellbeing. (IFSW, 2016)

Social work education in most modern multicultural societies is under pressure to equip social work graduates with a level of proficiency to start addressing the increasingly complex needs of a multicultural and multifaith client group. Accordingly, research literature emerging from less familiar cultural and regional contexts is a welcome addition to the dominant professional discourse of the global north in offering a wider and alternative view of human service work. A commitment to understanding and addressing cultural diversity holds an established place in social work curricula. How this enterprise should best be managed, however, remains open to debate and experimentation, and has been subject to various strategies in the discipline over the years.

Keating (2000) charts the development of anti-racist perspectives in their various evolutions in British social work education. Describing how this momentum paved the way for a more far-reaching examination of other forms of discrimination and oppression, he traces a pedagogic process to the adoption of anti-discriminatory practice and later, anti-oppressive practice (AOP). Today, in the UK at least, the latter has assumed the status of virtually unquestioned dogma. Yet in keeping with postmodernism's tendency to flatten hierarchies of oppressions to an equal weighting this has also eclipsed an emphasis on racism (Graham, 2009). However, anti-racism has undergone something of a revival in social work literature as holding a unique perspective in relation to the experiences of black and minority ethnic (BME) groups (Ashencaen Crabtree and Wong, 2012; Bhatti-Sinclair, 2011).

A further offshoot of both anti-discriminatory and anti-oppressive practice has been a commitment towards better understanding of minority cultures, endorsed as the 'sensitive' way forward (Payne, 2005). There has been criticism of such approaches, where it is argued that this may produce social work 'technicians' capable of responding to multicultural client groups within the status quo of existing state-run bureaucracies, but who operate in a politically and morally neutral vacuum (Williams, 1998, p 220). A further jeopardy for BME social work professionals is represented in the quest to 'be authentic as a practitioner', as Narda Razack (2001, p 220) claims, writing from the context of the US. This may occur where there is a personal need by such professionals to address oppressive experiences within the bureaucratic confines of predominantly 'white, middle-class, psychoanalytic' agencies (Razack, 2001, p 220). For such agencies, employing a 'token' social worker of colour in an otherwise all-white professional agency, can be read as offering a message of token interest in clients from minority ethnic (ME) groups, rather than offering a commitment to addressing the needs of such clients, including their insidious experiences of institutional and personal racism (Razack, 2001, p 224).

Tokenism results in personal and professional isolation. Individuals from particular backgrounds, in which the parameters and nuances of religion or culture are not easily comprehended, may be at greater risk of isolation. This may represent a particular concern for Muslim practitioners, if their worldview and social orientation differs markedly from non-Muslim fellow students and colleagues. Under these circumstances, such practitioners will find themselves pressed to advocate both on their own behalf as well as their clients'. The latter may in turn be lumped indiscriminately with other client/service user groups, who share apparent similarities (ethnicity, for example) but whose actual backgrounds are for the most part dissimilar. An alternative but equally likely scenario is one where the religious identities and cultural backgrounds of individuals are viewed as being so alien that the basic commonalities of human development, personal need and circumstances are overlooked.

Globalisation and social work

In relation to ethnic diversity, a further point for social work education lies in the obligation to adequately address the issues and dilemmas posed by globalisation. This is a matter of increasing importance if the profession is to be sufficiently poised to take advantage of the opportunities created by this phenomenon.

In discussing globalisation in the classroom setting, issues of 'difference and complexity' need to be sufficiently addressed (Suárez-Orozco, 2005). This, in theory, should not prove to be so very difficult in that social work purports to take these points into strong consideration as a matter of course. For globalisation incorporates not merely the ebb and flow of economies across international borders, but that of human migration as well and the adaption of cultural norms to new societies (Lyons et al, 2006). Additionally, globalisation indicates how cultural transformations develop, as manifested, for example, through the reforging of separatist ethnic identities, such as can be seen in Spain, the UK and the Balkan States.

A further effect is seen in the metamorphoses of cultural identities. Some countries may have partially assimilated values and practices from dominant nations along the axes of world power. In so doing, this is likely to generate some reconfigurations of traditional perspectives into the incorporation of new cultural identities and social interpretations. Where such transitions are taking place the effects are also often felt in relation to social welfare, thus giving rise to new forms of social work practice, melding established ideas with the new. These evolving responses in welfare provision thereby become examples of the processes of professional indigenisation, a topic that is further discussed.

In opposition to these paradigms are some ethnic and cultural groups that defiantly reject the encroachment of dominant cultural forms, as can be seen occurring in the Middle East towards principles, practices and policies deemed overly western or, specifically, American. These too have their ramifications for social work, in which the linkages between social work values and traditional or cultural values may be regarded as, at best, tenuous. A further example of incongruence between values may be found in relation to certain societies where a proportion of individuals are deemed of less worth and of lower status than others.

Globalisation in the global north seems for many a double-edged sword. In Britain the processes of globalisation raise fears over the perceived threat of immigration. It is often assumed in the media that there is a rising flood of asylum seekers who threaten to swamp either welfare services or the employment markets of the country of settlement. Yet it is equally thanks to globalisation that the diminishing ranks of personnel available to run essential parts of the UK health and social care sectors are swelled by trained doctors, nurses and social workers from overseas – a controversial issue of itself in terms of potentially poaching from nations whose resources are further drained.

A counter to the ethnocentric bias of European social work education (Williams, 1998) and the 'occasional responsiveness' towards internationalisation in US and UK HEIs, as critiqued by Lyons et al (2006, p 197), could be demonstrated by the British Higher Education Authority and the Joint University Council for Social Work, where both bodies express an interest in internationalised curricula. Additionally, across the global north international social work placements are increasingly popular among students (Ashencaen Crabtree et al, 2012; Parker et al, 2012). These externally facing interests challenge potential parochialism in social work 'training' or that potentially posed by rigid and unimaginative curricula.

A notable feature of most international placements hinges on regional, socio-economic privilege demonstrating an imbalance of student mobility across regions. It is primarily students from the wealthier and expensive global north who can afford to take up international placements and frequently in the less wealthy and cheaper global south (Razack, 2009). A deeper discussion of the issues and related implications arising from international social work placements lie beyond the scope of this book. However, the justification for these, irrespective of the imbalanced reciprocity of such arrangements are normally justified as enhancing cultural sensitivity in students, as well as exposing them to unfamiliar practices and values, which form part of the expansive collage that is international social work. In our experience this may indeed expand the minds, knowledge and ambitions of students greatly in revealing them to the unfamiliar and unique, or alternatively may lead to a reactionary dive behind the familiar sandbags of known and rarely questioned norms (Ashencaen Crabtree et al, 2015).

A basic tension can be discovered in social work curricula that serves to both equip students for practice in local settings meeting regional agendas, but also seeking to provide a global outlook, and hopefully transferrable skills that are relevant to an overarching international profession. In this vein, we can perhaps adapt and apply the observation by Brij Mohan (2002), following Leroy Pelton, who argues that commonalities need to be identified among individuals (or in this case, local social work bodies) that stand over and above the splintering of collective interests (or local agendas). Accordingly, restrictive social work curricula that aim to 'train' rather than 'educate' students undermine this broader, globalised remit, which in turn carries clear relevance for practitioners working in diverse societies. While great strides have been made to tackle oppression in many social work curricula, it is debatable how far this anomaly has influenced practitioners to fully embrace cultural diversity within societies in global transition. This is a particularly moot point as it is claimed that Islamophobia is a particularly powerful manifestation of a phobic reaction to multiculturalism per se (Marranci, 2004).

Dominant pedagogies

A number of useful teaching strategies have been developed across higher education internationally to facilitate student learning of diversity and multiculturalism. Reflective practice has become an essential component in social work education (Parker, 2010) and lends itself well to a personal and critical engagement with the clustered concept of culture (Johnson and Yanca, 2004). An embedded self-learning and self-governing tool in professional social work in many countries, reflectivity is arguably ill defined (Ixer, 1999), but nonetheless forms part of the educational structure of British social work (see, for example, the Professional Framework Capabilities model (TCSW and BASW, 2014, 2016)).

Ethnographic approaches have enjoyed a long and illustrious pedigree as a research methodology uniquely geared towards the understanding and decoding of cultures (Ashencaen Crabtree, 2013). As a tool for social workers in exploratory casework its virtues have yet to be appreciated in the profession, although it is now many years since the celebrated American medical anthropologist cum psychiatrist, Arthur Kleinman, recommended its use in hospital-based social work (1988). However, the use of ethnography is attested to as a means of providing an in-depth understanding of and empathy for the 'texture of the client's life', in relation to their experiences and the meanings attached to these (Thornton and Garrett, 1995, p 68). Ethnography is not confined to the personal only, but can in turn be linked to structural oppression across multiple and intermeshing levels of influence.

'Critical incident analysis', emerging from the Australian context, is now widely adopted as a valuable tool for reflective practice. It has been seen as particularly useful in practitioner encounters with unfamiliar cultural contexts or situations (Ashencaen Crabtree et al, 2012; Parker et al, 2012). Used in this way critical incident analysis is reminiscent of the 'cultural script portfolio', but is far more rigorous in terms of analysis, enabling premises, transformation and outcome to become explicit in the process of analysis and self-discovery (Fook, 1996).

In considering dominant pedagogies that inform understandings of cultural diversity and anti-oppressive practice, a 'culturally competent' approach holds a highly respected position. This in turn forms part of the prescribed professional value base of both American and now Australian social workers. Nevertheless while the general approach is familiar and commonly used in the UK, the term itself may not be. 'Cultural competence' relates to the practitioner's ability to work with sensitivity and knowledge across cultural boundaries. Naturally it is not possible to assume that working in a cultural competent fashion implies the ability to work across all cultures with equal facility. This notion would suggest a level of expertise and skill that would be virtually omniscient.

Rather, cultural competence indicates a conscious moving away from ethnocentricism of judging behaviours, values and lifestyles from the perspective of the practitioner and/or the dominant culture (Mlcek, 2014). Promotion of cultural competent social work can be found across a range of practice domains as well in social work education. Horevitz et al (2013) explores this in terms of medical social work in the US pointing out that ME groups generally carry a disproportionate level of health needs compared to the general population. Domestic violence among minority faith communities is also viewed as an appropriate area for cultural competent approaches (Stennis et al, 2015). Cultural competence has since moved beyond the issues of ethnicity to be applied to a wide range of other groups who also experience oppression (Abrams and Moio, 2009), although, aptly, Hodge and Nadir (2008) consider the low provision of cultural competent mental health services for North American Muslim minority groups.

Consciously adopting culturally competent practice, however, is by no means clear-cut, as Laird points out.

> Working towards cultural competence is difficult because it requires social-care professionals from the majority white population and other ethnic groups to step outside their own cultural context and relate to service users and carers within the frame of their cultural contexts... Cultural competence is not about presumption or the deployment of specific information about each ethnic group. Cultural competence is founded on a comprehensive understanding of the broad nature of potential differences between people of diverse ethnic backgrounds. (Laird, 2008, p 43)

Furthermore, in reference to underlying racism towards aboriginal peoples Mlcek (2014, pp 1990–1) defines the domains of cultural competence, as taught in the Australian social work curriculum, by delineating a range of considerations listed beneath domains. Thus, for example, 'respect for the person and his or her unique, cultural identity' falls beneath the domain of *developing cross-cultural competences – attitudes and values*, which holds a further four elements. Likewise, the first of four elements, 'a critical understanding of culture as a social constructed and contested concept', is subsumed under the overarching domain of *developing cross-cultural competences – knowledge*. The final and complementary domain of *skills* contains, for instance, the element of 'critically reflect on their (practitioner) personal and professional cultural identities and the influence they have in social work practice'.

Culturally competent approaches benefit from the use of culturagrams as a valuable addition to the toolkit of methods for skilled practitioners (Parker and

Bradley, 2014). Although originally developed in the US (see Congress, 1994) culturagrams are well adapted for employment in multicultural, multifaith modern Britain. Parker and Bradley (2014, p 65) suggest how this tool can be used to identify important domains of likely significance to migrant service users/clients in the assessment process:

- reason for immigration
- length of time in the community
- legal or undocumented status
- age at time of immigration
- language spoken at home and in the community
- contact with cultural institutions
- health beliefs
- holiday and specific events
- impact of crisis and significant events
- values held about family, education and work.

Despite the prevalence of cultural competence (and its variations) in social work pedagogy and practice it is not immune to critique. These refer to the potential for misplaced confidence in practitioners that it is possible to draw sweeping generalisations about beliefs and behaviour in ME communities based on learned stereotypes. In this vein, Ortega and Faller (2011, p 29) warn of the pitfalls associated with the misconception that ethnic differences can be understood as a 'set of observable and predictable traits'. Although obviously there are often aspects of truth in stereotypes, the homogenising of otherwise diverse groups of people forms the fallacy of *essentialisation*, where it is believed that the fundamental essence of the 'other' can be identified, captured and applied across those groups seen as 'the same'. Abrams and Moio (2009) thus argue that cultural competence does not of itself provide a critical route to understanding institutionalised oppressions, such as racism.

Alternative positionings have therefore been put forward as a means of avoiding the problems associated with the application of naive cultural competence.

Bridging models – CC plus AOP = CCAOP

In reference specifically to research, but with a clear application to practice, Danso (2014/2015, p 575) offers a combined model of cultural competence and anti-oppressive practice, labelled the 'CCAOP framework' which it is claimed builds upon the strengths of both models by combining the best elements of each. Thus, among other components we find the inclusion of i) social justice, egalitarian professional relationships, ii) genuine and holistic engagement in investigation, iii) a self-reflexive approach by the professional, iv) co-construction of knowledge with a participant/service user element together with v) accountability to individuals and communities served.

Critical race theory

Emerging from legal studies (Price 2009), critical race theory (CRT) has been described not so much as a theory but more as creating an 'intellectual movement' and a tool by which to understand how oppression is embedded across institutional structures in wider society (Treviño et al, 2008, p 9). Its primary virtue lies in its ability to offer the means of providing an 'analytical vertical dissection down the strata of macro-level social policy to the micro-level experiential layers of the personal' (Ashencaen Crabtree and Wong, 2012, p 3).

This perspective, along with anti-racist social work pedagogies, facilitates the foregrounding of racist discrimination as distinctive to and distinguishable from a range of multiple oppressions subsumed under anti-oppressive practice (Bhatti-Sinclair, 2011; Graham, 2009).

'Intersectionality', as conceptualised by Hill Collins (1998), enables us to understand the multifaceted nature of oppression as bearing down upon the individual in relation to factors like class, ethnicity, gender and national identity – to which we might pertinently add faith as well. CRT is argued to be not only clearly compatible with social work but manages to overcome some of the problems in cultural competence by promoting critical and intellectual engagement with structural oppression and individual responses to this.

In considering diversity in social work pedagogy Jani et al (2011, p 295) elucidate the concept of *intersectionality* as working at two levels: first, how 'multiple subordinating identities contribute to one's sense of self, perspectives and aspirations'. Second, intesectionality, as referring to how the individual actor takes on many social roles, in which they may act as both the oppressed and oppressor (Jani et al, 2011) – a perception that is presumably often experienced by practitioners working in the fraught area of child protection services.

A further conceptual development that marries the virtues of cultural competence with that of intersectionality is that of 'cultural humility', which advocates that practitioners should foster *self-awareness* in recognising the cultural lens through which they see and interpret the world (Ortega and Faller, 2011). In addition to self-awareness, the authors refer to the 'dimension' of *openness* in realising that full knowledge is not obtainable and that individuals are open to influences beyond them. Finally, *transcendence*, defined as an appreciation of the meta-reality of a massively complex and therefore unknowably dynamic world (Ortega and Faller, 2011, p 33), is a conceptualisation that obliquely resonates with recognisable understandings of spirituality.

Super-diversity

A particularly useful sociological concept is that of 'super-diversity', which, like 'intersectionality', offers a much more expansive and detailed vista from which to scrutinise familiar ideas of diversity. Using contemporary Britain as a case example, Vertovec (2007) observes the complexity of the multiple configurations of difference. Of course the UK historically speaking has always been the home of many cultures and has seen countless waves of migration from prehistory onwards, including aggressive invasion by both the Romans, the Saxons and later the Normans, as well as attempts at invasion (the Spanish Armada, the Napoleonic wars and the Nazi Third Reich). Yet Vertovec reminds us that diversity in the twenty-first century constitutes far more than merely noting ethnic markers, and that in London alone new migrants hailing from 174 different countries of origin can be found living at all socio-economic levels. Superdiversity therefore constitutes,

> a multiplication of significant variables that affect where, how and with whom people live. In the last decade the proliferation and mutually conditioning effects of a range of new and changing migration variables shows that it is not enough to see 'diversity' only in terms of ethnicity, as is regularly the case both in social science and the wider public sphere. In order to understand and more fully address the complex nature of contemporary, migration-driven diversity, additional variables need to be better recognized by social scientists, policy-makers, practitioners and the public. These include: differential legal statuses and their concomitant conditions, divergent labour market experiences, discrete configurations of gender and age, patterns of spatial distribution, and mixed local area responses by service providers and residents. The dynamic interaction of these variables is what is meant by 'super-diversity'. (Vertovec 2007, p 1025)

In consequence it is vital that the permutations of difference, as have been traditionally understood and taught in social work curricula, must now be conceptually stretched, and thereby *problematised* (as concepts subject to critical theorisation). This endeavour duly does justice to the exponential proliferation of social phenomena found in complex modern societies and conceptually encapsulated as 'super-diversity'.

Indigenisation, authenticisation and localisation

The terms 'multiculturalism' and indeed 'globalisation' are commonplace currency, although as previously discussed they refer to contested and fluid notions of diversity and social interaction. However, long before these, new phenomenasocial work was part of the transference of ethnocentric norms, practices and values across the globe in the form of cultural transmission.

Some decades back, James Midgeley (1981) gave a strong critique of how western social work models were implicated in modern day cultural imperialism in being transported wholesale to developing nations, primarily those of the global south. Midgeley's comments acted as a precursor to a number of further examinations of the incongruences of importing unfamiliar models and values into different cultural contexts (Baba et al, 2011).

This kind of energetic evangelism continues usually under the banner of 'enterprise' where established universities aggressively compete for business footholds through international 'partnership' alliances. Challenging this kind of colonisation is apparent in the drive towards *indigenous* and *authenticised* social work models. These two models are distinct in that indigenous models of social work may originally have derived colonising contexts but have been adapted over time to become fit for purpose to meet the needs of local populations (Ling, 2007; Munford and Saunders, 2011).

Authentication normally refers to the development of models that owe little to westernised social work practice and are instead closely grounded in the cultural knowledge and systems of local contexts (Baba et al, 2011). However, in reference to Islam and social work, Raqab (2016) unusually interprets authenticisation as an integration of religious knowledge with recognised practice, referring to this by the Arab word 'Ta'seel' – the search for personal roots. Owing to the hegemony of professional models and literature which continue to be dominated by authors and publishers from the global north, indigenisation and authenticisation are both primarily grass-roots phenomena. The collation of the 'Global definition of social work' by the International Federation of Social Work (IFSW, 2014) recognises the variations of interpretation in local/regional practices.

Finally, the lesser-known term, 'localisation', adds to the social work discourse on diversity and multiculturalism in promoting the adaptation or redefinition of social work intervention to the particular cultural context of the service user/client (Hugman, 2009). Graham et al (2010) consider how localisation can be applied to Muslim clients and service users in the professional encounter, although warn against homogenising assumptions. Localisation would thus involve embedding religious and cultural knowledge into services, as well as professional responses, in being sufficiently flexible to be tailored to individual needs (Graham et al, 2010).

Despite a wide range of pedagogic tools, it is nevertheless close to a truism to say that in the classroom setting dominant groups tend to impose dominant values (Taylor, 1997). In the west, for instance, epistemological concerns pertaining to the acquisition and generation of knowledge have favoured mechanistic (and, some would argue, masculinist) approaches (Bowers and Flinders, 1990).

Social work has traditionally tended to take a more open view of what may constitute knowledge. This has tended to emphasise the experiential aspect from both the client's and the practitioner's points of view in order to identify 'good practice'. However, this too has been under much criticism as being unscientific and of spurious value in terms of accountability towards the service users and the public purse. Instead, a much more quantifiable and positivistic approach has been demanded by some, in which evidence-based practice has been regarded as providing a much-needed correction to an assumed lack of rigour in the discipline. Many schools of social work are now committing themselves to teaching intervention techniques predominantly based on evidence-based practice, seen as congruent with a recognised and dominant form of validity as used in the 'elite' natural sciences.

Nevertheless, this move has equally been subject to some powerful critiques, in which even for its proponents there are obvious difficulties to negotiate. There is the problem of the dichotomy between an objective and quantifiable method of empirical data collection versus the subjective–interpretative experience that has traditionally underpinned person-centred social work (McNeill, 2006). Large-scale empirical data tell the practitioner nothing of individual differences, while intervention that is not tailored to specific requirements *and* the personal and cultural values of clients, is liable to prove alienating and ineffective (Humphries, 2003).

Humphries (2003, p 85) poses two important questions that encapsulate concerns for social work undertaken within broad multicultural parameters. The first question is: who can be 'a knower' of social work knowledge? Are there other ways of acquiring knowledge about client groups that work towards the goal of creating effective services that truly take into account both commonality of need and actual difference? The second question follows on: if we assume that we know what works in the west, in relation to the rest of the world 'what else *works* [and] to what end?'

Social workers internationally offer us examples of alternative practice with clients from specific socio-cultural backgrounds. Many of these practices offer a challenge to accepted social work ideas and values. In this book we attempt to address these questions through the critical engagement of social work values with practice issues, with the additional aim of attempting to achieve a fuller understanding of the belief systems and the wisdom of Islam to the further enrichment of the diversity that is social work.

Social work values

Social work is arguably more ethics-based and directly concerned with values than any other profession, including medicine and law (Reamer, 1995). Professional ethics, however, have a tendency to become enshrined into static lists of operational directives and prescriptions. They do not in themselves form a substitute for values, which are instead ideals made dynamic through application and analysis in an exercise of praxis (Hugman, 2005).

Professional values, in the main, are expected to become internalised in practitioners, and thus may come to be regarded by the owner as merely commonsense concepts operating towards good practice. Few practitioners are consciously aware all the time of how values inform their decisions and shape their intervention. Yet, clearly they do, and in so doing are subjected to amendment, reinforcement and deepening subtlety and complexity in a process that continues throughout the personal and career development of individuals.

In social work, practitioners regularly encounter situations that challenge held values; this is often the case with regards to conflict at multiple levels of engagement, often in relation to professional values, agency codes of conduct and personal values. Equally, in social work, most practitioners will have had experience of encountering paradoxical situations, where one value countermands the other, leading to an uncertainty about how to proceed. Under these circumstances social workers may opt for a teleological *Utilitarian* approach to the problem, in which the likely consequences (teleology) of actions are assessed and balanced in the selection of the best possible outcome for involved parties.

Nonetheless values and ethics change over time according to national priorities, social and political climates together with the organisation of social work services and – where such exist – regulatory bodies (Banks, 2006). For example, in the UK social work values and ethics occupy a sliding scale according to the level of professional expertise or leadership role an individual attains (see TCSW and BASW, 2014, 2016).

Two main issues have become more prominent over time in relation to social work values and ethics. The first lies in the awareness of cultural diversity within society, inevitably meaning that at least some of the values held by one dominant group will not necessarily be shared by others. This has ramifications for social workers when working with groups who hold alternative values and belief systems, as well as for those wishing to practise social work, but without necessarily accepting all the values held by the profession or agency by whom they are employed. The second, as we will see, is an awareness of the spiritual needs of clients (and indeed practitioners as well, in many cases), and how these should be addressed in training and service delivery.

Internationally, we can find examples of social work driven by values that are not prominent within a western context. Al-Krenawi and Graham (2001), for example, discuss the use of an informal 'cultural mediator' to intervene in the growing discord between a social worker and his Bedouin Arab clients in Israel. The problem revolves around four families, all of whom are closely related. Due to a quarrel one husband banishes his wife from the family home, retaining custody of the children under traditional prerogatives. This gives rise to offence in the second family and retaliation in which the second wife is ejected; and the exact same response is enacted in the third and fourth families respectively. The social worker, himself an Arab, intervenes, demanding the immediate return of the children to their mothers under Israeli law. This threat escalates tensions still further and it now becomes a tribal dispute, until, that is, the mediator is brought in to work with the families and the social worker, when order is restored.

The choice of the mediator in this social context stands in keeping with cultural notions, being a highly respected, male senior of recognised community standing and pious outlook. He is therefore equipped to address traditional cultural issues pertaining to family honour and male prerogative, while juxtaposing these powerfully with Islamic principles. These fortunately are congruent with Israeli law in believing that young children, under these circumstances, are in need of their mother.

Apart from being an instructive anecdote, the main point in using this example is to demonstrate how the values evidenced by the client groups and cultural mediator offer an alternative set of priorities, from which the reader may learn that it is not the welfare of the children that is of paramount consideration here, nor the equal rights of access to children by both parents. Instead, what is considered more important within this cultural context is the balance and harmony of the immediate community. Thus relations of power between the families, according to status and position, should be symmetrical for equilibrium, as Al-Krenawi and Graham (2003) point out in a later paper on this topic. The initial quarrel creates an imbalance that triggers off a chain reaction of equivalence, which is at first negative, but then finally works towards an outcome of positive restoration and united families.

Despite being of Arab heritage, the social worker in this case had been trained in models that are not indigenous, the results of which are clearly shown to be a disastrous mismatch of values, and indeed communication styles, between himself and his clients, which serves to inflame rather than alleviate the situation. The authors, not surprisingly, draw from research literature to contend 'that Israeli social work education "does not orient students towards reducing prejudice or enhancing their cultural sensitivity"' (Al-Krenawi and Graham, 2001, p 670).

A further example that is pertinent to social work is taken from the same region, and involves the education of Arab children in Israel. This serves to highlight some of the incongruence in values based in a traditional culture versus those of the majority Israeli culture. Marwan Dwairy (2004, p 428) argues that the prevailing self-orientated, individualistic ethos in services, in which young people are encouraged to be assertive, is directly in conflict with collective values prevalent in Arab communities, where 'assertiveness is frowned upon as a rude, selfish or even aggressive behavior', being one that is liable to expose perpetrators to family rejection and punishment.

A level of assertiveness, however, is required in the interests of pursuing autonomy and self-determination, both of which are highly prominent values in social work. Consequently, these are promoted by western-trained social workers in work with clients. However, apparently some thorny paths must be negotiated first if Israeli social workers are to work successfully with Arab clients who may be unfamiliar with professional frames of reference that are normally western-orientated and individualistic, as is the case in the Israeli context. Such considerations are not likely to be confined to Arab client groups alone, obviously, but instead hold wide-reaching implications for minority groups living within cultures with alternative and dominant discourses.

Islamic values

The issue of cultural diversity apart, the principles governing Islam are often regarded as being essentially compatible with social work values. This presents a viable challenge to some of the very negative Islamophobic notions that abound, as

David Hodge (2005) points out in reference to the 'denigrating images connoting ignorance, oppression, fanaticism and violence' (Hodge, 2005, p 7).

A further challenge to Islamophobia, which is often noted as a xenophobic fear of the Muslim 'other', is further offered by Naina Patel et al (1998) in the clarification of some of the beliefs that underpin Islam. These are viewed as overlapping the professional value-base of social work, and are paraphrased in Table 1. Patel et al's observations (1998) are next aligned with a slightly truncated version of the principles of Islam and daily practices in Table 2. This is complemented by the daily and universal ritual practices of Muslim devotees, as defined in Table 3. In the following sections we discuss the values, outlined by Patel et al (1998) in relation to the principles of Islam, as described by Barise (2005), with a further analysis of the suggested congruence between these two discrete canons. An exception is made with regards to a discussion of equality between the sexes. This is a large and complex area and is unpacked in more detail in Chapter Four.

Table 1: Professional and ethical domains

- *Respect for dignity and worth of all human beings*: includes promoting the rights of individuals and groups towards self-determination.
- *Promotion of welfare or wellbeing* of service users and society.
- *Promotion of social justice*: including addressing inequalities, and fair distribution of goods and services towards individuals and groups.

Source: Banks (2006, pp 47–8)

Table 2: Islamic values

- Emphasises the wellbeing and welfare of the community.
- All people (men and women) are regarded as equal.
- There is a relationship between individual freedom and the community's obligations to the individual.
- Conscience and conformity dictate the individual's sense of responsibility and obligation.
- Consultation between people is important in relationship building.

Source: Patel et al (1998, p 199)

Table 3: The six pillars of faith

1. Belief in Allah (God) being the One Creator and Sustainer of all beings.
2. Belief in and reverence of the angels who never disobey Allah, unlike humans.
3. Belief in all of the revealed scriptures of Allah (including the original books revealed to the Prophet Moses and Prophet Jesus).
4. Belief in and reverence of all Prophets of Allah from Adam to Mohammad (peace be upon them) without discriminating among them.
5. Belief in the Hereafter.
6. Belief in human free will as well as the fact that nothing can happen without Allah's permission.

Source: Adapted from Barise (2005, p 4)

Welfare of the community

In relation to the topic of well-being and welfare, Banks (2006), in addition to other writers, is concerned not only with the empowerment of the individual, but the demand for social justice towards the community in the shape of social welfare.

In Islam there is an equal concern to balance these two claims in which an individual should strive for perfection through selflessness, altruism and giving happiness to others as a pious Muslim (Al-Krenawi and Graham, 2000). Nowhere are these ideals shown in collective action more succinctly than in the Islamic conception of welfare.

Zakat forms one of the five pillars of faith in Islam. This requires that Muslims pay a proportion of their wealth to the community for the purposes of providing public assistance to the needy (Barise, 2005). This moral imperative is of course not solely confined to Islam; much the same can be found in Christianity and Judaism, for example. However, in the Christian context, the parting of goods is a private and pious, but essentially charitable, act. Hartley Dean and Zafar Khan (1997) argue that, by contrast, atonement is not the purpose of *zakat* in Islam. This has a more altruistic purpose altogether, for it is social justice itself that is served by a redistribution of wealth among the *ummah*. The very word 'zakat' indicates its rationale in meaning both growth and purity.

The hoarding of wealth is believed to lead to economic and social malaise. *Zakat* purifies the wealth of the individual, but it also keeps the social, economic and political body – the structure of the *ummah* from deterioration. To employ a metaphor that is often used for the purpose, *zakat* taps the parts of the body where the blood is congested and transfers it to those parts that are weak or anaemic (Dean and Khan, 1997, pp 197–8).

In the pre-Victorian Christian tradition, the beneficiaries of charitable donation had no specific rights to assistance and the act of charity therefore bestowed virtue on the giver. However, in the Islamic world this is not the case and so the needy, as equally worthy in their own right, have every right to claim from wealthier sections of society.

This has implications for citizenship issues, specifically in terms of the rights of the individual and the community's obligations towards them, a further point mentioned by Patel et al (1998). In terms of welfare assistance, it may also explain the generous welfare provision extended to citizens in the affluent society of the United Arab Emirates (UAE), for instance. There an affluent Muslim state can offer easily accessed welfare provision towards its underprivileged citizens, such as Emirati widows and divorced women, as well as other designated individuals; public assistance usually exceeds any comparable state welfare that can be found in the west. However, it is fair to note that such public assistance is the right of Emirati citizens solely and is not normally extended beyond those parameters.

Individual freedom and social conformity

Islam, as in the Judaeo-Christian tradition, emphasises the interplay of the conscious mind in relation to the governing of conscience and the awakening of insight. These forces are instrumental in enabling individuals to exercise their choices as moral agents in society.

Equally, the monotheistic triumvirate of Islam, Judaism and Christianity all emphasise the importance of social concern and commitment by the individual that in turn leads to social conformity and justice (Burr, 2005).

With reference to Muslims in particular, to go against the overarching principles of society and religion is in effect to behave as a bad Muslim – a most serious indictment. Thus for Muslims, while hypocrisy may exist naturally, there should be no psychological or ontological gap for tensions to exist between social accountability and the individual inclination, as Dean and Khan so eloquently put it:

> It [Islam] eschews the dualism of the Western Enlightenment and thereby the inherently ambiguous distinctions between body and soul; between the secular and the religious; between state and church; between politics and morality; between public obligation and private belief. Islam is at one and the same time a religion and an ideology. (Dean and Khan, 1997, p 194)

Others would argue against this definition of singularity, in wishing to add that Islam does distinguish between body and soul or spirit (as in, *ruh*: 'prayer is food for the soul'). For fasting in Ramadan is a way to distance oneself from the physical body and to concentrate on prayer and spiritual nourishment through the strengthening of one's relationship with Allah. Finally, there also exists a distinction between sacred time, which is eternal, and profane time, which is temporal and earthly.

Furthermore, conflict is open to resolution, ideally through informal as well as strategic consultation. To aid these processes, the social networks in the *ummah* are reinforced through the processes of spiritual connection and socialisation. An excellent example is the in-mosque greetings of peace during major feast celebrations. Even enemies are compelled to be cordial. The feast seasons often provide the context for settling instances of marital or family discord, very often with the assistance of concerned family members, neighbours or friends (Al-Krenawi and Graham, 2003, p 296).

A final point is that to be a Muslim, one must act as one; and this of necessity means adhering in full and proper measure to all the expectations and prescriptions that are attached to the state, which include a declaration of faith (*shahadah*), as the first of the five pillars (Barise, 2005).

Conflict in values

What has been argued so far is that outwardly it would seem that the principles of Islam fit well with normative social work values. However, there are some significant points where there is a departure, and one of the more prominent may lie in relation to the social work values of 'respect for individuals' and the ethos behind anti-discriminatory stances. This becomes particularly prominent in relation to clients whose personal lives or orientation may be unacceptable to some practitioners adhering to particular religious points of view.

Islam, for instance, is not in principle tolerant of homosexual orientations, although obviously as a personal issue it may be practised in private. This, however, most clearly does represent a problem area for social work, as prejudice in this area stands in obvious violation of non-oppressive practice. Nor, too, is apostasy considered to be acceptable and can bring unforgiving punitive ramifications in its wake – although Al-Krenawi (2012) argues for apostasy as a human right.

Indeed, there are many issues that may be offensive to Muslims (as well as others), including abortion, some forms of single parenthood, premarital sex, some types of adoption and euthanasia, to name but a few contentious areas. Social workers, however, are expected to work with most, if not all, of these aspects without discrimination. To attempt to force the issue that certain problems or client groups are not acceptable according to a practitioner's personal brief is to attempt to redefine the basic core values of the profession in most countries where social work is established.

When there is a yawning gap between the practitioner's principles and the professional ethos, many would argue that it seriously militates against achieving effective work with clients and service users. Unsurprisingly some in the profession may feel that under these circumstances the onus would be on the objecting practitioner to find an alternative outlet where they could practise within their own personal boundaries, such as faith-based NGOs and pastoral care (Crisp, 2014; Jawad, 2012).

It could also be suggested that such practitioners should be reserved for work within mainstream social work with client groups who share their belief systems. However, this tends to assume that service users who lead lifestyles unacceptable to devout Muslim practitioners will not be encountered. Michael Merry points out the fallacy in such thinking in discussing a similar issue for educators in the US (Merry, 2005).

Similarly, if we assume that religious customs and beliefs are basically innocuous and seek merely to promote the good of the community through articulated beliefs we unavoidably participate in the oppression of gay and lesbian Muslims (Merry, 2005, p 29).

This observation is a crucial one, for many Muslims would argue about whether a gay or lesbian individual can at the same time be a Muslim. This is an issue explored in Chapter Five. Yet moving faith practitioners out of mainstream social work practice and education, unless they can commit themselves completely to a non-oppressive professional ethos to all clients without distinction, diverts a difficult problem into a socio-religious, cultural cul-de-sac but does little to resolve matters satisfactorily.

Conflict between religion and social work is not confined to any one specific faith group. In discussing a new social work programme offered to ultra-orthodox Jewish women in Israel, Garr and Marans (2001) cite the reaction of one student towards the issue of a client's unwanted pregnancy, which was to immediately wish to discuss the matter with the student's own rabbi. The authors reflect on this reaction in the following way:

> The student focused on her own religious value system. As social work educators, the authors focused on identifying the client's needs. Dilemmas such as this emphasized the need for an effective method to teach that the best interests of the client must determine the treatment plan. With this student population we found a greater resistance than usual in changing the focus from themselves to the client, their needs and value system. Our presumption is that this resistance was reinforced by the centrality of religion in their lives. (Garr and Marans, 2001, p 463)

Putting service user/client needs first is another essential social work value that fundamentally underpins good practice; however, as the Israeli authors point out, this can be problematic, and is a point that is thoughtfully considered by Malaysian Muslim psychiatrist Ramli Hassan (1993). Here he summarises a paradox: that of the professional ethos of unconditional acceptance of the client in the counselling situation versus his moral obligations as a Muslim working with Muslim clients. This, he believes, should be to shepherd them back onto the correct path according to the dictates of religion: 'In such a relationship, the Muslim psychiatrist is first and foremost a Muslim and a psychiatrist second.... It obliges him to adopt a therapeutic attitude that may entail abandoning the detached, morally neutral and emphatic stance that he has been taught' (Hassan, 1993, p 94). A challenge to this stance, however, was previously set by a colleague and fellow Muslim, who in reference to this very point deplores curtailing the autonomy of clients, and with it opportunities to explore their options in full, through 'moral preaching and defining the right path for the client. Such practices create an authoritarian image of counselling that may be hard to get rid of' (Soliman, 1991, p 9).

The argument of what constitutes the correct obligations of the Muslim professional towards a Muslim clientele will no doubt continue, particularly as the label 'Muslim' encompasses a veritable diversity of individual opinions and intellectual perspectives. However, what is needed in the meantime is a more critical evaluation of social work values, which could usefully revolve around at least two particular points: first, that of respect for persons and second, non-judgemental acceptance. Regardless of cultural and religious context, some students find these values difficult to relate to in any case. They question whether one really can respect people who commit offensive acts, whether towards others, the community or themselves. This kind of dilemma in fact disguises a basic misconception, in that it is not the action that commands the social worker's respect, but rather, taking a Kantian philosophical point of view, the moral agency of the client to make decisions for themselves, as an autonomous human being, according to the value of self-determination.

The Rogerian person-centred approach clarifies the issue to some extent by positing that all living organisms strive towards self-actualisation. Everyone makes decisions occasionally that may on the surface appear unwise. Yet these actions are often steps that wend progressively towards a more complete wholeness, if only through trial-and-error, and increasing insight into self-motivation and needs. While this actualising process may not lead to a complete achievement of defined goals, social work by its very nature remains optimistic that the self-determined path undertaken towards this end is one well-travelled.

For Muslim social workers working with clients who do not necessarily share their beliefs or adhere closely to their practices, this does not need to be a bar to effective work. Nor does it mitigate the need to extend respect towards clients and suspend negative judgements of them. Judgement in social work is a necessary component, but should be employed only in the evaluation of intervention and outcomes, not personal condemnation (Banks, 2006).

The equivalent of non-judgemental acceptance is tolerance, and this is a quality that is much demanded in social work practice. Tolerance is also a quality that is not highlighted in the media as being a notable strength in the wider Islamic community; in fact the usual depiction is quite the reverse. These corrosive messages are consequently filtered down through society at all levels, including schools, creating suspicion and dread of the Muslim 'other' (Richardson, 2004).

The accusation of rampant intolerance by Muslim groups, however, is a blanket stereotype that is unfair. Interesting ethnographic evidence contradicts this derogatory assumption, where tolerance is shown to be a most important attribute in the conservative Arab Muslim communities of Oman in the Arab Gulf, where commendable pains are taken to avoid labelling others as sinful (Wikan, 1991).

In conclusion, however, the threat of a clash of values between the profession and faith groups is not going to instantly dematerialise, but may well come increasingly to the fore. There are two reasons for this: Islam is one of the fastest-growing religions in the west, and other religious groups also share some of these same prescriptions. There is a need for more open and sensitive discussion in the classroom setting regarding social work ethics and values, and the potential conflict for practitioners of faith, as well as others. A sound justification for this educational strategy is that the ethical base of social work is the cornerstone of the profession, and therefore merits as much critical discussion as do intervention strategies.

Finally, the entire dimension of spirituality and religion is increasingly being emphasised in social work literature as a neglected aspect of life that should be adequately taken into account, not only for the benefit of practitioners, but, what is more important, for those upon whose behalf they work.

Spirituality, epistemology and cosmology

As indicated, attempting to draw a distinction between the spiritual aspects of Islam and secular considerations is a futile task, since Islam offers a unified ideology that permeates all aspects of daily life seamlessly. This will be a somewhat difficult concept to grasp for many readers, given that for historical and political reasons such divisions are embedded in the very fabric of societal institutions in the UK and France. Although faith-based welfare organisations supplement state-run social services in the UK, the latter has long since lost touch with its religious and charitable origins (Crisp, 2014; Jawad, 2012; Payne, 2005; Proschaska, 2006).

For non-Muslims practitioners a useful list of key Islamic dates, festivals and holy days is offered in Table 4, which are observed by most practising Muslims, although institutionalised religion and ritualised practice varies significantly within and across communities and families. To be 'Muslim' is as fluid a concept as for any of the other major religions.

For Muslims, as Al-Krenawi and Graham (2000) explain, the ritualised observance of prayers five times a day enables the devotee to adhere all the more closely to the pillars of faith. Group prayer is deemed to be more effective than solitary prayer in consolidating a sense of being part of the universal community of believers, and is subject to the same rules. They also maintain that prayer acts as a safeguard against 'anxiety and depression' (Al-Krenawi and Graham, 2000, p 297). This point is more obliquely made in a cross-cultural study of Pakistanis across the UK and in Pakistan, regarding the correlation of prayer with mental health – a finding that tallies with Christian faith groups, and presumably others as well (Khan et al, 2005).

As Barise comments, however, 'Anyone can face hardships, but Islam allows practicing Muslims to perceive and respond to problems through the teachings of Islam and by God's help' (Barise, 2005, p 8). Since in Islam it is accepted that nothing can happen against Allah's will, this enables Muslims to view hardships as having some intrinsic meaning and purpose. The following extract highlights

Table 4: Islamic holy months, festivals and holy days

Hijri Year	Muslim calendar is based on the lunar cycle
Muharram	1st month, significant for Shi'a Muslims
Ramadan	9th month of fasting from just before sunrise (*Fajr*) to sunset (*Maghrib*)
Djulhajj	12th month in which *hajj* is performed at the *Ka'aba* in Mecca, Saudi Arabia
Eid al-fitr	Three-day celebration after month of *Ramadan*
Eid al-adha	Three-day celebration after annual pilgrimage: the *hajj*
Friday	Holy day for many Muslims (mostly men) who attend congregational prayers and listen to weekly sermon

this point well, and is taken from an ethnographic study of family care-giving of children with disabilities in the United Arab Emirates:

> Acceptance of Allah's will in this regard brings not merely compensations but actual blessings upon the home; and thereby piety, as construed in this positive way, represented dominant forms of strength and resilience in such families. Thus three of the families described themselves as reaping the rewards of their compliant conduct through dramatic changes of luck or continued prosperity and tranquillity. One child with severe disabilities was described by her mother as: 'A gift from Allah. He is testing us. Allah gives everyone problems. Sometimes they are financial and sometimes to do with health. He gives us these problems to see how we will overcome them. Since we always look after X [child] and love her too, Allah will protect us. He gave us a lot when he gave X to us.' (Ashencaen Crabtree, 2007b, p 56)

In attempting to comprehend the scale of the Islamic framework, and its interaction with social work, it is important to acquire a basic understanding of two important areas influential in the perceptions of many Muslims. The first addresses how people know what they accept to be true (epistemology). The second point considers which agencies or forces exist in the universe that in turn may assist or subvert human endeavours to live a principled life as a Muslim (ontology).

Education, according to Islamic principle, should not only be accessible to both sexes, but is considered a demonstration of *Imaan* (religious faith) (Haw et al, 1998). However, as Barise (2003) explains, in the Muslim faith knowledge is acquired from Allah as the true source, and is divided into two distinct areas: that of revealed and acquired knowledge respectively. This knowledge may be certain or speculative from the human point of view; however, there is no basic contradiction between revealed and acquired knowledge at the level of ultimate authority: Allah. Where any contradictions are perceived this is due to human ignorance and frailty only and would be resolved by consulting the revealed knowledge contained in the holy Qur'an and the sayings of the Prophet Mohammed (Barise, 2003).

In terms of ontology, there are once again two main areas: *shahadah*, which corresponds to the western notions of sensory data, and which can be known via acquired knowledge, and *gayb*, that which cannot be known through the senses and is only known through revealed knowledge. As Barise explains:

> The human environment includes both the seen and the unseen creatures such as jinn and the angels. From the Islamic perspective, all creatures exist in compliance with God's will. All creatures, from the tiny atoms to the mighty galaxies, worship God and thus co-exist harmoniously according to God's will. When one accepts Islam,

one becomes part of this harmonious co-existence *willingly*. Being a Muslim thus necessitates revolving on an assigned course (just like the electrons and celestial bodies do) without transgressing boundaries and infringing on the rights of the self, the environment, and God. (Barise, 2003, p 8, emphasis in original)

According to Barise therefore, the goal that Muslims are meant to strive towards is 'all-encompassing peace' and to this end they are guided by the pillars of faith and of ritual practice, with Allah as the 'ultimate Helper' (Barise, 2003, pp 8–10).

In seeking to live a life that will keep them 'on the straight path' to Heaven and in Allah's good grace, Muslims seek guidance from multiple sources. Apart from the Qur'an, Muslims refer to the *hadith* (the sayings and actions of the Prophet Mohammed, considered to be authenticated, as the chain of transmission is verified and documented under the authority of recognised Islamic scholars). These *hadith* offer practical guidance on a range of issues and assist many Muslims in interpreting contemporary issues and in reaching decisions on how to behave and act in a particular situation. Accordingly, *hadith* are referred to by most Muslims but not all, while some scholars might question their authenticity.

Straying from the straight and narrow path of piety is, however, a hazard for all humans. For Muslims, as for many Christians, *Shaitan's* (Satan) influence is at the basis of wrongdoing, and it is he 'who capitalizes on human weaknesses as lassitude, desire for immediate gratification, tendency to forget etc.' (Barise, 2003, p 10).

If Allah empowers Muslims, Shaitan in turn attempts to enfeeble them. Barise goes so far as to claim that clients' help-seeking, and the subsequent development of a good professional, working relationship between social worker and client, comes about through the omniscience and omnipotent agency of Allah. This insight by the Muslim client can be used therapeutically to reinforce the intervention process. This positive motivator is not cancelled out if the social worker is not a Muslim, for such practitioners are nonetheless providentially sent during a time of need.

Assessments and cultural diversity

David Hodge (2006) strongly endorses normalising the idea that spirituality forms an important source of strength for service users/clients, who may see no reason why their beliefs cannot be integrated with social work intervention. In so doing he duly offers some useful open-ended questions that social workers might adapt for assessment purposes (Table 5).

While culturally and historically there may be a greater awareness of the centrality of religion for individuals and communities in the US, it would be unfair to assert that social work in the UK has been unaware of this important aspect and makes no allowance for it. Yet, it would certainly be correct to say that this holds a lesser priority than, say, assessing for cognitive and physical

Table 5: Assessing for spirituality

• I was wondering if spirituality or religion is important to you?
• Are there certain spiritual beliefs or practices that you find particularly helpful in dealing with problems?
• Are there any spiritual needs or concerns I can help you with?

Source: Hodge (2006, p 319)

functioning and consequently assessments of spirituality and religion appear to occupy marginal spaces. However, it is encouraging to see that there have been a number of important developments made in this area over time (Parker et al, forthcoming). In respect of this Holloway and Moss (2010) identify four kinds of assessment that social work practitioners may employ:

1. Generic approaches

   Generic approaches that recognise the importance of spirituality in the lives of clients/service users require a good level of self-awareness by practitioners of the significance of spiritual domains in their own lives. Such assessments can articulate with autobiographical approach (see Hollinsworth, 2013), in being sensitive to revealing social and cultural priorities in individuals.

2. Measurements for spirituality

   This uses a systematic measurement of the degree and significance of spirituality, including spiritual need and as a coping mechanism. This quantitative instrument is common in the US, but it is not one used in the UK outside of nursing and relies on a scoring system of a list of indicators.

3. Biographical approaches

   This type of assessment, qualitative in nature, encourages the client to engage in creating their personal story. This holds the latitude to move from open-ended questions to an in-depth charting of life journeys towards spiritual maturity (Hodge, 2005). Spiritual histories, life maps, ecomaps and ecograms may be used in such assessments (Furness and Gilligan, 2010) with culturagrams added to the mix (Parker and Bradley, 2014).

4. Holistic approaches

   These can include the overlapping domains of the individual's ecology (see Skalla and McCoy, 2006). The Mor-VAST model incorporates a number of spiritual ecological domains and dimensions in terms of:
   • Moral authority – self-management
   • Vocational – life purpose
   • Aesthetic – beauty and creativity
   • Social – relatedness to others
   • Transcendent – sense of awe and sacred (Parker et al, forthcoming).

Assessing religiosity

Furness and Gilligan (2010) identify a range of models setting a backdrop from which to assess religiosity and the importance of religion in the lives of service users/clients. These include (i) Howell's (1982) four-stage model of development and learning moving from unconscious incompetence to conscious competence; (ii) Campinha-Bacote's (1999) ASKED (awareness, skills, knowledge, encounter and desire) model, promoting sensitivity to one's own beliefs and developing through a reflective cycle to other aspects of sensitivity; (iii) the transactional model of cultural identity (see Green, 1999), which seeks to move beyond traits and characteristics to a relational understanding of diversity and complexity; and (iv) awareness and sensitivity to difference (see Papadopoulos, 2006) which represents a four-stage model to examine own beliefs and the impact of these on others. The four stages of the latter comprise promoting cultural awareness, gaining cultural knowledge, becoming culturally sensitive and demonstrating cultural competence (Parker et al, forthcoming). In this vein, one such framework is proposed as including the following:

- awareness and reflexivity about one's own religious or spiritual beliefs or their absence
- asking whether people have sufficient opportunities to discuss their religious and spiritual beliefs
- asking whether the social worker listens sufficiently
- inquiring where a person's expertise in respect of self is recognised
- questioning whether the social worker is open and willing to revise assumptions
- asking if the social worker is building a trusting relationship that is respectful and willing to facilitate the wants of the person
- probing the capacity of the social worker to be creative in response to an individual's beliefs
- ensuring that the social worker has sought sufficient information and advice about religious and spiritual beliefs (Furness and Gilligan, 2010).

Furthermore, in keeping with the unitary perspective of Islam, Barise offers an indigenised Islamic social work model (Figure 1).

Barise's model addresses the metaphysical transformations of Islam, as well as the procedural mechanisms of the profession. Rooted in Islamic concepts, which are admittedly not always easily accessible to non-Muslims, Barise is at pains to demonstrate how compatible the essential framework of social work is with Islamic perspectives. From the initial help-seeking stage by the client, to the assessment process, to goal-setting procedures, then on to outcome and finally, evaluation – each step is commensurate and compatible with both the context of Islam and that of social work. This alliance holds in relation to shared values, mutually agreed intervention and a successful outcome.

Finally, Barise's vision highlights certain attributes and attitudes, regarded as typical of Muslims, which are acquired through virtue of their religious conditioning. These, as collated in Table 6, can be usefully exploited by social workers, in their various roles as change agents, in formulating intervention strategies.

Despite providing food for thought, we might query how far Barise's model is germane in relating to the Muslim experience as a whole. Furthermore, it could be argued that the esoteric nature of the model does not easily provide a practical basis for task-centred social work intervention. One telling critique that can be levied against the model is that it does not address one of the more important issues in the UK, which revolves around a sufficient understanding and awareness of the help-seeking behaviour of ME individuals. For while a Syrian or Somali refugee and a British Pakistani might have a faith in common, their migration motivations, experiences of migration, housing, settlement, skills, employment and other distinctions are more likely to play a greater role in terms of access to appropriate service provision.

Figure 1: Islamic social work model

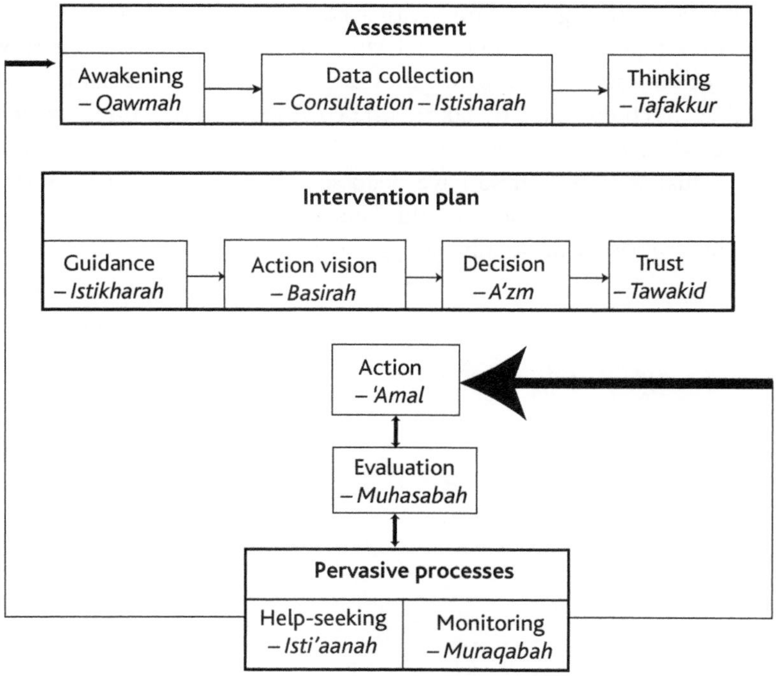

Source: Barise (2005, p 13)

Table 6: Complementary social work strategies

Some attributes of Muslim families:

- flexibility
- optimistic outlook
- resilience
- family orientation
- responsibility towards vulnerable family members
- neighbourhood and community ties
- consultation and mediation traditions

Commensurate social work intervention:

- emancipatory
- strengths-perspective
- capacity building
- networking
- broker
- advocate
- mediator

Source: Adapted from Barise (2003; 2005) and Dorfman (1996)

In conclusion, it would seem that there are more commonalities to be discovered between the professional canon of social work and the Islamic faith than actual points of difference. Although certain areas between the two remain open to debate, and are duly treated as problematic in this book, they do not negate those numerous areas of compatibility. Nor do they divert from the essential message that social work is much enriched by taking on board some of the unique visions of Islam, particularly where these beneficially influence debates on social well-being and individual welfare. These have been social issues of great import in the historical and traditional Muslim world, and retain their relevance as much as ever in the contemporary multicultural, global community.

FOUR

Gender relations and the centrality of the family

Family morphology

The family in the Muslim world is the central institution in society, in being the primary one where social, cultural and religious values will be communicated to the growing child. In common with Christianity and Judaism, the Muslim family is predominantly patrilineal, where family membership and descent are followed down the male line (Warnock Fernea, 1995). This almost invariably indicates that, in common with the other major monotheistic religions in their traditional guise, Muslim families tend to be patriarchal. The greatest authority is consequently vested in the oldest male, be that father, husband, brother or son, on whom also lies the main responsibility for earning the family's living.

Typically, the role of breadwinner and protector of women and children is one endorsed by Islam as falling to the husband. While a wife may earn an income, Islamic principles dictate that this money cannot be viewed as forming part of the family budget but is hers alone, whereas the income of a husband is viewed as *the* family livelihood (Siraj, 2010). This asymmetry therefore carries ramifications for how gender roles are enacted in families, as well as providing the rationale for the unequal division of inheritance between sons and daughters under *shari'a* law, where sons will inherit a larger percentage than their sisters given the assumption of heavier financial responsibilities.

Nonetheless the morphology of Muslim families globally is diverse, with many different permutations, some of which are likely to be unfamiliar to many readers. A wide diversity of family structures can be found in the Middle East and some parts of the Indian subcontinent where families may adopt nuclear, extended or polygamous arrangements. This very much depends on the cultural context of that particular society, as well as the prevailing socio-economic climate, since these domestic arrangements may often be dependent on the financial standing and means of livelihood open to members. Wealthy, industrialised societies, like those of the Arab Gulf, embrace a variety of domestic models: from those perceived to be traditional, extended networks, to nuclear and urbanised cohabiting units, typical of the west.

The archetypal family arrangement in many Muslim societies has been that of the extended family. Such an arrangement may be extremely large, in which several generations of both married and unmarried children live in the parental home along with grandparents. Ideally this ensures that the young, the old and the infirm receive support at all times from a pool of available adults. However, it should be noted that this has not always been the case, for sometimes a married woman's role has been to serve her husband's parents while attending to her own family unassisted

In extended families an income might be swelled by a concentration of wage-earning members; yet, alternatively, individual incomes might be retained for personal use without the necessity of duly providing for the communal pot. Finally, although the extended family system seems to vary widely, the ultimate rationale behind such arrangements has traditionally been to provide sufficient and necessary care for family members in societies with a weak, or indeed non-existent, formal welfare system.

It is true to say, however, that such models are being replaced by smaller, nuclear families due to the forces of modernisation and urbanisation, militating against the building of properties capable of housing a number of interconnected families. Furthermore, welfare state provisions in some countries may obviate the need for such intensive family support. The lack of privacy inherent in the extended family system is also seen as a good reason to maintain discrete households in communities where there have been wide-reaching social changes accompanied by exposure to western lifestyle models. Furthermore, when a communal family model (which often includes help from neighbours) is interrupted by migration to the west, this can disrupt the former and lighter parenting role to one that feels more burdensome and isolated in the new cultural context (Stuart et al, 2016).

As Marwan Dwairy (2004) points out, a nuclear arrangement does not necessarily indicate greater privacy or independence for reproductive families, since often such groups live in very close proximity to relatives, in which patriarchal norms may still exert a powerful influence on the shaping of the normative behaviour of individuals.

The extended or nuclear division, therefore, is not one that can be viewed as clear-cut as families may remain very tightly knit, whether they live beneath the same roof or not. An interesting example is one raised by Jørgen Nielsen (1999) in discussing the issue of *purdah*, referring to the practice of keeping women secluded from non-related men, as occurs in villages in Northern India, Pakistan and Bangladesh. This is regarded as a form of protection, and thereby, as the author suggests, is consequently not one that imposes hardship on women where they are surrounded by a large network of helpful relatives. Nevertheless, in the event of migration to the west, *purdah* can be transformed into a deeply isolating experience where women are placed in urban housing with unknown neighbours and removed from the interwoven matrix of extended family (Nielsen, 1999).

The issue of isolation obviously carries implications for social work, particularly as this can have a significant impact on mental health. In their qualitative study of Pakistani and Bangladeshi women, Ravinder Barn and Kalwant Sidhu (2004) identify social isolation as a contributory factor in the problems female participants experience in relation to daily coping, as well as in the process of adjustment to British society. The civic space is often perceived as foreign, threatening and largely inaccessible to the women in the study, not least due to language problems (Barn and Sidhu, 2004).

Social isolation carries other risks as well: it is, for example, a factor in domestic violence, an issue discussed further in the next chapter. On a wider scale, isolation can become part of a minority community's protective response, where neighbourhoods may become ghettoised due to the perception that the inhabitants' ethnic and religious differences are incongruent with the values and conduct of the wider society. A perception of being besieged by bigotry and racism or Islamophobia is likely to lead to the erection of social barriers, which serve to segregate individuals still further, making access to educational and employment opportunities even harder to achieve.

To return to the subject of family morphology, under Islam a man is permitted to take up to four wives on the condition that he can provide for them and their offspring equally, in terms of material goods, time and attention. Polygamy is viewed as acceptable in religious terms in having been practised by the Prophet Mohammed in his lifetime and whose wives are often viewed as female role models by contemporary Muslims.

Polygamous marriages are for the most part not recognised as legal in the west, with a few exceptions; however, they are practised in a different form among the Mormons in the US. The right for Muslims to practise polygamy in Britain has been argued for at times, but to-date there has been no accommodation of this practice in law.

Immigration to western countries of polygamous unions is a common means for bringing the issue to the fore. Marriages contracted for the purposes of immigration are not deemed to provide legal entry to the UK, for instance. Danish immigration authorities interpret serial, rather than polygamous marriage, as a manoeuvre by immigrants who marry nationals in order to establish residency rights, only later to divorce them and bring in their original spouse and family into the country (Charlsey and Liversage, 2013). However, as the authors also note, *de facto* polygamy can still take place through the strategy of acquiring one wife through a western civil ceremony and the other through *nikah*, the Islamic marriage ceremony, which is not legally recognised in countries like Britain. Al-Krenawi and Jackson (2014) comment on how polygamous unions in the US can be retained by applying for civil divorce but keeping *nikah*-acquired marriages.

The reasons for polygamy in Muslim societies have been put variously forward as, first, constituting a safeguard for women during times when the male–female ratio may have become imbalanced in society due to war and widowhood. In addition, polygamy is seen to be acceptable in a barren union (on the wife's part) where children are desired, as is invariably the case, which we discuss later in the chapter. Polygamy is also viewed as acceptable where the first wife is too infirm to be able to participate in normal sexual relations within marriage. In these cases, polygamy is viewed as a better alternative for women than that of divorce or celibacy on the part of the husband. Furthermore, it has been asserted that polygamy preserves the moral order of Muslim society, since it is commonly regarded as instinctual for men to desire women other than their wives (Mernissi, 1975). However, Fatima Mernissi goes on to argue indignantly that polygamy may have a very different effect on the self-esteem of men and women respectively, in that it tends to boost that of men, but has the reverse outcome for women: 'Polygamy is a way for the man to humiliate the woman as a sexual being; it expresses her inability to satisfy him' (Mernissi, 1975, p 16). Mernissi points out that while polygamy is acceptable under Islam, polyandry (the taking of more than one husband by a woman) is forbidden (although arguably male infertility undermines the polygamy-only patriarchal notion).

Some Muslim women would disagree that polygamy represents a disrespectful move on the part of men towards women, as Moxley Rouse (2004) makes clear:

> Islam requires the drafting of a marriage contract prior to legalizing the union, and this contract can specify that polygyny [polygamy] is unacceptable. Therefore, it is claimed that Muslim women view polygyny as the choice of both the man and the woman, and if a husband breaks a contract forbidding polygyny, a woman has a legitimate reason for divorce. (Moxley Rouse, 2004, p 68)

It could nonetheless be argued that many women are unaware of their rights to make such stipulations or would be hesitant to demand specific provisions in a contract. However, whether this constitutes a genuinely free choice on the part of all women of polygamous unions, the research evidence does appear to indicate that polygamy involves some negative outcomes for wives and families, particularly in relation to the first wife.

In Arab communities it is a common experience for the first family to feel supplanted by subsequent wives and their offspring, if not in terms of material needs, in terms of time and affection devoted by the husband (Al-Shamsi and Fulcher, 2005). Although there is little research into this phenomenon, polygamy has been associated with poor mental health outcomes for first wives and their adolescent sons (the situation for daughters remains unknown) (Al-Krenawi et al, 2002). Additionally, polygamy, as practised by Muslim families in the US, is also associated with spousal abuse when this is seen as a means to marginalise and tyrannise wives in these unions (Hassouneh-Phillips, 2001).

It would be misleading to suggest that the three main forms of domestic arrangements discussed here constitute the only morphology to which Muslim families may conform. The patrilineal model associated with Islam is not one that is universally embraced when it is juxtaposed with longstanding traditions that accept bilateral kinship, such as is the norm in many multicultural communities in Southeast Asia, where a child is regarded as descended equally from the mother, as well as the father, irrespective of Islamic precepts (Errington, 1990).

Uxorilocality is the final form of family morphology we will consider here and is a feature found in some communities in Southeast Asia, including Muslim ones. To summarise, on marriage a man will go to live with his wife and her family in their family home and will supply labour to his wife's kin. This is an interesting reversal of patriarchal systems where almost invariably a woman must leave her kin to join her husband and his family. The advantage of this kind of matrilineal system for women is that they are held in high esteem through the strengthening of mother and daughter ties (Rousseau, 1991, p 404).

Adult sons, therefore, as opposed to daughters, are transient in such communities in passing from one household to another. This refreshing difference serves to challenge dominant patriarchal notions of gender norms. As such, the relocation of a man from his mother's home to that of his wife has been somewhat caustically described as 'trafficking in men' (Peletz, 1995, p 85).

Indeed, in many Southeast Asian communities matrilineal lines of descent coexist with patriarchy, creating interesting areas of ambiguity and paradox. Among the Muslim Minangkabau of West Sumatra, Indonesia, inheritance is traced through the mother's line, along with lineage (Blackwood, 1995). Kling (1995) additionally reports that some Malay Muslim communities in Peninsular Malaysia also practice matrilineal systems described as *adat perpatih* (customary law).

Inheritance practices are closely correlated to the norms and principles that govern cohabitation within communities. Consequently, matrilineal systems provide an intriguing variation on the Islamic norm that permits daughters to inherit roughly half the portion allotted to their brothers (Al-Khateeb, 1998). By contrast, among the matrilineal Minangkabau, although married sons have rights to inherit land for cultivation, their portion will return to their mother and sisters on their death (Blackwood, 1995). A similar system exists among the Malay communities in the Malaysian Peninsular State of Negeri Sembilan, in which the rights of daughters to inheritance of property are emphasised *over* those of sons, due to their greater parental responsibilities and the perceived limits of their ability to exploit an alternative livelihood (Peletz, 1995). As in the practice of uxorilocality, such inheritance rules ensure that a woman and her female descendants are considered the true guardians of ancestral lands.

Thus, unlike in the Indian subcontinent, in Southeast Asia the birth of a daughter does not necessarily imply the ruinous allocation of scarce resources through the entrenched dowry system. Consequently, a daughter is not likely to be viewed as being a commodity that will be taken over solely by the family she marries into, as may occur for many women in Pakistan and China, for instance (Mohammad, 2005). The result being that in Southeast Asia the birth of a female Muslim child is likely to be viewed as a significant asset to her family and community.

These examples provide a most empowering notion of the role and status of daughters in contrast, for example, to the cultural preference for boys, which remains unabated in families of Arab (Muslim or Christian) heritage (Al-Krenawi and Jackson, 2014). A study of Muslim women's perceptions of equality in Saudi Arabia notes the inferior status of Muslim women compared with that of men: 'Having a baby boy is a source of pride and honor, while having a baby girl is a source of sympathy and consolation. If a woman has many boys, she feels happy and proud. But when she has many girls, people look at her with pity and sympathy' (Al-Khateeb, 1998, p 118).

Under Islam, however, the rights and value of Muslim women are said to be affirmed. To highlight this point comparisons have often been drawn with the apparent lowly status of females in pre-Islamic Arab societies, of which it is said that widescale infanticide of female infants was practised by burying them alive. Other scholars contest this version and claim that pre-Islamic societies were much more accommodating than have been portrayed (Mernissi, 1975):

> Pre-Islamic marriage customs were flexible and some of them gave women considerable independence and control over their own lives. In such cases, women tended to remain within their kin family circles after marriage. The husband, if not related to the wife, visited her at her home. Sometimes there were several husbands at the same time, for polyandry existed. When the wife bore a child, she summoned her husbands and announced which of them she believed to be the father, and her word was law. (Karmi, 1996, p 77)

Such accounts obviously tend to diminish the liberating and life-saving effect of Islam on females and are therefore somewhat controversial. The accepted Islamic version is, however, that with the acceptance of Islam, the value of daughters was asserted by the Prophet Mohammed and the rights of women were duly elevated and infanticide consequently condemned (Jawad, 1998).

The rights of women over those of men, as illustrated in some Southeast Asian communities, are explained through the dichotomous but intertwined relationship of *adat* ideology (as it is uniquely manifested in Malaysia and Indonesia) and Islamic interpretations. *Adat*, or traditional, indigenous (customary) practice, is viewed as upholding women's autonomy and authority in societies where Islamic ideology asserts the prerogatives of men (Ong, 1995). Consequently, the dominance of Islam through state control in Indonesia creates 'contradiction' for the Minangkabau who both seek to retain their cultural matrilinear beliefs, while as 'devout' Muslims they attempt to adhere to the prevailing attitudes towards women as primarily subordinate to husbands in the domestic and civil spheres (Blackwood, 1995, p 140).

The diversity of family structures in the Muslim world and their underlying rationale can be seen to be very wide, where the influences of culture and religion create some intriguing permutations. The dominance of each is often dependent on the forces of state and law, as well as the dynamic ties of tradition and social change. In relation to gender norms, these create patterns of interesting variation that add to the heterogeneity of the experiences of the *ummah*.

Marriage

Regardless of the adaptation of the family, there are values for Muslims that remain unchanged across social contexts. Marriage is considered very important as the legitimate means of channelling sexuality, since chastity is also highly valued (Moxley Rouse, 2004). Muslim women are generally committed to marrying within the faith, but Muslim men may choose wives from other religions, although often these wives will convert to Islam on marriage. The Qur'an states that a Muslim can marry someone who is of 'the people of the book': namely, Christians and Jews who venerate sacred texts, and these are not required to convert, although conversion is required for all other faiths. That said, the Canadian example is instructive. Canada is viewed as having a particularly hospitable host culture for immigration and where Islam is the fastest growing faith group in the country. Nonetheless, Canadian Muslims are apparently the least likely to marry out of their faith than other religious communities (Cila and Lalonde, 2013).

Among the Pakistani community in Britain, marriage is assumed as an expected outcome in a person's life, and unions may have been planned by parents from a daughter's infancy: 'Often, women are prepared for their roles as wives and mothers from birth. Farah, aged 16, whose engagement for marriage was decided by her parents on birth, comments, "Women are sold at an early age"' (Mohammad, 2005, p 188).

To-date 'arranged marriages' have been regarded as the 'community ideal' among British Muslim Asians (Lyon, 1995, p 53). Although as Anitha and Gill (2009) point out owing to potential family pressure on girls to consent to such marriages, the divide between arranged and forced marriages may at times be very narrow.

Arranged marriages are subject to wide permutations, in terms of the form of the arrangement, in both the west and in modern countries of the Middle East, like Lebanon (Nasser et al, 2013). Young people may be permitted to get to know each other first before consenting, or they may be brought together for the first time during the wedding. Furthermore, migrant families may negotiate an agreed union through local contacts in their adopted country. Otherwise children, most frequently daughters, may be sent to the parental land of origin to contract a marriage with someone from a known community. Although some adult children will find their own partners independently, the background assumption has been that the spouse will then be entitled to be brought into Britain to facilitate the marriage and to maintain transnational kinship ties. Yet this is a practice that, as Lyon says, the immigration authorities view with deep suspicion (Lyon, 1995). Current British immigration laws demand that a foreign non-European Union spouse wishing to enter the country on spousal resident visas pass an English language test (Elgot, 2016). Additionally, a UK resident spouse must also achieve a specific level of income in the UK (regardless of marital assets or income outside of the country) and where the amount increases with each child born. Former Prime Minister, David Cameron, made a recent controversial announcement that wives on spousal visas could be deported if they failed to have acquired sufficient

English after 30 months of residency. This threat was widely viewed as targeting Muslim migrant women with poor English (Sparrow, 2016).

According to the African American Muslim participants in Moxley Rouse's study (2004), the ideal husband, in common with notions elsewhere in the Muslim world, is pious, responsible and financially able to support a wife and family. However, in her similar study, McCloud states that the favoured 'Muslima' African American bride is apparently one who has never been married before and has no children; McCloud goes on to say that well-educated women and those with prominent careers may have difficulties finding a husband, regardless of their right to employed work under Islam (McCloud, 1995). This indicates therefore that such personal competencies are not considered to be particularly attractive to prospective partners, who are evidently seeking other attributes in brides.

Moxley Rouse (2004, pp 152–3) in turn quotes a participant who clarifies the rights of wives in relation to husbands:

> The right to know where his wife is going every time she leaves the house (but not the ability to restrain her) and the right to sex when he so desires. She has other rights, including the right to distribute her husband's income how she sees fit, the right to work, to keep all her earnings for herself, to own property, to inherit, to educate and raise the children the way she wants.

With the exception of the sexual access a man may enjoy with regard to his wife, which is in keeping with Islamic rules, this, on the whole, is a liberal interpretation within the milieu of a particular westernised cultural context. Research into Arab families indicates that wives, of all ages, may be expected to seek permission from their husbands in order to go out and if this is denied, she has little choice but to submit to his decision (Ashencaen Crabtree, 2007c). The same situation is true of employment outside of the home, in which no automatic right is conferred on women to be able to take up waged labour.

In traditional Arab society (as well as for many South Asian communities), marriages are arranged by parents or by the child's male guardian. Although a girl has a right to refuse a suitor under the principles of Islam, generally she was expected to waive her objections. Such filial submission has been expected as an indicator of a daughter's respect for her parents' judgement, as well as her owing to her perceived ignorance of what was best for her, in addition to her maidenly unfamiliarity with men.

The ideal suitor was a first cousin, and he was tacitly assumed to have greater rights than other men to make an offer of marriage to a girl. Moreover, he often had had a strong obligation to propose such a marriage, particularly if the couple were the children of brothers (Zlotogora et al, 2002). The reasons behind this are that consanguineous unions maintain patriarchal kinship and tribal connections (Kenan and Burck, 2002) tend to retain the bride within her own community and certainly within her own extended family, and this has been viewed as a wise safeguard. A bride, it was felt, would be less likely to be maltreated by her husband were he to be related to her by blood and subject to the influence of two parental households whom he had known since infancy. It had other benefits as well, by safeguarding the future care of elderly parents and ensuring that wealth remained within the family network (Dhami and Sheikh, 2000). In the UK, unions between first cousins are still common in families that originate from certain parts of the Indian subcontinent and probably for very similar reasons. Nevertheless the benevolent aspect of consanguineous unions is challenged by Fikree (2005), who claims that domestic abuse is very likely to be perpetuated in marriages with a generational history of violence. Furthermore, it is also claimed that consanguineous marriages in India are more likely to result in separation and divorce than non-related marriages (Saadat, 2014).

Parenthood and child-rearing

Islam regards wedlock as the only acceptable route to parenthood, and a natural and pleasurable consequence of this relationship. Marriage and parenthood remain important objectives for Muslim couples. The marital union is a crucial step in a young adult's life; however, it is, in fact, the birth of children that confers adult status, as procreation is considered a very important religious obligation (Al-Krenawi and Jackson, 2014; Warnock Fernea, 1995; Sharifzadeh, 1998).

For Muslims, therefore, children are highly prized and practically always wanted in a marriage. This is unlike the situation in the west where couples may decide to remain child-free and with reducing social disapprobation attached to these decisions. Consequently, Muslim families have traditionally been large, and often remain so globally, despite the progress of industrialisation, education and career opportunities for both sexes (but particularly for women), and improved mortality rates in many Muslim nations.

As indicated in Muslim families, men and women hold clearly defined and often immutable parental roles in the raising of children. In Arab families, infants and young children are cared for predominantly, and often solely, by the mother and other female relatives, including the child's sisters. Furthermore, the husband is not normally expected to be present during his wife's postnatal visits or during the birthing process itself. Birth and child-rearing are seen as essentially the domain of women where a man's presence is generally not considered necessary or appropriate (Bouhdiba, 1977).

Tove Stang Dahl (1997) points out that in Islam men and women are regarded as standing in a complementary position to each other. This, however, should not be understood to mean that gender is irrelevant, symmetrical or even similar, as is the perception among many in the west, as well as several ethnic groups in Southeast Asia, for example (Monnig Atkinson, 1990). Rather, the essential natures of men and women mean that each holds qualities that make them particularly fitting for specific duties and responsibilities. Thus the sexes are regarded as occupying a polarised, as well as hierarchical, position in the continuum of human nature (Stang Dahl, 1997).

This view stands in some contrast to the struggle of non-Muslim women in the global north attempting to share childcare and domestic burdens more equally with men, in view of women's greater participation in paid employment and civic society. Instead, although Muslim women in many regions of the world are increasingly undertaking successful careers, this is often seen as an addition to, and of less consequence than, their domestic duties (Al-Khateeb, 1998). The 2011 UK census shows that although 43 per cent of full-time Muslim students are women, their participation in the labour market is low (28 per cent) in comparison to the overall female employment rate. Waged work is seen as an addition to, and of less consequence than, their domestic duties (Al-Khateeb, 1998), which takes priority even over that of attending the mosque. While the high rate of participation in full-time education may shift attitudes to working outside the home, structural barriers and discrimination may be a counteracting barrier.

Within traditional households young Muslim children inhabit a world dominated by women. Their physical needs, together with many of their educational ones, will usually be met within this maternal milieu. Writing from the UK Scourfield et al (2013) recognise the importance of establishing a religious foundation for children as part of Muslim parenting without specifically noting gender differences between parents. Beyond this, however, the general nurturance of children, including social training and the implanting of normative knowledge, together with religious values and conduct, is seen as primarily the mother's role and will be extended towards her children throughout their childhood (McCloud, 1995). An articulated ideal of Muslim motherhood is offered by a participant from a study into Swedish and American converts to Islam:

> I think in Islam it is strongly recommended for women to be home with the children, it is not a law or a rule but it is promoted. There are so many blessings and *hadiths* saying that it is beneficial for everyone to have roles that are designated. That the man is the head of the household. (Mansson McGinty, 2006, p 122)

For these particular converts the attractions of being affirmed in their wish to stay at home and immerse themselves in motherhood is a very important aspect of their Muslim marriage. It is also a point of view that stands at odds with many prevalent feminist dialogues on the nature of equality in marriage and wider society, although these equal opportunity stances are also being challenged within western feminist discourses.

The values that are promulgated within Muslim families may be very different from a child or adolescent's non-Muslim peer group, as well as being seen as oppositional to those of society in general. Such contrasts can provide further areas of contention within the family setting and typically may occur across generations. Although, as has also been noted, a commitment to conservative and politically extreme interpretations of Islam can be viewed as a characteristic of some Muslim youth living in western societies, regardless of parental influence, and is consequently one that is often viewed in many quarters as problematic and threatening.

Sexuality

Here we discuss sexuality in terms of heterosexuality, while homosexuality is considered in the next chapter. Bouhdiba (1997) remarks that psychologically the domain of the secluded feminine is one some Muslim men may yearn for as representing the lost Eden of their innocent infancy. Unlike their sisters, men are unable to return to this comforting female environment, which later takes on a level of mystique. The physical separation of male from female is followed by a masculine psychological rejection of attributes regarded as belonging to the feminine: the soft, emotional, irrational, dependent and physically weak (Bouhdiba, 1977; Al-Khateeb, 1998).

The Arab male's nostalgia for a delicious haven of feminine pampering is not dissimilar in some ways to that which corresponds to the male westerner's idea of the harem. This notion has historically captured the imagination of the west, having been reproduced in erotic and erroneous detail many times in paintings and films. However, historically the harem carried different connotations in the Middle East, in which it was a very real, forcibly enclosed establishment in which incursions from outside or escape were prevented. The very name originates from the word *haram*: that which is forbidden by sacred law (Mernissi, 2001).

The westerner's sexual fantasy of the harem is effectively debunked by Mernissi, who throws cold water over the fiction, for having been born in one herself she regards it as 'synonymous with prison' (2001, p 2). Far from being a bower of orgiastic delight filled with beautiful and sexually submissive women, she states that 'In Muslim harems, men expect their enslaved women to fight back ferociously and abort their schemes for pleasure' (Mernissi, 2001, p 14).

Mernissi (1975; 2001) has long focused on the topic of sexuality in the Muslim world, and uses the conceptualisation of the harem to engage the reader in a learned discussion on gender. She points out that the idea of female sexual passivity, which in the west is quintessentially manifested through the notion of the harem, is a castrating concept towards women, and is furthermore one that is not recognised by Muslims. In fact, Muslims view female sexuality as a powerful and dynamic instinctual force and therefore place much importance on the mutual sexual satisfaction of couples within the boundaries of a lawful married relationship.

Sexual frustration is seen as mischievous and contributes to social disorder, a belief that stands in stark contrast to early Christian ideals in regarding the celibate life as the noblest path that can be followed, since sexual urges are viewed as inherently sinful.

Mernissi (1975) accordingly takes issue with the Christian concept of sexuality and states that Islam takes a stance similar to that of psychoanalysis in viewing raw instincts (libido) as neutral energy, neither good nor bad, but subject to, defined and channelled by the restraints of laws. Consequently, she puts forward a powerful argument that female sexuality from the Muslim perspective is seen as in need of curbing through social and physical restrictions. Thus an active female sexuality, as comprehended in Islam, can result in the patriarchal strategies of seclusion and surveillance. This is further indicated in the double-entendre term, *fitna*, which refers to feared chaos, as well as meaning a beautiful woman (Mernissi, 1975, p 4).

In the west, the presumed disinterest and sexual passivity of women, as it has been historically framed in sexist discourses, requires no such coercive measures as the harem. This traditional view is constantly challenged by an increasing western emphasis on female sexuality as dynamic and multifaceted. Yet, the Madonna–whore/good girl–bad girl dichotomy is not yet dead and buried, for as any British female teenager knows, to be labelled 'a slag' remains the ultimate insult to a girl's or woman's reputation. Even for those who regard themselves as sexually liberated, they have yet to win a total and enviable freedom. For, as Mernissi (1975) argues, contemporary western women are subject to the tyranny of merciless standards of accepted feminine beauty as devised by the male-dominated fashion and beauty industries. This is a domination that shackles women at least as much as the harem system in Mernissi's view, but is not one that Muslim women need be oppressed by.

Conforming to gender norms

The western convert to Islam is in a unique position to be able to consider gender norms from different perspectives, particularly those who come from more secularised nations, like those of northern Europe. First, it should be pointed out that seen from an Islamic perspective the label of 'convert' is a misnomer, for dogma dictates that all individuals are born Muslims but that social and cultural influences divert many from the right religious path. Therefore, converts are more correctly considered to have *reverted* to Islam, rather than *converted* (Mansson McGinty, 2006).

The greatest majority of converts are women, and they often find that the acceptance of a Muslim identity and lifestyle creates problems, where families and friends may overtly reject their choice to a certain extent (Mansson McGinty, 2006). Equally, their new lifestyle will require adopting many new forms of socialisation in which, for instance, platonic male friendships will not be sustained on a one-to-one basis due to gender propriety. This carries ramifications for male social workers who are apt to discomfit or cause offence to Muslim clients if their encounters invade the space of propriety. Since such contact between the sexes, albeit seen as perfectly innocent by social workers, is also likely to inhibit effective professional intervention, it cannot therefore be regarded as helpful to the professional relationship. Such considerations, furthermore, may apply to

Muslim males in relation to female social workers. Religio-cultural sensitivities obviously demand a more congruent accommodation in terms of the matching of worker to client wherever possible. However, professionals should not pander to cultural practices or individual prejudices that are discriminatory and contrary to the law of the land. A typical case, for example, relates to a Muslim family who refused to be allocated a Hindu social worker.

To return to the topic of conversion, entertainment such as clubbing and social drinking will usually be abandoned entirely in favour of appropriate, female-only gatherings (Rehman and Dziegielewski, 2003). Converts will usually be obliged to seek friendships and relationships that are compatible with their faith, and logically these are most likely to be found among those who share their beliefs. Yet, converts may also have to struggle to find their place within the Muslim community and to be accepted as genuine, and can therefore find their identity and integrity questioned on both sides of the religious divide.

Modesty and propriety

The approach to adolescence is a time of great change for daughters in many Muslim families. Accordingly, she will usually be expected to suspend friendships with boys other than her brothers, if indeed she had been allowed such playmates in the first instance. As we have seen, these forms of restriction will often extend throughout her adult life. Her close contact with males should now be confined to her *mahram*: those males who are not lawfully able to contract marriage with her due to consanguinity or marital bonds (Rehman and Dziegielewski, 2003).

The dress of a child will be transformed to the garb of adult, although in some societies even very young girls will have begun to adopt a form of adult female dress by adopting loose, long clothing and covering their hair. We learn that in the presence of her *mahram* a female 'does not need to cover her hair, neck or chest area' (Rehman and Dziegielewski, 2003, p 35). Although, as elsewhere, there are variations to this practice in which covering the head as a daily ritual is not prescribed by all denominations.

Modesty in dress is promoted for both sexes but the enveloping robes of some Muslim women, and in particular the use of veils, are the most conspicuous elements of certain forms of Muslim dress. Depending on ethnicity and how conservative a family is, women may cover most of their hair with merely a fashionable scarf. Veiling may also involve a complex arrangement of materials (including cloth and even leather or wood) that completely covers the head and all of the face with the exception of the eyes. In the case of Afghani women (particularly under the Taliban regime), the *burqa* incorporates even the concealment of a person's eyes where women are only permitted to squint through a small, restrictive window of crochet.

These concealing outer garments will be worn outside of the home or in the presence of strange men. In some Arab societies this outer robe and veil will be ubiquitous even in university settings, especially when there are male members of faculty present. However, it should not be assumed that this is a general practice in all Muslim countries, for some, like Malaysia, tend to place much more emphasis on student security issues that are not best served by facial concealment.

In European countries with established Muslim communities the issue of secular school uniform and the demands from Muslim girls to replace these with customary robes has aroused controversy. In defence of its Republican secular values, France has banned the wearing of *all* religious symbols by pupils, including veils, crucifixes and skullcaps. Since the ban several French Muslim students have transferred to British educational establishments, although school policies have also been challenged as discriminatory. This was highlighted in a court case, where it was argued that a British schoolgirl had the right to attend school wearing Arab dress (the *jilbab*) instead of a school uniform that was modified to meet the requirements of culture and religion. In another case, a school assistant was sacked for refusing to remove the *niqab* (her full veil) after pupils claimed they had difficulty understanding her. The education secretary of the time, Alan Johnson, stated that he expects schools to ban the wearing of full veils on 'safety, security and teaching' grounds (Wintour, 2007).

In 2011 France passed legislation to ban face concealment in public. This includes the *niqab* and carried with it a fine and mandatory lessons in French values. Legislation in Belgium soon followed, accompanied again by a fine or up to seven days' imprisonment. Local bans exist in Italy, Spain, Switzerland and Russia. The contentious nature of veiling and face covering is not restricted to countries in the west. In 2015, citing the bans in France and Belgium, the city of Urumqi in the predominantly Muslim region of Xinjiang, China, banned the *burqa* noting that it was not the traditional dress of Muslim Uighur women. Syria, Turkey and Tunisia are among a number of Muslim nations where national debates have been on-going. In France, much energy and legislators' time was spent on legislation that applied, in 2010, to only 2,000 women. The success of the French ban is questionable – fuelling Islamophobia and encouraging extremists, but has been backed by the European Court of Human Rights.

Few items of clothing proclaim a stronger commitment to a set of values than the veil for Muslim women. Post 9/11 such values may be regarded as antithetical to those of the dominant culture in western societies, and often arouse strong and very negative emotions in the general public. These circumstances were duly considered by Lord Ahmed of Rotherham, the first Muslim peer in Britain. His comments were quoted by *The Guardian* newspaper as, 'The veil is now a mark of separation, segregation and defiance against mainstream British culture' (Press Association, 2007). Similarly, in France, wearing the *burqa* since the ban has become a symbol of resistance, particularly among coverts to Islam: 'For them it is an act of resistance against the state, just like the punk or skinhead movements. That's why they are happy to pay their 150 Euros fine' (*The Local*, 2015).

In the west, in general the complexities of appropriate clothing for Muslim people, and women in particular, have yet to be fully comprehended. Indeed, the veil has become a contested symbol, in which it is seen as both oppressive to women and conversely as empowering; as a strategy of segregation of women from civil society and as a means by which women may safely negotiate it. Given these great contradictions it is hardly surprising that the issue of the veil arouses such strong emotions between Muslims and non-Muslims, and where, to confuse matters still further, in each camp may be found both ardent Muslim proponents of the veil and its fierce opponents.

Basharat (2006) provides a useful historical context for Islamic dress for women as signalling the right to their chaste inviolability, in contrast to the sexual availability of uncovered enslaved women. The origins of the veil (the *hijab*) come from a literal reference to the Arabic word for a 'curtain'. This relates to a verse in the Qur'an when the Prophet Mohammed wished to separate himself and his bride from the presence of a male visitor (Mernissi, 1991). To clarify this account Anna Mansson McGinty (2006) explains the huge significance of this event and the later extrapolation to the veil, in which it provides not only physical privacy from the eyes of men, but in addition creates the necessary distance between the sexes for propriety.

The veil acts as a form of *purdah*, in that it is worn in public, which, as Mernissi argues, 'is a male space. The veil means that the woman is present in the men's world, but is invisible' (Mernissi, 1975, p 84). Accordingly an interesting observation is made by Robina Mohammad (2005) that *purdah*, in terms of the wearing of a veil, has been practised in a more extreme way in Bradford than in Bangladesh. While Haideh Moghissi quotes one male Pakistani commentator as saying that the veil constitutes one of the 'basic principles of human rights in the Islamic world' (Moghissi, 1999, p 27).

So it has been argued that the veil permits a Muslim woman to conduct her business in the external world in a literal and metaphysical space that represents decorum as well as personal safety. Writing from Malaysia, it is now some time since Ong (1995, p 180) observed that veiled Muslim Malay women benefited from being able to participate in the 'social milieu' of the upwardly mobile and professional classes, without insult to their morality, or overtly offering a challenge to male authority. This situation is equally true for young Muslim women in the Middle East in seeking educational and career opportunities that were often denied their mothers, but without offending cultural, gender-related mores.

The political implications of the veil are also made apparent, however, particularly in relation to its modern usage. Mansson McGinty (2006) refers to studies of Javanese women who by donning the veil consciously use this as a strategy of self-transformation demonstrating their outward commitment to Islam. The wearing of the veil in this Indonesian context is also regarded as a crucial means towards a remaking of the social order in the closer image of Islam. In this vein Haleh Afshar (1996) clarifies the use of the veil as a political statement: 'Islamist women are particularly defensive of the veil…[Nevertheless], many Muslim women have chosen the veil as the symbol of Islamisation and have accepted it as the public face of their revivalist position' (Afshar, 1996, p 201).

This, however, is precisely the point that has been raised by politicians in Britain who claim that the wearing of the veil in this fashion is designed to imply a separatist stance in society. Predictably, this may then be regarded as not only a gesture of alienation towards western values, but as actively hostile towards those of the prevailing culture. Under these circumstances it is hardly surprising that moderate Muslim voices in Britain, such as Lord Ahmed, raise concerns regarding the wearing of the veil, and the safety of the wearer.

Afshar (1996, p 201) alternatively argues that for many Muslim women the veil is seen as liberating in that women become 'the observers and not the observed'. They thereby become freed from being regarded as sexual objects by men. In her study of female converts to Islam, Mansson McGinty describes the physical and metaphysical liberation that participants feel in adopting conservative Muslim dress:

> Fatima understands the veil as something that keeps the spiritual energy inside. An image of veiled power emerges; the experienced space of safety implies a sense of control and power. The power of being 'invisible' but observing, the power of controlling sexual energy from both outside and inside. Understanding the veil as 'protection' from 'guys eyeing you' instead of as oppression, she thus reverses the power perspective. By donning the veil she disciplines her own body and sexuality as well as strengthens her Muslim sense of self. (Mansson McGinty, 2006, p 121)

Revealing, western-style clothing for women is frequently castigated by the participants in this researcher's study as demeaning to the wearer by exposing her to the sexual gratification of men. Nevertheless, it is also noted that converts in particular have also been verbally attacked by Muslim women for acceding to a form of dress that these fellow Muslims regarded as anachronistic and decidedly oppressive, based on their cultural experiences in Iran, for example (Mansson McGinty, 2006).

This is not an isolated controversy, but is one that is analysed by Haideh Moghissi (1999) who powerfully refutes the idea that veiling forms a protection for women from rape, assault and murder within Muslim societies. Instead, following El Sadaawi, she points out that:

> Women in Islamic societies are caught between the globalized image of femininity or female beauty as a commodity in the west and the Islamic notion of femininity 'protected' by men and hidden behind the veil. In fact, 'veiling and nakedness are two sides of the same coin,' in which women are manipulated into serving agendas of control by others. (Moghissi, 1999, p 46)

In this vein Moallem (2008, p 130) offers an analysis of gender, patriarchy and imperialism in reference to dominant symbolic icons constructed in opposition to each other within this problematic socio-religio-cultural discursive space: those of the ubiquitous 'Muslimwoman' and the 'Westoxicated' woman. However, as Ashencaen Crabtree and Husain (2012) point out, toxic stereotypes of the degenerate western woman versus the oppressed, veiled Muslim woman are merely the flip side of the same patriarchal coin, where women embody and are therefore burdened by being the symbolic vehicles of cultural values and gendered norms.

The use of dress as signifiers of socio-cultural values is hardly a new phenomenon and has intrigued observers across cultures since clothing was first donned. A sartorial witticism concludes this discussion where the headscarf now seems to have been part of a socio-cultural uniform adopted in the late twentieth century by young Muslim women living in the west. As Afshar et al (2005) points out this has permitted them to create an ideological statement without jeopardising contemporary style in reconstructing a new tradition of the hijab combined with jeans, jackets and kitten heels.

Feminism and Islam

The rich and diverse debates in feminist scholarship focusing on the political relationships between men and women demonstrates the plurality of feminisms, in which the perspective of white, middle-class feminists has been dramatically challenged by women from alternative ethnic, cultural and class identities. Malik (2005) for instance, takes issue with western feminists who adopt a masculinised and orientalised stance towards 'the other': the (inferior) non-western woman who is viewed as being steeped in and bound by dogma and oppressive tradition.

In turn Moghissi (1999) claims that there does not exist a unified, coherent feminist philosophy in the Muslim world, where although the term 'feminism' may not be regarded as appropriate, concerns for greater equality between the sexes and the representation of Muslim women in public life do exist and have done so since the nineteenth century. Mir-Hosseini (1996) remarks on how women's issues abound in the literature on Muslims and Islam. Furthermore, women's contributions to social development are now more fully recognised in the Muslim world than ever before and concertedly harnessed in many regions (Ashencaen Crabtree, 2007c).

Moghissi takes care to delineate one crucial point: that there is a difference between 'Islam as a belief and personal choice, and Islam as law, as state religion' (Moghissi, 1999, p 139). Political activists and scholars may promote a secularised Muslim vision of equality between the sexes and a self-identification as Muslim that can be read in a cultural and spiritual sense, but without necessarily personally endorsing Islam as a state religion and legal framework.

To comprehend this point better, Fatima Mernissi offers the following clarification: 'To understand the dynamics in the Muslim world today, one has to remember that no one contests the principle of equality, which is considered to be a divine precept. What is debated is whether Shari'a law inspired by the Koran, can or cannot be changed' (Mernissi, 2001, p 22).

Etin Anwar (2006, p 221) draws out the 'metaphysical, social, ethical and eschatological grounds' for equality between the sexes, in an examination of relevant verses of the Qur'an (Table 7).

Table 7: An Islamic egalitarian gender system

• Both men and women, by virtue of their being in the world, are God's (Allah's) creatures.
• Men and women as persons (selves), partners, members of society, and servants of God are obliged to respect each other.
• Men and women will receive rewards according to their actions and behaviour.
• Men and women are jointly responsible for preventing evil and promoting good.
• Men and women as persons, partners, members of society, and God's creatures and servants are, therefore, equally expected to maintain each other's rights in order to be recompensed in the hereafter

Source: Anwar (2006, p 21).

Thus it may not be state law that is opposed, but the interpretation of *shari'a* law, as it currently stands. The well-known Malaysian women's social activist group 'Sisters in Islam' (www.sistersinislam.org.my) targets a range of issues which have an impact on Muslim girls and women nationally, including child brides and domestic violence. Sisters in Islam challenge the prevailing gendered interpretation of the Holy Qur'an, which they argue has been wrongly understood by male theologians, in reducing women's status under Islam to that of inferiors. Such views have been articulated by prominent female theologians like Dr Amina Wadud, who was reported by a Malaysian newspaper as saying that: 'What we have seen are fourteen centuries of traditional exegetical works that were exclusively written by males. This historical legacy established a male advantage.... It tends to marginalize or deny outright women a first-hand representation in discussions of basic paradigms on which much of the Islamic perspective rests' (Hamzah, 1996).

Much more puzzling to western feminists, however, is the claim that Islamic 'fundamentalism', as it is viewed in the west, attracts many Muslim women. The girls and young women drawn to the cause of Daesh being a case in point, whose fate (apparently embraced at the outset as a romantic ideal) is a rapidly arranged marriage to a jihadist soldier followed by strictly confined life of domestic drudgery and pregnancy. Examination of social media among the Mulan (female followers of Daesh) picked up this message from such a convert:

> I have stressed this before on twitter but I really need sisters to stop dreaming about coming to Shaam and not getting married. *Wallahi* [I swear to God] life here is very difficult for the *Muhajirat* (female migrant) and we depend heavily on the brothers for a lot of support.

> It is not like the west where you can casually walk out and go to Asda/ Walmart and drive back home ... even till now we have to stay safe outside and must always be accompanied by a *Mahram* [chaperone]. (Hoyle et al, 2015, p 23)

The appeal of fundamentalism seems a particular conundrum because such movements might otherwise be seen as instrumental in victimising women religiously and culturally. The stereotype of women living under deeply conservative Muslim regimes is, to quote Moghissi, that of 'veiled, secluded, ever-passive ... mute, immobile and obedient creatures' (Moghissi, 1999, p 138).

As Haleh Afshar points out, however, in Islamic terms so-called fundamentalism is seen by the zealous as 'revivalism' and symbolises a return to a purer and 'golden age' of Islam — and thus this vision is framed as empowering to women: 'They argue that Islam demands respect for women and offers them opportunities, to be learned, educated and trained, while at the same time providing an honoured space for them to become mothers, wives and home-makers' (Afshar, 1996, p 200).

It is claimed that these female advocates of revivalism apparently despise feminism as manifested in the west, because feminism is associated with foreign colonialism, as well as offering spurious freedoms to women in the west that are themselves dubious and illusory. The argument therefore runs that feminism has ultimately failed in its mission to alter the labour inequities between the sexes, but is instead culpable in having contributed to the devaluing of the benefits of matrimony for women (Afshar, 1996).

A full investigation of the paths Muslim women may take towards self-actualisation in terms of the politics of gender, as well as those of religion lies beyond the scope of this book. However, social workers working with female Muslim clients would be well advised to realise that the issue of gender equality is a highly complex one, as well as being deeply contested terrain. Muslim women who oppose conservative interpretations of Islam need empathy, and should not be subject to the undermining of their personal identification as Muslim, which may be owned in a cultural and spiritual sense.

Muslim critics of conservatism may or may not include those who embrace the principle of living under Islamic *shari'a* law. Those moderates who accept the principle may instead seek a reinterpretation that is not seen as contaminated by fallible and male-orientated discriminatory attitudes towards females. However, this does not mean that the former secularist group should necessarily be regarded as apostates, even if, as in Moghissi's words, 'The ultimate goal of the secular reformers is not to modify *Shari'a*, but to do away with it altogether' (Moghissi, 1999, p 130).

In conclusion, it is apparent that the Islamophobic stereotype of Muslim women generally being forced to live in bondage under a totalitarian, culturally oppressive dogmatic regime is largely unfounded for the majority of Muslims. Albeit, abusive circumstances for individuals undeniably exist, as will be discussed later. However, what is apparent is the complexity and heterogeneity of the Muslim world, where symbols such as the veil, for example, carry a multiplicity of meanings and defy a simplistic definition. Likewise, the convoluted and esoteric conceptualisations of gender and equality span numerous interwoven discourses and that the easy assumption of a polarity between progressive secularity and oppressive religiosity is a flawed distinction. While social workers cannot be expected to appreciate all the subtleties of the distinctions of the Muslim perspective, as has been introduced briefly here, it is important to avoid assumptions that reduce the multiple dimensions of human experience in the Muslim world to that of a single, misinformed and therefore misleading one.

FIVE

Working with families

In this chapter various issues relating to conflict within a Muslim family are discussed, including divorce and spousal abuse, as well as more extreme forms of domestic violence towards other family members. Later, we also consider child welfare issues with respect to child protection procedures and the accommodation of children. Throughout this chapter we seek to examine the assumptions and beliefs that underpin family behaviour and responses in conflict situations, as well as highlighting the implications for social work practice.

When discussing traditional means of resolving family conflict, we must differentiate between that which is promoted in the Qur'an, and other methods that have evolved across cultural groups. In Chapter Three we saw how the use of mediation by a respected, senior male authority figure can help to resolve an otherwise entrenched and deteriorating inter-family war of attrition within an extended Arab family (the *hamula*) (Al-Krenawi and Graham, 2003). In Arab Muslim societies there are many other forms of peaceful resolution, including one of the most important, the concept of *sulh*: a form of reconciliation using mediation (Al-Krenawi and Graham, 2003). According to Süleyman Derin (2005–06) *sulh* is associated with Sufism, whose mysticism, in common with many other spiritual philosophies, is fundamentally non-violent, and was in turn inspired by the accounts of the Prophet Mohammed:

> The Prophet (pbuh) displayed the greatest examples of this clemency and compassion. For instance, when the people of Taif stoned him, instead of asking for their punishment, he asked for their forgiveness. In fact, he never prayed to God for the destruction of the people who harmed him: even when he was pressed to do so he replied: 'I was not sent to this world for condemnation; I was sent as the Prophet of Mercy.' (Derin, 2005–06, p 2)

Although essentially a religion of reconciliation, Islam also accepts the idea of vengeance, and it is said that this signifies a restoring of the status quo, rather than being moved by vindictiveness (Al-Krenawi and Graham, 2003). These authors refer specifically to 'blood vengeance', which is described as an 'obligation to kill in retribution for the death of a member of one's family or tribe', through which family pride (*Ar*) can be restored (Al-Krenawi and Graham, 2003, p 284). This is a practice commonly accepted throughout Arab Bedouin culture where it is regarded as an established guarantee of security that members of a *hamula* extend towards each other (Al-Krenawi and Graham, 2003). They go on to describe the distressing case of a Bedouin family who flee into the desert where they live under conditions of extreme stress, dire poverty and utter isolation in an attempt to avoid a death sentence at the hands of a neighbouring *hamula*. Whatever the purported motivation behind blood vengeance, the consequences appear very similar to the enactment of the 'blood feud' or vendetta of Southern Europe.

Working within cultural parameters, the author Al-Krenawi, a former Bedouin social worker, is unable to offer any real protection to the adults or even the deprived and disturbed children in this family when working within cultural parameters. The best that can be done is to supply them with some material goods to alleviate their present distress (Al-Krenawi and Graham, 2007).

Although it is evident that blood vengeance retains a hold in contemporary Bedouin culture, in the UAE this has been replaced by 'blood money' (*diya*), in which a family may choose to be financially compensated for the killing of a relative. So prevalent is this arrangement that all motorists, Arab and non-Muslim expatriates alike, make sure that they are well insured for a substantial payout of *diya* in the event of a fatal road accident.

It seems fitting to conclude this section on traditional conflict resolution, however, by returning to the Sufi approach in which sinfulness and crime are viewed as closely overlapping, and where for Sufis, at least, the criminal is viewed as a sick person who requires, above all, compassion and mercy (Derin, 2005–06).

Contemporary family conflicts: changing gender roles

As has been pointed out, there are many variations of family life among the *ummah* and therefore no single example can serve as typical of the whole. Muslim family life is often said to be rigorously hierarchical and with clearly defined, gender-specific roles. Particularly so in relation to wage-earning and child-rearing duties, yet even here this depends on a wide range of factors governing the needs of individual family units, as well as the influence of culture. Modernisation is also changing the face of the Muslim family internationally, and specific roles may become more permeable and flexible as opportunities in society widen for both men and women. Modern Emirati women, for example, appear to have little in common with female kin of previous generations, due to a radical transformation of the social landscape and the need for nationalised education and skills in society. For a large number of Middle Eastern women, juggling careers and family commitments will become the predominant factor in their life that it is for many women in the west.

Although these changes are beneficial both to society and for women seeking greater empowerment in and beyond the home context, change often involves a certain level of transitional tension; thus family conflict may emerge from within and across generations and gender divisions. Conflicts leading to domestic violence can therefore occur where migrant families attempt to impose transported cultural values to keep certain members of the family under tight control. Such strategies tend to have the hardest impact on the younger females of the family, for reasons that will be explored further in the section on spousal abuse in Muslim communities (Ammar, 2000, p 8).

Problematic parenting

The implicit belief that most parents can be trusted to do a reasonably good job without state interference is increasingly under question in certain western countries, creating a climate of distrust concerning the values which impressionable children are imbibing within some minority ethnic (ME) communities.

In the UK, however, suspicions of dysfunctional parenting are being focused on Muslim parents. The recruitment of English born and bred young Muslims to extremist Islamist causes, as exemplified in the 7/7 London bombers and the hundreds of Britons attracted to Daesh to become jihadists, has fuelled suspicions regarding the adoption of such alien and nihilistic values. This is not viewed as just a British problem: the Madrid bombers, for example, were assumed to be socially integrated into Spanish society, albeit as Maghreb immigrants (Ashencaen Crabtree, forthcoming; Jordan et al, 2008). Although in the UK distrust is now being extended to the role of mosques as potential sites of radicalisation and where the perceived lack of muscularity among moderate Muslim voices to counter extremist views is viewed as a public concern.

As Fathi and Hakak (forthcoming) note, in consequence the private domain is now viewed as subject to social policy strategies and surveillance by professionals as part of a risk prevention approach (Fathi and Hakak, forthcoming). To this end, as part of the British counter-terrorist strategy 'CONTEST', the 'Prevent' programme (discussed in further detail in Chapter Eight) attempts to target radicalisation by monitoring a range of services and organisations including education, faith, health, criminal justice, charities and the internet (HM Government, 2011). Self-policing lies at the heart of the strategy, where self-monitoring is expected by organisations and reporting to authorities in the event of suspicions of radicalisation. Indeed, the latest expectations are that parents should police their children and apply to the state to have their passports confiscated if they suspect possible abscondment to extremist groups – with the threat that failure to do so would raise suspicions of parental complicity. The Prevent strategy has unsurprisingly been heavily criticised and is viewed as exacerbating an already combustible situation of state-enacted Islamophobia (UK Gov, 2015). The entire concept of 'radicalisation' would appear to be highly flawed as well, where the articulation of any views that can be constructed as 'radical' are now viewed as intolerably subversive to the state. To be facetious, extreme views are typical across the lifespan of angry youth, disillusioned and jaded middle age, and, finally, disgusted and furious old age. The dangers of making illicit freedom of speech in a supposed democratic state is clearly apparent and therefore need not be laboured here.

Family crisis due to 'unlawful' sexuality

Threats to family cohesion leading to family conflict can be found in many forms. Sometimes these may be manifested through individuals demanding the right to choose a marriage partner, irrespective of the choice of parents. Occasionally this may involve opting for a lifestyle and values that are regarded as very different from, and indeed even incompatible with and antagonistic to, the traditional culture in which the previous generation was raised. Such a case could typically revolve around the development of a gay or lesbian identity.

Homosexuality is an issue of huge controversy in the Muslim world for religious reasons. The international gay community has monitored over the years the number of gay Muslim men murdered for their sexual orientation. The press also report the occasional murders of western gay men by Muslim offenders and have taken sensational note of notorious film clips of lurid atrocities enacted by Daesh showing gay men in Syria being hurled to their death off tower blocks.

In common with other life variations, however, attitudes towards lesbian, gay, bisexual and transsexual (LGBT) people vary across the Muslim world. These range from the outright condemnation and rejection typified by the Islamic context in Somalia, and much of the Middle East, to partial acceptance in Malaysia along the lines of 'turning a blind eye', which, despite moving towards greater conservativeness, has been regarded as relatively liberal. In Malaysia the transsexual *pondan* ('boy–girl'), can still obtain a recognised and even respected niche in society (Ashencaen Crabtree and Baba, 2001; Mahamud-Hassan, 2004).

It would also be wrong to claim that homosexual eroticism is unknown in the Muslim world; for example, the Faithful are assured that they will be served by young men as perfect as pearls in Paradise. Many Sufi texts are lyrically erotic in this regard, although this is viewed as a spiritual allegory rather than incitement to the gay lifestyle (Halstead and Lewicka, 1998). Furthermore, it would be incorrect to say that homosexual love has not at times been practised and celebrated in Muslim societies (one thinks of the photographs taken of Taliban soldier lovers in this respect), as well as in pre-Islamic Arab culture.

Although there is insufficient data regarding the issue of sexual orientation among the Muslim *ummah* living in the west, there is a clear indication that this is an area of tension. For example, Jaspal and Cinnirella (2010, p 849) note that 'the dominant view among many Muslims is that LGB (lesbians, gays and bisexuals) identity is incompatible with Islam'.

The Old Testament parable of righteous Lot ('Lut' in Islam) and the cursed, sinful cities of Sodom and Gomorrah is one also rehearsed in the later Qur'anic texts, while the *hadith* cite Prophet Mohammed deploring homosexual behaviour (Yip, 2004). Homosexuality as carnal conduct is considered a form of *zina*[1] and is therefore unacceptable in Islam. Consequently, the internet abounds in warnings about and rejection of homosexuality, often wrapped in the language of compassion as well as hard rhetorical questions regarding whether such people can even be considered real Muslims at all.

In respect of non-heterosexual Muslims, Yip (2004) describes how homosexuality, being viewed as *haram* (forbidden), may be constructed as an example of 'westoxification', where it can be primarily deemed a western aberration. Afzal (2014) examines the tensions which American Muslims may experience owing to the embracing of LGBT rights into the national citizenship agenda, where individual alignment with constructions of nationhood would also imply acceptance of the equal status of these groups. This is by no means a problem for the US alone but raises a spectre of the same conflict bedevilling most liberal democracies.

Based on this evidence it is clear that a stigmatised sexual identity, coupled with perceived experiences of Islamophobia, is likely to add to a deeply troubled dynamic leading to multiple oppression of affected Muslim individuals. Rejection at various strata of the ecological context of the individual, especially at the fundamental level of home and family, inevitably creates situations of high risk for mental and physical health (which could be particularly injurious in vulnerable youth). Such family rejection may include a hasty arranged marriage and violence as well. Yip (2004) notes how one gay British participant in his study describes being beaten so severely by his elder brother that he was hospitalised for three months. The dangers for lesbian and bisexual young woman can be equally if not more hazardous: where physical abuse can be accompanied by forced marriage, imprisonment within the family, repeated rape and unwanted childbirth. Despite these alarming prejudicial attitudes and reaction, the LGBT Foundation estimates that there is likely to be around well over a 100,000 non-heterosexual Muslims in Britain alone (LGBT Foundation, 2016). Although undoubtedly insufficient in number to cater for the need there are some useful British resources offering support, such as the Safra Project catering for Muslim lesbian, bisexual and/or transsexual women, while Muslimyouth.net offers a forum for discussions and NAZ offers advice on the sexual health and wellbeing of Muslim LGB people.

The religious rejection of active homosexuality in Islam (which, incidentally, is similar to the views of several other conservative interpretations of faith) requires caution in relation to social work intervention with families in crisis. To this end, Mallon (2005) offers some useful nuggets of advice to social workers dealing with such situations summarised in Table 8, although they should be considered critically, alongside several caveats in relation to Muslim clients that are subsequently discussed.

The attitude of Muslim individuals towards their own sexual unlawful orientation may run along a continuum of self-loathing as being under a curse imposed by *Shaitan* (Afzal, 2014; Jaspal and Cinnirella, 2010). Or by contrast, sexuality as a condition unaccountably bestowed upon them by Allah, from which paradoxically emanates all perfection. As research indicates, because the primary identity for the individual is that of a Muslim, rather than of a LGBT individual, the scope for emotional turmoil is consequently ample and the struggle to achieve psychological congruence may be equally great (Jaspal and Cinnirella, 2010).

Table 8: Families in crisis: working with homophobia

- Defuse the crisis through relationship building and calming of family tension (particularly in relation to stigma).
- Identify and work with the most uncomfortable individual first.
- Work on changing attitudes through discussion and the use of informative reading material ('bibliotherapy').
- Link the family into any appropriate, informal support groups (Mallon, 2005).

Additional and interrelated points to incorporate are:

- Involve the most senior member of the family at the beginning, from whom the other relatives are likely to take their cue.
- In Muslim families, fathers should be listened to first, unless they are clearly indicating a deferment to another member of the family, for example, the mother.
- Rapid construction of a supportive partnerships around vulnerable youth (of both sexes) using a coalition of social work networks, youth services, community-based advocates and teaching professionals.
- Being aware of and prepared for extreme reactions in the family setting, in relation to the protection of minors and vulnerable youth. This risk factor relates to child protection and domestic violence procedures.

In relation to social work intervention with Muslim families, it is important to bear in mind that attitudes towards homosexuality can vary widely and combine faith, cultural and community overtones together with being influenced by class and education. As such some family attitudes may prove impervious to moderation towards the rejected individual, while others may be more accommodating, provided that the family honour is not publicly disgraced. There are practical issues to consider as well. It is unlikely that social workers would be able to conduct much in the way of 'bibliotherapy' (Mallon, 2005) in Muslim families, since there is little in the way of specific and helpful information on the subject, which unfortunately is outnumbered by condemnatory, religiously based tracts, viewing the homosexual act as an abomination.

There is, however, a crucial and potentially very helpful dichotomy for practitioners to recognise and exploit in any potential intervention in this area. The concept of a 'gay identity' is a nonsensical construct for many Muslims families and therefore unhelpful (Halstead and Lewicka, 1998). This is owing to the neat distinction frequently drawn by Muslims between the forbidden act and inclination, which differs markedly from the Christian position on sin. This is made clear in this statement clarifying the theological stance: 'In other words, in Islam, we are not held accountable for *desiring* something sinful. We are held accountable only for *acting on* something sinful' (MM, 2014).

To clarify therefore, right across the Muslim world individuals that under other circumstances would generally be viewed as having apparently adopted a gay identity, voluntarily marry into cohabiting, heterosexual unions without any social censure or family concern whatsoever, but rather with complete social approval (Jaspal and Cinnirella, 2010). In consequence, illicit desire, as it is deemed in Islam, is much more likely to be acceptable to families provided it does not actually translate into action. This position, although it may contradict the practitioner's personal and codified professional values, provides a potential starting point for constructive family negotiation using cultural sensitivity, which is particularly important where young LGBT people are dependent in many ways, including emotionally, on the family support system.

Divorce

Divorce is permitted in Islam but is not encouraged; both men and women have the right to initiate a divorce but with different conditions attached. Muslim communities have developed different social attitudes towards divorce, and in some Muslim societies, such as certain Arab communities, it is more acceptable than among South Asian Muslims. The attitude of this latter group may be a result of cultural influences from living alongside Hindu communities, which consider divorce to be impossible according to the Hindu Laws of Manu.

In Islam there are many different forms of divorce, the most common being *talaq bil tal*, which occurs when a man pronounces 'I divorce you' three times to his wife. The *shari'a* states that this has to be pronounced in front of two adult male witnesses, and between each pronouncement there has to be a gap of 30 days. This time lapse is to enable the husband to reflect and rethink his decision, as a divorce does not become final until the third pronouncement. The *talaq* therefore provides a 90-day respite in which discussion, mediation or resolution can take place.

This type of divorce has at times been distorted, with stories of a husband pronouncing 'I divorce you' in rapid succession without a time gap or witnesses present. Such a divorce does effectively dissolve the marriage but is termed a *bi'da*: an undesirable innovation but legally binding within Islamic law.

Women, on the other hand, have to either stipulate their right to divorce in their marriage contract, or otherwise they need consent from the husband to divorce. A stipulation in a marriage contract is often problematic as most women are unaware that they have this right, and even armed with this knowledge some might be nervous about commencing marriage with a request of the right to divorce.

When a woman requests a divorce it is called *khul*. A husband can refuse to consent, but is still free to polygamously remarry. It is, however, more problematic for a woman whose husband refuses to consent to a divorce. Here legal action would need to be taken by the wife through a *shari'a* court and/or intervention of an *imam*.

A divorce, according to Islam, does not entail spousal support payments but the husband is obliged to repay the *mehr* (a form of dowry, but one held in trust for the wife in the event of divorce), as designated in the marriage contract. In the case of children, the father is responsible for supporting the children. In many patriarchal traditions children are considered to 'belong' to the father. This of course can differ greatly from one Muslim society to another and will depend on how embedded *shari'a* law is in any specific society.

In the context of minority Muslim communities in the west most couples will need to formally register their marriage, as Muslim marriages may not be considered legally binding. Therefore, in the event of a marriage break-up the national family courts will be involved, and couples might have to obtain two divorces: one secular and the other religious. There have been publicised cases where some divorced Muslim women have not realised that they also need to obtain a *talaq* and have tried to remarry, only to find out that they require this before they can contract another Muslim (not civil) marriage.

Divorce carries deep stigma for women particularly in South Asian communities. While divorced men may rapidly remarry, a divorced woman is considered a pariah, is often rejected by her family and community, and ultimately is blamed for the break-up. Some support groups have been set up in the UK aimed at South Asian communities in order to reduce the level of isolation experienced by divorced women. The social stigma attached to divorce means that women may often prefer to remain in an unhappy marriage; and in general divorce rates in Muslim communities are relatively low compared to the rest of the population. However, there is little research generally to quantify the number of divorces in Muslim ME groups and to investigate the circumstances and experiences of divorced individuals, especially women.

Domestic violence: forms and features

Domestic violence is a shorthand term covering a wide range of abusive situations that includes some or all of the following factors: physical, psychological/emotional, neglect, sexual and financial abuse. The dominant feature, however, is the victimisation of one or more individuals by other members of the family, as opposed to abuse in other settings, such as residential institutions.

In the west, the general assumption is that domestic violence is synonymous with spousal (or partner) abuse. In other cultural contexts the victim may be the sibling, the child, the daughter-in-law or the parent of the abuser, to name but some relational variations, as will be discussed further.

With respect to spousal abuse and Muslim families in general, there is a growing body of literature, although in terms of other forms, such as elder abuse, there is scant information. However, it seems that it is older women, in common with their younger female counterparts, who are more likely to be abused in domestic settings than men (Women's Aid, 2015). Additionally, one of the few references emerging from the affluent nations of the Middle East in relation to elder abuse relates to that of an older woman suffering from physical neglect and psychological abuse. Accelerated social modernisation is regarded as eroding the extended family network, leading to atomised family units where traditional respect for, and care of, elderly parents is on the wane (Barise, 2005).

Physical abuse

The issue of spousal abuse is, as Ibrahim and Abdalla (2010) point out, a universal problem, which inevitably also implicates Muslim families, despite the Qur'anic ideal of marriage in Islam as the foundation of love, mercy, responsibilities and rights for both sexes (Faizi, 2001). Details of the home life of Prophet Mohammed are often used as primary exemplars of marital harmony for Muslims, to an extent that may deeply surprise many non-Muslims who may be quite unused to thinking of the literal and prosaic domestic arrangements of holy figures like Moses, Jesus Christ or Buddha. Thus it is claimed with absolute assurance that the Prophet willingly shared domestic chores with his wives and never beat them (Ibrahim and Abdalla, 2010). Faizi (2001) points out how the Prophet strongly disapproved of ill treatment of wives and points to a body of evidence in support of this statement.

Nevertheless, international studies provide evidence that for many Muslim women the realities of marriage can be far from this respectful ideal. Douki et al (2003), for example, argue that domestic violence is endemic in Arab societies. Haj-Yahia (2003, p 203) sums up his research into 'wife beating' in Arab society in Israel by concluding that justification for spousal abuse in this region is 'considerably more prevalent than in Singapore, the US, or Australia'. Wives are blamed for provoking the attack through 'careless' or 'provocative' behaviour as well as 'behaving in a way that is not appropriate for a woman' (which may include questioning and self-assertion) (Haj-Yahia, 2003, p 203).

Elsewhere, research data into domestic violence in Bangladesh reveal it to be a common hazard for women (Koenig et al, 2003). While Fikree and Bhatti (1999) ascribe domestic violence, with associative physical and mental health consequences, as affecting one third of their population sample of Pakistani women living in Karachi.

In relation to Arab Americans Nawal Ammar comments on how cultural stereotypes influence police procedures when investigating domestic violence. Accordingly, in the US Arab males are portrayed as 'particularly violent, controlling, and exceptionally oppressive of women'. In contrast, Arab women are viewed as conforming to the feminised image: 'submissive, veiled, helpless and accepting of all forms of oppression' (Ammar, 2000, p 58). It should be noted, however, that Ammar is not denying the extent of domestic violence in the Arab American community, which she regards as serious, but only the cultural caricatures that prevent the police from making the most appropriate judgements in attempting to help victims. Her plea is for a 'criminal-justice system ... that is culturally sensitive and respectful of Arab-American cultures' (Ammar, 2000, p 66).

Two particular issues emerge from Ammar's paper. First, that the criminal act of domestic violence is undermined within the discourse of the 'sacred-religious', across the Abrahamic religions. Second, she considers the way domestic violence is used by migrant families settling in the west as a means of distancing themselves and their female kin from the perceived negative ways of the new environment (Ammar, 2000). Accordingly, it is interesting to note that in the majority of discussions touching on the issue of domestic violence in Muslim families or societies, the same Qur'anic verse (Sura 4, Verse 34) will invariably be quoted with varying interpretations attached, as for example (Faizi, 2001, p 212):

> Men are the protectors/And maintainers of women, because God has given/The one more (strength) than the other, and because/They support them/From their means. Therefore the righteous women/ Are devout, obedient, and guard/In (the husband's absence). What God would have them Guard. As to those women/On whose part ye fear/Disloyalty and ill-conduct/Admonish them (first)/(Next) refuse to share their beds/(And last) beat them;/But if they return to obedience/Seek not against them/Means (of annoyance): For God is most High, Great.

It is, however, asserted by some that this should not involve leaving marks on a wife's face or her body (Doi, 1992). Ibrahim and Abdalla (2010) scrutinise the meanings of chastisement the Prophet advocated for adulterous wives. Kort offers an interpretation from a 'cyber-mufti' suggesting that the beating should involve no more than a symbolic tap (Kort, 2005, pp 376–80), while others state that this verse is altogether misinterpreted (Bucci, 2012).

Yet this verse has for the most part been used to justify spousal abuse as a form of legitimate correction of women, to the extent that assault administered 'with good intentions', and provided it is not to the face or is fatal, cannot be punished under Egyptian criminal law (Ammar, 2000, p 62). In recent years, Pakistan's lurch towards religious extremist voices has seen the Council of Islamic Ideology (CII) that advises the government on the compatibility of law with Islam, declare as un-Islamic a law that criminalises violence against women (*The Express Tribune*, 2016). This has led to demonstrations by women's groups and human rights activities and mockery of the CII in Pakistan's leading online satirical newspaper (*Khabaristan Times*, 2016).

Satire apart, however, justifications can equally be found in the UK, according to Fikree (2005) reporting a Bradford study of Muslim men and women, which found that Islam was used as justification for violence by male participants. By contrast women referred to their faith as a source of strength to cope with domestic violence.

Obtaining help

The exact figures relating to domestic violence towards ME women in the UK are hard to quantify given the lack of comprehensive research in this area, but they are assumed to be large. Southall Black Sisters have long campaigned for women subject to domestic violence and living under stringent immigration rules to be better catered for. The Domestic Violence, Crime and Victims Bill 2005 has afforded greater protection to such individuals; although in the UK, like in Italy, immigrant women experiencing domestic violence are made vulnerable to further domestic violence through immigration rules (Bucci, 2012), similar to the British Two Year Rule, where those entering the country under a spousal visa can be deported if they leave the marriage within that timeframe.

For ME women fleeing domestic violence the issue of finding a suitable refuge is problematic, with insufficient mainstream provision to cater for religious and cultural needs such as a space for prayers or facilities to store and cook halal food (Bhatti-Sinclair, 1994; Pryke and Thomas, 1998). Others may have difficulties in the first place accessing refuges through public funding owing to their current immigration status, which may preclude this.

Faizi (2001), writing from the context of the US, discusses refuge initiatives and their successes. She compares two different refuges: one based in Georgia maintains links with *imams* but offers liberal house rules regarding Islamic religious observation. The other, based in Texas remained open for only 18 months. During its short lifespan the 'shelter' imposed very strict Islamic-based guidelines on the conduct of its residents, which included enforced prayers and restrictive demands that residents would not be employed where they might encounter men outside their immediate family *mahram*; and jeopardised confidentiality by seeking permission from the local mosque prior to admitting any individuals.

Confidentiality breaches are by no means a trivial business when one recalls two shocking cases where a couple of British South Asian women were murdered by their abusive spouses while supposedly being in places of safety. In 1985 Balvant Kaur's trail was traced to Brent Women's Refuge with tragic consequences, while in 1991 Verduna Patel was actually killed inside Stoke Newington police station (Pryke and Thomas, 1998).

Culturally sensitive or separatist refuges, like the UK Refuge's South Asian services have increased due to demographic and social needs over the past decade, assisted by the professional recognition for a need for more inclusive services for women and their children. Nonetheless, because of the extremely disempowering nature of domestic violence, it requires great desperation and determination to decide to leave an abusive marriage and where flight may finally be prompted by fear for the victim's children, as much as, if not far more than for themselves.

Research findings also show that ME women may have additional particular problems accessing places of safety in terms of feeling able to speak of their experiences in the first place. It was only in 2015 that a UK national helpline was launched to support British Muslim women and girls experiencing sexual violence. 'Certainly a battered woman's ability to disclose abuse, and thereby receive instrumental and emotional support, is critical to her survival' (Yoshioka et al, 2003, p 171).

In the UK, Bhatti-Sinclair (1994) notes that many abused Asian women in her study had hardly ever voiced their experiences to anyone, not even to close members of their family. She notes in particular a lack of cultural community support, to the extent that sharp criticism may be levied against abused women who speak out, and even towards the natal family if they attempt to intervene on their daughter's behalf. Furthermore, many South Asian participants face enormous challenges in terms of disclosure due to a sense of loyalty to family or cultural families, as well as a pronounced sense of shame: 'These dynamics give rise to issues such as whether to remain silent in order to maintain family honour (described as 'izzat' within some communities) which can subsequently act as a barrier to seeking help' (Reavey et al, 2006, p 174).

Writing from the US, in comparing South Asian, African and Hispanic women subject to domestic violence, Yoshioka et al (2003, p 172) comment on the shared ethos of 'familism and collectivism', in which the emphasis decentralises the individual over the unity of the family and the collective wellbeing of the whole. In specific reference to South Asian women, these authors comment that the severing of the connection with the abusive spouse through divorce is considered a very undesirable outcome by participants, a conclusion equally shared by Bhatti-Sinclair (1994), with Faizi (2001) commenting on how hateful in the eyes of God divorce is for Muslims.

Wiper (2012) argues that intersectional understanding of overlapping oppressions is critical to tackling violence against South Asian women in relation to gender, ethnicity, together with (one would infer) education, class/caste and position in the family hierarchy. Women's status in the family and immediate community is also linked to domestic violence, although this too remains a contested area, where research data worldwide provides an unclear picture. Koenig et al (2003), citing Jejeebhoy and Cook (1997), report that although in some Indian States high levels of autonomy among wives reduced the risk of domestic violence, in more conservative areas this proved not to be a protective factor. In the Philippines the risk for wives of violence is higher when they dominate decision making in the home than where husbands enjoy the head of household role. These authors also cite findings that show that women's involvement in group credit and saving programmes in Bangladesh commensurately decreased the risk of abuse, although this also depended on the continuum of liberal/conservative normativity in the villages studied (Koenig et al, 2003): 'More autonomous women, at least initially, are likely to violate established norms concerning gender roles and call into question the larger family's honor and prestige and, as a consequence, to incur a higher risk of domestic violence' (Koenig et al, 2003, p 10).

This has some clear implications in relation to faith communities in Bangladesh, since the authors point out that, regrettably, religious affiliation is a further factor that influences domestic violence, whereby higher levels of violence were found among Muslim households than among Hindu families (Koenig et al, 2003).

The issue of religion is inextricably bound up in the unpalatable one of domestic violence, although it should be emphasised that many would argue that justification for abuse is based on a misinterpretation of religious principles. In this vein, Faizi offers the following chilling account of an American Muslim woman who feels compelled to remain with her abuser:

> The woman was willing to jeopardize her own life, as well as the lives of her three children, because she believed that leaving her husband would damn her to hell. Usually, one of the major obstacles to leaving is not having anyone to turn to within the family. The irony in this situation was that the wife's family, including her father and brothers, had encouraged her to leave the abusive relationship and offered her refuge. Nevertheless, she was determined in her religious convictions and remains with her abusive partner to this day. (Faizi, 2001, p 18)

Sexual abuse

Forced sexual relations in marriage are by no means confined to Muslim marriages. It has only relatively recently been framed as marital rape and a form of domestic violence in the west, when once it was commonly viewed as the unspoken but accepted fate of many women. Islam, however, can create particular areas of ambiguity and difficulty in this respect, since a woman's submission to her husband's sexual demands is considered one of her marital duties. Etin Anwar makes this clear in quoting a part of the following Qur'anic verse al–Baqarah (Surah 2, Verse 223) going on to adjure men to purify themselves before sexual acts with their wives: 'Your wives are your tilth; go, then, unto your tilth as you may desire' (Anwar, 2006, p 73).

The metaphor of women as ripe and open fields for man's use and (if the pun will be pardoned) 'husbandry', is one that Shakespeare also employed where the blunt soldier Agrippa, commenting on the sexually fertile union between Julius Caesar and Cleopatra, states,

> 'She made great Caesar lay his sword to bed;
> He plowed her, and she cropped.'
> (*Antony and Cleopatra*, Act II, Scene II)

Alluring Queen Cleopatra's consent to seduction by the great Roman emperor (or debatably vice versa) is of course never in question. However, in reference to marital rights in Islam, Mernissi points out that while mutual sexual satisfaction is important in marriage, the primary issue is that wives cannot refuse sexual intimacy without fear for their souls:

> If the wife refuses to have intercourse with her husband she is penalized both on earth and in heaven. The Prophet, according to Imam Bukhari, said a woman 'who is asked by her husband to join

him in bed and refuses to do so is condemned by the angels who throw anathemas on her until daybreak'. (Mernissi, 1975, p 24)

Wives therefore can be regarded as completely sexually available within marriage, and would seem to be denied any legitimate right to refuse to be used in this way. Thus it not surprising that according to British research findings (Reavey et al, 2006), it is extremely difficult for abused women in these circumstances to seek help in relation to sexual abuse, over and above that of physical violence. The following case studies exemplify the deeply isolating position of Muslim women in obtaining help due to religious and cultural beliefs that assert the male prerogative over that of the female's.

Case study 3: Marital rape, Malaysia

A Muslim Malay woman, Aini, working in the Malaysian health system, was informally referred for clinical social work practice by a medical consultant who had become aware that she was a victim of domestic violence. Aini was very reluctant to be interviewed at first and presented as a very anxious, tearful individual. She disclosed that she had been subject to many years of physical, psychological and sexual abuse by her husband. Although, she said, she had once been reasonably content in her marriage and had borne several children but that matters had seriously deteriorated between the couple to the extent that she claimed to be regularly raped by her husband. She said that he regarded sexual congress as his absolute right and would resort to violence if she attempted to avoid his advances. She also said that he regarded her reproductive organs as belonging to him in which to plant his seed (this couple already had six small children), and wished to keep her in a state of constant pregnancy and childbearing.

In desperation she had tried to talk to her relatives about the problem but this had led to no resolution. She then tried to get an *imam* to mediate on her behalf, but he had not appeared to be at all sympathetic to her, and had made it clear that he believed her husband was acting within his rights. Finally, she surreptitiously tried to lodge a complaint with the local police. The results were catastrophic: two relatives of her husband working in the police force quickly become aware of her presence. Before having the chance to make her complaint, she had been forcefully escorted back home into her husband's keeping. Aini's case was finally referred to a fringe, Muslim, woman-oriented legal service who attempted to help her and her children escape from her abusive marriage.

Case study 4: Marital rape, UK

Noora called a national telephone helpline for Muslims in a state of panic and distress She had just been raped by her husband and not for the first time. She expressed deep feelings of dishonesty, betrayal and oppression. She also expressed anger and wanting to take justice into her own hands. She sounded emotionally drained and wanted reassurance that she was not going insane. She would simultaneously express anger at her husband, while blaming herself, demanding to know of the telephone counsellor whether she was believed or not. Noora needed reassurance that forced sexual intercourse was abusive and talked through her sense of trauma, belittlement and impurity were normal, as well as her anger at her husband's denial of her feelings. Expressing shame about telling her alienated family, who had not approved of the marriage in the first place, her increasing vulnerability was discussed further, in view of her husband's knowledge that she has no one to support her or confide in. Comfort and options were offered to Noora to enable her to gain more control of the situation. The worker suggested that asking for guidance from Allah in prayer would also be helpful. Finally Noora was signposted to various specialist organisations with the required cultural and religious sensitivity to meet her needs. Finally, she was asked if she was aware of the importance of gaining confidential proof of her rape through medical examination. It was hoped that this intervention would give Noora more information to help her decide whether to leave her abusive marriage in the future.

Sexual abuse may not be identified by victims as a type of domestic violence, but only as the general exploitation of the disempowered female self. The following quotation from an advocate working in a South Asian women's organisation illustrates the problems related to helping and protecting victims by prosecuting offenders:

> She [abused wife] didn't acknowledge it was rape but she said he forced her to have sex that she didn't want to. And they said ok, that's rape but she didn't understand the concept of rape so when it came to court, she couldn't go into court and...talk about rape coz she didn't believe that it was...she felt it would make her look bad as a wife, so she couldn't do it. (Reavey et al, 2006, p 177)

These authors add that the reluctance of South Asian women to speak out on the topic of sexual abuse was related to the trivialisation, and even, in some cases, normalisation, of the female experience of coerced sex in marriage as rooted in cultural and faith-based interpretations. The authors argue that instead, owing to the intertwined dynamics of familism and collectivism, the women regarded their experiences as merely another manifestation of power play, where women living in strict hierarchical and patriarchal structures regarded themselves as effectively powerless to resist. The very act of speaking out was seen to damage the family *izzat* (honour) and cast a bad light over the women's reputation in consequence, rather than that of the perpetrator's (Reavey et al, 2006).

Some might argue that if a woman does not frame forced sexual intercourse within marriage *as* rape, then the psychological and emotional consequences, at least, would not be as severe as on those victims who define such acts precisely in this way. Research findings, however, show that domestic violence, including sexual abuse, is a factor in mental health problems affecting South Asian women, as is the case for other population groups (Dienemann et al, 2000; Chew-Graham et al, 2002).

Additionally, a review of research findings in the UK shows that among young South Asian women domestic violence contributes to self-harm and suicide (Chew-Graham et al, 2002; Reavey et al, 2006). Ominously, many of these women felt unable to approach health agencies and social services precisely because they felt that their referrals would come to the attention of people from their own community working in such settings who would then betray them to their families.

For these women, more work needs to be done by the mainstream services in relation to building trust through reliable, culturally competent and strictly confidential outreach work that targets vulnerable groups discreetly, flexibly and, above all, effectively. A corollary is the need for streamlined, integrated services able to swiftly assess risk and offer support and appropriate places of safety to women and children at risk of domestic violence, without need for further unnecessary delays and exposure to hazard. Where professional assessments indicate a significant risk for clients the model of intervention needs to be one of rapid 24-hour, crisis management.

Forced marriage *is* domestic violence

Improved outcomes for clients are considerations that the UK government and the police force also have to consider in relation to the more unfamiliar or extreme forms of domestic abuse. While arranged marriages are a long established and valued cultural norm in many Asian cultures, serving to bind extended families together, there is a clear distinction between genuinely consensual arranged marriages and forced marriages. It is the latter form that this section explores as a type of domestic violence.

Coerced (or forced) marriages of young females have become a matter of increasing concern internationally where there is growing recognition that forced marriages of girls conforms to aspects of human trafficking (Eskind Moses and Russ, 2014). Every year in the UK alone hundreds of girls are removed from school by their families for the purpose of marriage. The extent of forced marriages is unknown; however, it is feared that there are many. A survey carried out by Bradford City Council over a decade ago tracked 1,000 schoolboys and an equal number of schoolgirls from primary school to secondary, to find that only 860 schoolgirls were still on the school roll in secondary schools at the time of investigation. These missing youngsters had apparently been taken out of Britain back to Bangladesh and Pakistan for the purpose of marriage (Tickle, 2006);

India, Somalia and Afghanistan also receive numbers of young, female British citizens brought into the country for this purpose. In 2015 the Forced Marriage Unit (FMU) received 1,200 referrals, although few from victims themselves, and it is believed that this number represents only a small proportion of actual cases of forced marriage (Travis, 2016).

Case study 5: The non-consensual arranged marriage

Raha's family are forcing her to go abroad to marry someone in Pakistan. She is unhappy about this as she already met someone that she wants to marry but he is not an acceptable choice to her family. Raha fears losing her family if she chooses not to go ahead with the marriage. Her loyalty to the love, care and attention they have provided her over the years leaves her feeling torn about how to deal with this decision. She feels there is no compromise and that this is a cycle being repeated in her family as her mother, sisters and various cousins have all had arranged marriages. Raha does not feel strong enough to challenge her family and contacts a youth helpline to speak about the pressure she is under by female members of her family who did not sympathise with her predicament.

The response to forced marriage internationally varies widely. Law enforcement and social services in the US currently lack the necessary knowledge and experience to properly support those under threat or experiencing forced marriage (Eskind Moses and Russ, 2014; McFarlane et al, 2016). France by contrast uses a raft of existing but not specific social policy and legislation to protect and prosecute (Gill and van Engeland, 2014). Australia is also confronting forced marriages as a public concern and employs the existing Commonwealth Criminal Code Act 1995 as a legislative tool. The UK has the longest experience of this phenomenon among these nations for historical reasons and has now established specific legislative measures to address the issue, this being the British Forced Marriage (Civil Protection) Act 2007 for England and Wales. Like the Australian approach this carries a penalty of up to seven years' imprisonment for forcing someone to marry against her (or his) will (gov.UK, 2016a).

In forced marriages unless she (typically females rather than males) acquiesces to pressure she may be subjected to harassment, threats, imprisonment in the home and physical abuse. This constitutes an unacceptable breach of human rights. The FMU liaises closely with British consulates overseas with a view to helping to rescue girls and women from deplorable domestic conditions where they may have been kidnapped, held captive and subjected to rape by the stranger 'spouse'. Prevention, however, is considered the best way to tackle the problem of forced marriages, and consequently the FMU also engages in outreach work in targeted areas of the UK.

Support may also be found from a number of independent charities and NGOs, while some *shari'a* law experts, such as the Islamic Sharia Council in Leyton, will take on the role of 'releasing' Muslim women from enforced and bad marriages in general. In addition to *shari'a*, their divorce rights are of course protected under British jurisprudence in any case. However, for concerned Muslims wishing to conform to Islamic family law, the *shari'a* ruling spiritually ratifies the situation under Islamic principles, in addition to the legal weight of UK law. Satisfyingly, both civil and spiritual law are in mutual agreement with regard to enforced marriages being indefensible (Bell, 2007).

Murder, 'shame' and domestic violence

Finally, we consider the phenomenon of so-called 'honour' based violence (HBV), which encompasses probably the most extreme forms of domestic violence. Included in HBV are forced marriages according to the definitions used by the London Council Women and Girls Network (WRC and WGN, 2011), as girls may have been promised to suitors from early childhood (or may lack capacity to consent owing to learning/intellectual disabilities). The breaking of betrothals may be viewed as constituting a disgrace for the families involved, leading to HBV. Crimes that fall under the category of HBV refer to occurrence in certain ME families where the real or imagined conduct of a family member, invariably female, is viewed as bringing the family's reputation into disrepute and thereby becoming a question of *izzat* (honour).

> These causes are clearly linked with the concepts of honour and shame, which many Asian Muslim families are reluctant to let slip and they will go to any length to keep intact; although such reticence apparently may extend to the community at large. The concern of honour and shame for the victims of abuse becomes nothing more than a form of social control designed to protect the abuser. (Irfan and Cowburn, 2004, p 96)

The conduct of the victim is interpreted by her family and/or community as running counter to the normative values of the original cultural mores – although usually this behaviour is not considered either illegal or particularly immoral (indeed, often the conduct is considered perfectly normal) in the adopted country, such as this example from the UK exemplifies.

Case study 6: The forbidden chat

Fatima, a young college student, called a Muslim helpline sobbing desperately. Her brother had been beating her for the past two days as he had seen her speaking to an old school friend. She was on her way home from college when her brother saw her and dragged her into the car. He then drove straight home and locked her in her bedroom. Returning with a belt he started beating her until she passed out from the pain. Fatima said to the helpline worker that her parents were too afraid of their son to intervene. He finally stopped and let her out of the room to eat something. Since then he has forbidden her from returning to college or leaving the house unaccompanied, telling her that he will kill her if she does not obey. Fatima expressed how scared and hopeless she felt and wanted to know if such violence by her brother was accepted in Islam. Upon being reassured that Allah does not want anyone to be punished unjustly, she was given the number of the local social services office and that of a local *imam* in her area from whom she could seek confidential advice.

The cultural belief governing a brutal family response to their relative's behaviour is that the violence, including murder, of the offending individual somehow cancels out any supposed disrepute on the honour of the family. In this oppressive gendered construction females embody the normative values of an entire cultural community and therefore pay dearly for any perceived betrayal or transgression of these values.

The very term 'honour-based' violence is descriptive of these transported cultural values, which are alien to the new societal context and as such is a terminology highly disputed as potentially 'othering' the phenomenon. In this process HBV becomes distanced in the minds of the general public as serving only to demonstrate an example of exotic barbarism in unfamiliar and backward communities. However, the term can also serve to exculpate the perpetrator's crime to an extent as culturally justified in the transgression of established mores by the victim who effectively 'brings it on herself'. Worse, the dramatic phrase 'honour killing' does a serious disservice to victims in that it tends to disguise the brutal truth, which is essentially, domestic violence taken to the extreme of murder. Finally, in response to the remorseless killing of Farzana Parveen, a pregnant woman in Pakistan murdered by her family for choosing her own marriage partner, Navi Pillay, High Commissioner for Human Rights, disgustedly retorted to the media 'I do not even wish to use the phrase "honour killing": there is not the faintest vestige of honour in killing a woman in this way' (UN News Centre, 2014).

Whichever term is used, whether 'shame killings' as advocated by UN General Secretary, Kofi Annan, or 'femicide' or 'patriarchal killings' (Dias and Proudman, 2014), it is sobering to grasp the scale of such crimes, where the Honour Based Violence Awareness Network, following UN figures, reports that there are 5,000 women killed annually under the excuse of salvaging family honour (HBVAN, nd). Although the Indian subcontinent is often implicated in such crimes, Tripathi and Yadav, comment that this is a commonplace feature of patriarchal control in the Middle East as well.

> Thousands of women and girls are stabbed, burned or maimed every year by husbands, fathers or brothers who believe they have brought dishonour by being unfaithful, seeking a divorce, eloping with a boyfriend or refusing to marry a man the family has chosen. When the victims do not survive, the crime becomes an 'honour killing', a term that has come to symbolize the cruel irony of a conservative

Islamic society that purports to shelter women, yet often condones savage violence against them in the name of male and family honour. (Tripathi and Yadav, 2004, p 64)

An international campaign to prevent violence against women living under Muslim Laws (www.violenceisnotourculture.org/home1) reports on the rise in coerced suicides in Turkey on the orders of their family as another sinister variant of HBV. Depressingly the rise in apparent suicides and accidents of girls and women is a calculated strategy by abusers designed to avoid prosecution of family offenders directly, owing to tougher Turkish legislation seeking to protect female victims.

Although Muslim majority societies are implicated in HBV across Asia and the Middle East, it is by no means exclusive to these nations, however. It is thus very important not to essentialise heterogeneous groups by erroneously assuming this is an Islamic custom, which is not the case, but rather to see it as fundamentally embedded in patriarchal culture. To this end, Lila Abu-Lughod (2011, p 22), in reference to Bedouin Arab communities, explores how daughters are cherished by loving parents where they the girls are likened to 'gazelles' and unfettered 'falcons'.

Examples of HBV occurring in modern liberal democracies are illustrated by three tragic examples in the UK. Academically ambitious 17-year-old Shafilea Ahmed was physically abused for years by her conservative Pakistani parents for her perceived westernised ways and resisting an arranged marriage. Although a social work referral was made by Shafilea's school it was closed shortly afterwards at the girl's request. Shafilea was eventually murdered by her parents in 2003 by being suffocated with a plastic bag forced into her mouth while being pinned down.

The body of 20-year-old Kurdish woman, Banaz Mahmod, was found in a suitcase in 2006 months after being subjected to hours of rape, beatings and then finally garrotted at her South London home by family members. Her crime was to walk out of an abusive arranged marriage and then later falling in love with a Kurdish Muslim boyfriend, who was not from the same village. What was particularly appalling in the case of Banaz was that all her previous attempts to alert the local police to her danger were not taken seriously by the local police, even though Banaz accurately named her future killers (McVeigh, 2007). Once Banaz was reported missing by her boyfriend, the London Metropolitan Police took over the case and spent several determined years pursuing her killers through an evidence trail obscured by obfuscations and false evidence from the local Kurdish community, going to the extent of organising a previously unprecedented extradition of two of her murderers from Iraq. Eventually her uncle, father and two male cousins were given life sentences for her brutal murder. Her grieving boyfriend recently committed suicide and her elder sister, whose evidence helped to convict the murderers, remains in hiding for fear of her life. Remarkably since then discovered film footage from Banaz' police interview formed the basis of an extremely powerful and moving documentary, which is highly recommended viewing (see www.youtube.com/watch?v=VepuyvhHYdM).

In 2004 Heshu Yones, a Kurdish girl aged 16, was savagely stabbed 17 times before having her throat slit by her father in the family's West London bathroom, following months of beatings owing to her wish to lead a normal life in the west. An anonymous letter by someone in the close-knit Kurdish community in West London had been sent to her father accusing her of behaving like a prostitute as she was going out with a boyfriend of Christian Lebanese heritage. The father's reaction was explosively and mercilessly terrible (Butalia, 2003; Bedell, 2004). After an attempt at suicide the father later attempted to blame Heshu's murder on an Al-Quaeda break-in. It also became apparent that he was being protected by members of the local Kurdish community attempting to pervert the course of justice, such as in the Mahmod case.

It was, however, the abominable Shafia case in Canada that went on to grab the attention of the world press when Afghan migrants, Mohammed Shafia, his polygamous second wife Tooba and their son murdered the couple's three teenage daughters aged 19, 17 and 13, along with his unhappy, polygamously married first wife, Rona Amir Muhammed. The victims' bodies were found in a submerged car in a canal in Ontario. Convicted for murder in 2009 the offenders are currently appealing against the verdict on the grounds of cultural prejudice in the Court hearings.

Three main lessons can be drawn, namely that these cases are not committed in the heat of the moment but are normally pre-meditated and organised conspiracies that rely on collusion in the family and community, as in the Yones and Mahmod case. Second, that health workers, social workers, teachers and the police need additional and specialised training to understand the risks involved for vulnerable girls and women from ME cultures, as became poignantly apparent in the Mahmod case, where there were many errors made prior to the London Metropolitan Police taking over. Third, that procedural guidelines need to be firmly in place to respond appropriately with a view to immediately protecting those at risk.

One concern that has been raised in relation to teachers, but can just as easily apply to social workers and the police, is that of actually instigating violent family responses. This may occur when taking the otherwise routine steps of contacting the family to discuss areas of concern which they have in the care or management of the girl in question. Avoiding contacting the family openly may tend to conflict with the professional outlook of both social workers and teachers, who usually seek to involve families with a view to resolving problems (although in the case of Banaz Mahmod such a fundamental error was made by one of the police officers). In the case of schoolgirls at risk, caution, confidentiality and security needs to be the first professional responses, while proper risk assessments are rapidly undertaken which are grounded in cultural awareness and knowledge.

The issue of cultural sensitivity, together with a focused person-centred approach, is therefore of paramount importance, since the client may have no other resource to fall back on except that of the abusive family itself, as was the case for Banaz Mahmod. She may also feel excessively guilty about betraying the family through the very act of seeking help out of a need for self-protection, as seems to have been the case for Shafilea Ahmed.

It is important therefore for both professionals and their clients to be able to distinguish family and cultural norms from that of faith. Yet there is also a tremendous need for concerted outreach work to bring the seriousness of the issue home to targeted communities, in order to enable them to take collective responsibility for the attitudes that generate violence. A change of terminology to remove the 'honour' from foul and cowardly deeds is an important step forward in driving that message home. Innovative social work initiatives such as 'Projekt Heroes' in Germany involves inviting immigrant youths to training programmes to reflect on issues of gendered norms and violence via discussion and role-play. The aim is for these youths to take on championing roles to alter community attitudes incongruent in the new country of settlement (Schuster-Craig, 2015).

The necessity of maintaining open discussions are clearly apparent, when according to a 2006 poll undertaken for the BBC's Asian Network one in ten young British Asians believed that murders committed in the name of family honour could be justified (BBC, 2006). Table 9 offers some guidelines for intervention in domestic violence when working with Muslim families.

Table 9: Working with domestic violence

- Improved multidisciplinary risk assessment procedures and rapid response protocols.
- Effective, early collaboration between professionals involved in the care and protection of girls and women at risk of domestic violence.
- Improved training of professionals to work more effectively in this area.
- Ensuring the immediate safety of the possible victim before contacting the family, if required.
- Enlisting the help of culturally knowledgeable, faith-informed, community-respected mediators to advocate on the victim's behalf with the family of origin, if this is what the client wishes.
- Obtaining legal advice and guidance for the victim via British jurisprudence and, if desired by the victim, *shari'a* experts.
- Ensuring that victims cannot be taken out of the country against their will.
- Ensuring that their wishes, circumstances and safety have been adequately investigated and that the victim is not being coerced into closing cases prematurely.

Abuse of children

Over the years there has been a wealth of information written about child abuse and neglect, as well as a large quantity of material on professional protection procedures and guidelines. It is not our intention therefore to offer a lengthy explanation of Child Protection as an area of social work practice and its legal implications, since it is assumed that readers unfamiliar with this very important area of social work are best served by referring to texts dedicated to the subject.

Instead, our discussion here revolves around how social workers may consider these issues in relation to Muslim perspectives on the subject, as well as offering some examples from the global community of the *ummah* regarding how child abuse allegations have sometimes been dealt with internationally.

As with domestic violence, research data pertaining to child abuse tend to classify cases along broad ethnic lines rather than faith. This can disguise evidence-based data that may be highly relevant to Muslim families, as opposed to, say, Vietnamese Buddhist ones. It is therefore difficult to tease out specific examples of how social work assumptions may have had a negative impact on intervention with Muslim families specifically.

The prevalence of Muslim families involved in UK child protection cases is therefore notoriously difficult to ascertain where data is scarce (Chand and Thoburn, 2006). However, the problems confronting social workers regarding insufficient knowledge of religio–cultural differences, language barriers and the appropriate accommodation of Muslim children by social services continue to bedevil practitioners.

In a review of research literature Chand and Thoburn (2006) claim that white children and those of Asian origin are under-represented in the statistics for children receiving formal child protection work. Although the authors also state that by contrast the combined group of African Caribbean and African children were given an average representation in the same data.

Turning their attention to discipline issues among Bangladeshi parents, Chand and Thoburn cite research data that suggest that physical abuse is tied to punishment strategies, and these are once again used as means to curb westernising tendencies in adolescents (Chand and Thoburn, 2006). By contrast, mothers from the Punjab appear to rarely use and even disapprove of corporal punishment (Chand and Thoburn, 2006). A further interesting piece of research from Irfan and Cowburn (2004) indicates that examples of harsh corporal punishment may be found among some Pakistani parents in the UK, where a sample group of Pakistani youngsters had experienced the following forms of discipline at the hands of siblings, mothers and fathers. A statistical proportion of 65 per cent of young people in this study had experienced being slapped, and 50 per cent had been punched, with a further 42 per cent hit with a shoe by their mother. In addition, some forms of rare and unusual punishment were indicated, which included cold–water immersion, suffocation and Chinese burns.

Despite this, less than half of the respondents considered being spanked or hit with a shoe as constituting abuse, and regarded their parents as loving but occasionally driven to exasperation, or even a more serious loss of control such as a case of HBV where a 15–year–old British Pakistani girl was beaten with an iron rod (Irfan and Cowburn, 2004).

Chand and Thoburn (2006) refer to a 1997 survey of British casework where the majority of children suffering from neglect in Britain were white, standing at 32 per cent, followed by children of African Caribbean descent at 26 per cent, and finally Asian families taking up the rear at 11 per cent. However, the issue of child sexual abuse among Asian communities was scant and therefore Chand and Thoburn (2006) refer to data going back to 1991 where several Bangladeshi boys came to the attention of social workers in the then underprivileged area of Tower Hamlets, London. One crucial point highlighted by these authors refers to the inhibitions that Asian families and communities may feel towards sexual abuse issues over and above the abhorrence felt by the general public. This impression was also confirmed in a study of Gilligan and Akhtar (2005) of British Asian families in Bradford,[2] where sexual abuse was considered both unmentionable and unbelievable:

'People in my community think that sexual abuse doesn't happen, there is no way that a family member would sexually abuse a child, [adding that] if it is disclosed, the child is making it up or has provoked it'. [Another wrote] 'Maybe some people are aware, but most people would disregard or dismiss the idea that things like these happen in our community.' (Gilligan and Akhtar, 2005, p 272)

Such huge reservations relating to any reference to the topic altogether for both cultural and religious reasons are beginning to slowly change (Gilligan and Akhtar, 2005), but it is still evident throughout much of the Muslim world, and here useful lessons could be learned from Malaysia, which has well established child protection procedures (Munir, 1993). Thus, it is true to say that there is only a minute amount of research literature that refers to sexual abuse among Muslim populations at all. This is likely to be closely associated with the perceived distastefulness of the subject altogether, to the extent that nations may be in total denial that such social problems exist in their particular society (Crabtree, 2006).

One of the rare exceptions to this general silence is a paper written by Abu Baker and Dwairy (2003) discussing cases of incest in a Palestinian community in Israel. Accordingly, they note survey findings where 20 per cent of 12-year-old Palestinian boys and 11 per cent of girls had made reports of sexual abuse, whereby 40 per cent were perpetrated by relatives and neighbours (Abu Baker and Dwairy, 2003). It is interesting to note that the issue of the gender disparity of the victims is not discussed in their paper, raising speculations of the potential higher risk for boys or the greater secrecy surrounding sexual abuse of girls.

These authors go on to critique the social work intervention strategies used in one particular case study: that of a 12-year-old female victim of sexual abuse perpetrated by her paternal grandfather, who was imprisoned for the crime. However, this outcome created huge conflict between the paternal and maternal extended family network, where the child was regarded as tainted and her suffering ignored (Abu Baker and Dwairy, 2003). The subsequent rejection of the child by her family is viewed by the authors as a fundamentally punitive means of displaying the collective anger at the dishonour brought on the family reputation, as well as being a form of disassociation.

In the case of incest, institutional (state) intervention threatens the family structure and therefore the family members are enlisted to protect the family unity and reputation, even at the cost of sacrificing the victim. In some cases, the family may even go so far as to kill the victim as an attempt to 'save' the family honor...Arab society blames females for not being able to protect themselves from sexual intercourse out of wedlock, even it happens as a result of brutal rape. (Abu Baker and Dwairy, 2003, p 113)

In other parts of the Middle East the procedures for child protection remain at a more rudimentary level than that shown in the Israeli–Palestinian context. For instance, the UAE offers a prime example of a progressive welfare state, but is only just beginning to publicly air concerns that sexual abuse constitutes a relevant social problem. It remains unclear whether the deeply inadequate child protection protocols referred to in the first edition of this book have yet been replaced or whether tertiary social work education has altered its absolute allergy to discussing sexuality whatsoever, outside of heteronormative relations in wedlock. The repercussions of inadequate training in this respect means that future social workers in the UAE are not properly equipped to tackle abuse cases when they come to their attention, as the following case study graphically illustrates.

Case study 7: Child sexual abuse in the Arabian Gulf

A 14-year-old Emirati girl with genital injuries was brought to a United Arab Emirates hospital by her mother. In private the girl informed a social worker that she was being repeatedly raped by her brother. She asked the social worker not to disclose this to her family, as she was terrified of their reaction, saying that they would kill her if they knew of her plight. The social worker called the police and informed the mother of the girl's allegation. The mother angrily denied her daughter's claim and instead accused their gardener, a disposable Asian migrant labourer. The daughter persisted with her allegations against her brother, but the police were powerless to act unless the mother pressed charges. This she adamantly refused to do. After treatment the daughter was sent back home into the abusive family situation without any charges being pressed or her safety guaranteed in any way. No further information is known regarding her fate (Crabtree, 2006, p 234).

Taboos, 'political correctness', cultural sensitivities and collective collusion – minefields in practice

The allegation of sexual abuse of children is always an emotive issue for families to contend with. The challenges for social workers are often compounded where there are cultural and ethnic differences to take into account in relation to the nature of the alleged abuse, the intention of those involved and the psychosocial context for the victim and its family.

Case study 8: Cultural collusion in child abuse, UK

AB, an 11-year-old girl, is found to be heavily pregnant, but no child protection investigation commences, either at this time or after the baby is born and accommodated by social services. It is decided not to investigate the case since the mother's reasoning was accepted at face value: that a police investigation would jeopardise her daughter's future chances of marriage. A year later, AB bumped into her former social worker just after the girl has had another pregnancy terminated. This procedure was quietly arranged by her general practitioner (of the same cultural background as the family) and the obstetrician, neither of whom raised alarms over her continuing sexual abuse. At this point AB was accommodated and reveals that her brother was her abuser, a fact she claims was known to her family all along (Webb et al, 2002).

In considering good social work practice in the western context, the cultural context of the child is frequently emphasised, and professionals involved in child protection cases are urged in the first instance to closely consider the context of the allegation. For example, it is considered important to differentiate between traditional, cultural practices that are actively harmful, and those that are merely different and innocuous, like co-sleeping with babies and children (Gough and Lynch, 2002).

Harran (2002) follows Chand's definition in urging practitioners to understand the motivation behind the use of certain cultural practices. This permits practitioners to be able to discern whether such practices are actually considered harmful to the child's wellbeing within that cultural context. As Chand explains: '[C]ultural differences in the way families rear their children should be…respected, but where child abuse does occur it should be understood that this particular family has gone beyond what is acceptable not only in the British culture, but in their own' (Chand, 2000, p 75).

Yet this suggestion is also problematic. Chand's advice appears to take a firmly relativistic view of child abuse: that is, whether something can be viewed as abusive is dependent on whether it is viewed as such in the originating culture of the family (Webb et al, 2002). On the other hand, child abuse could also be argued to be subject to more universal definitions regardless of culture, since, as some critics have pointed out, certain cultural practices, whether well intentioned or not, are evidently harmful to children, such as female genital mutilation (Webb et al, 2002). Or, to give another example, the unusual and very unpleasant punishment, apparently practised among some West African families, of placing hot peppers or ginger root in the anus or vagina of older children to inflict suffering (Koramoa et al, 2002).

Consequently, there are a number of hazards facing social workers dealing with child abuse issues among ME groups. Chand (2000) highlights two main areas in relation to cultural deficits: hesitancy to intervene due to fears of insufficient cultural knowledge to evaluate the home situation accurately; alternatively, anxieties felt over possible unnecessary intervention, based once again on the practitioner's cultural ignorance.

Two cited cases of British Muslim children illustrate these concerns. The first relates to the physical abuse of a five-year-old boy by his mother, who had previously been the subject of professional concern in connection with neglect of her older children. The case conference was hampered by the liaising link worker, of the same cultural background, who refused to believe that the mother could be capable of the offences committed. This view appears to be based less on the mother's personal attributes but rather on some generalised cultural notions of idealised motherhood (Webb et al, 2002).

The second case is that of 'EF', a British child of Arab heritage with multiple disabilities, who was seriously neglected by her parent. This neglect was consistently overlooked by social work practitioners, despite clear indications that the child's health and wellbeing obviously were in jeopardy in the home situation, and that the young mother herself was coping poorly due to an on-going history of mental illness:

> EF's name was not entered on the child protection register. She was seen by social services as a child in need rather than a child in need of protection; health staff argued that both applied. Instead of a protection plan, an assessment was resolved on. Five years on, there has been little change. The family continue to live in conditions of extreme socio-economic deprivation. EF is intermittently excluded from school for health and safety reasons because of recurrent cockroach infestation of her wheelchairs, clothes and hair. (Webb et al, 2002, p 401)

Finally, it is inevitable that social workers will sometimes be unjustly accused of discrimination when carrying out their legitimate duties in relation to child protection. Understandably most people would wish to shy away from such accusations, and instead would like to show that they are culturally sensitive individuals. However, where practice involves double standards for ME families, leading to some children receiving less statutory protection than the norm, practitioners need to rethink their priorities. As Table 10 indicates, cultural competence does not only mean sensitivity towards difference, but also disallowing inconsistencies to infiltrate vital assessment and intervention processes for fear of appearing Islamophobic or racist.

The fear of racist accusations appears to have been one of main fears inhibiting local authority workers from effectively investigating well-known local problems seen on the municipal streets, as will be discussed in further detail. Serious crimes implicating members of ME background often draw unwanted attention to their communities as the cultural harbours from which such reprehensible individuals have embarked. Speaking objectively this seems less than fair, yet

Table 10: Anti-discriminatory practice versus cultural deficit attitudes

- Reflecting on faith-based and/or cultural stereotypes that militate against a non-judgemental, objective professional attitude.

- Avoiding poor practice, for example, the failure to evaluate the needs of ME children and families using similar risk assessment strategies, as used for children from more familiar cultural/ethnic backgrounds.

- Distinguishing between culturally relative practices, which may be regarded by perpetrators as non-abusive, and any *actual* harm to children, which should be evaluated on broader definitions of abuse.

- Addressing any possible collusion impeding effective practice where practitioners (including all members of the multidisciplinary network) share similar cultural assumptions and beliefs to that of the family under investigation.

recently the terrible revelations in the press of repeated abuse of young white girls in Northern English towns by gangs of primarily Pakistani men inevitably generated a whirlwind of recriminations and agonising about how so many children could have been so blatantly abused and cruelly exploited over many years with apparently complete impunity.

Although the UK Child Protection and Online Exploitation Centre (CEOP) (2011) states that the majority of perpetrators in child abuse cases are white, in relation to the phenomenon known as 'street grooming', or more accurately 'localised grooming', a different demographic begins to emerge. This shows that offenders are more likely to be younger than the average older paedophile and proportionally it is also noticed that there is a high percentage of Asian men implicated in this type of crime. Furthermore, the ethnicity of victims in localised grooming is weighted towards white female children, although this may be that victims from other groups remain currently less visible.

Localised (or 'street grooming') is described as organised and calculated grooming of children by (usually) groups of offenders working in concert who meet children in public places (such as takeaways and other popular outlets) in order to establish a relationship prior to sexually exploiting them. The child may be led to regard the offender as their actual 'boyfriend' and is then likely to introduce friends to the offender group who will then go on to take advantage of this fresh meat in the same way (CEOP, 2011).

Organised criminal networks of localised grooming was the basis of recent high profile trials of offenders who were found guilty of serially abusing young white girls primarily over decades. The extent of these crimes together with the levels of sadism and depravity uncovered profoundly shocked the British public, and has led to further inquiries and investigations. It was found that minors from underprivileged backgrounds were being targeted by gangs of local men, who terrorised, controlled and abused them horrifically. Many of the victims came from troubled backgrounds and were consequently in care. Others lived with their families but for one reason or another, these were unable to protect the girls from networks of violent sexual predators and often did not know about the abuse.

Although the problems of child sexual exploitation in the area was known by police and social services the scale and nature of it was not sufficiently recognised and little was done to tackle it in any concerted and determined fashion.

Rochdale in the Greater Manchester area became notorious, where ten men (eight Pakistanis, one white Briton and one Afghan, aged between 24 and 59 years old) received long prison sentences in 2012 for their crimes in serious sex abuse enacted between 2005–13. The female victims, aged from 13 to 23, were groomed for sex, plied with alcohol and drugs to incapacitate them, subjected to threats and violence, multiply raped and forcibly prostituted. The charged offenders were named as Abid Khan, Afraz Ahmed, Choudhry Ikhalaq Hussain, David Law, Kutab Miah, Mohammed Dauood, Mohammed Zahid and Rehan Ali, while the oldest member of the gang, Shabir Ahmed, was named as the ringleader.

The 2014 Independent Report, *Real Voices* by Ann Coffey, referred directly to the Rochdale case in an investigation of the risks posed to young local girls particularly those living in more deprived neighbourhoods. The report documented numerous accounts of the daily and menacing sexual harassment and molestation of young schoolgirls by men in the Greater Manchester area to the extent that the children thought it futile to report molestation to either their teachers or the police.

In the notorious Yorkshire Rotherham case, deeply debauched sexual exploitation of minors finally came to light following years of complaints to the police by some victims, parents and concerned individuals. By 2013 South Yorkshire police had received 57 complaints concerning localised grooming. This finally resulted in the trial and conviction of the Pakistani gang leaders, brothers Arshid, Basharat and Bansas Hussain, along with their uncle Qurban Ali and white female accomplices, Karen MacGregor and Shelley Davies who were charged with 55 cases of serious crime involving exploitation and abuse of 15 young girls between 1987 to 2003.

In terms of the Rotherham scandals an *Independent Inquiry into Child Sexual Abuse in Rotherham* under Professor Alexis Jay, estimated that the number of actual victims over these years in question was conservatively estimated to be in the region of 1,400 children (of both sexes, although female minors appear greatly in the majority). Of those children identified, the reports of their suffering was harrowing,

> In just over a third of cases, children affected by sexual exploitation were previously known to services because of child protection and neglect. It is hard to describe the appalling nature of the abuse that child victims suffered. They were raped by multiple perpetrators, trafficked to other towns and cities in the north of England, abducted, beaten, and intimidated. There were examples of children who had been doused in petrol and threatened with being set alight, threatened with guns, made to witness brutally violent rapes and threatened they

would be next if they told anyone. Girls as young as 11 were raped by large numbers of male perpetrators. (Jay Report, 2014, p 36)

Following the Jay Report, the National Crime Agency began investigations with a view to bringing potentially up to 300 or more child sex offenders in the Rotherham and Oldham areas of Yorkshire and Lancashire to justice, possibly including certain town councillors and police officers. In the meantime, a number of police officers have been suspended.

In the serious case review of the Rotherham sexual abuse cases Jane Booth, chair of the Rochdale Borough Safeguarding Children Board, described the findings of the investigation as shocking. The Report described an institutional culture of resigned complacency about the sexual exploitation of children largely seen as incorrigible guttersnipes immersed in perverse lifestyles and, in short, effectively voluntary child prostitutes. Children in care regularly absconded and were found returned to old haunts. Incredibly others were picked up from care homes and foster parents by colluding taxi drivers and driven to their rendezvous with rapists. One detail captures the grotesque subversion of all normality where one child victim was allowed by her foster parents to go to meeting places arranged by her abusers provided she was back no later than 10pm. In short the brutal conditioning the children experienced at the hands of their abusers and the lack of effective protection by the police or social services trapped them into lives from which they felt they could not escape or be rescued from.

The level of professional apathy and dismissal, irrespective of any collusion, as described by the Safeguarding Report makes it clear that this was a situation where no one in authority, among the police, the CPS and social services believed that any change was possible or worth seriously pursuing.

The explicit ethnic dimensions that seem integral to the Rochdale and Rotherham cases have generated much considerable controversy in the UK. Several high profile commentators in the media attempted to play down the ethnic aspects of the cases, arguing reasonably, if somewhat tangentially, that abusers come from all ethnic groups. The fear that any focus would primarily exacerbate racist and Islamophobic antipathies by extreme right wing groups has proved to be realistic. Nevertheless, this also smacks of disingenuous apologism, given that the Jay Report of the Rotherham case makes it quite clear that the cross-ethnic factor was a conspicuous aspect of the cases.

By far the majority of perpetrators were described as 'Asian' by victims, yet throughout the entire period, [town] councillors did not engage directly with the Pakistani-heritage community to discuss how best they could jointly address the issue. Some councillors seemed to think it was a one-off problem, which they hoped would go away. Several staff described their nervousness about identifying the ethnic origins of perpetrators for fear of being thought racist; others remembered clear direction from their managers not to do so. (Jay Report, 2014, p 2)

Additionally, Judge Gerald Clinton, summing up at Liverpool Crown Court on the Rochdale case, made it clear that he believed that the girls were treated as utterly dehumanised and worthless owing to overt ethnic and religious prejudice on the part of the perpetrators of Pakistani origin with one of Afghan origin in the following quote, 'One of the factors leading to that was the fact that they were not part of your community or religion' (BBC, 2012).

Tufail (2015, p 33), however, scornfully challenges the findings in the Jay Report of police inaction to intervene effectively owing to fear of racist labels as completely implausible on the partial grounds of British ME groups being 'over-policed and under-protected', also pointing out that the ethnicity of white paedophiles generally pass without mention in the media.

The Islamophobic and racist implications implied in Tufail's (2015) critique is located on the sharp end of exoneration of Muslims as generally socially deviant, where the obvious other argument is that such frightful abuse constitutes a complete perversion of Islam, which, to clarify, emphasises tolerance and the protection of women and children. Yet simply rehearsing this sound principle sadly falls far short of directly addressing the implications involved in child sexual exploitation as highlighted in these cases. More is clearly needed.

Accordingly, given the cross-ethnic particularities of the Rotherham and Rochdale cases, these could be viewed as constituting alarming levels of xenophobia coupled with vicious predatory opportunism by the perpetrators. However, the Jay Report also refers to research undertaken by the UK Muslim Women's Network, which brings to light the horrifying levels of sexual abuse inflicted on young Asian girls by men from their own community, where the greatest majority of the victims are Muslims aged below 16 years (Gohir, 2013). In this report entitled *Unheard Voices*, we learn that some young Muslim girls may initially believe that they are entering into a *nikah* (Muslim marriage) until they are abused and trafficked. Commonly, others are raped by their older male relatives before being passed on to other men. Some may experience their first assaults in school by older aggressive boys, or will be initiated into the grooming process online or initially groomed by older boys on behalf of other men (who may otherwise play the role of respectable pillars of the local community), or indeed by their own complicit female school friends. Blackmail is very common where the rapes are often filmed with subsequent threats of exposing the details to the victim's family unless she obeys orders. This is an important consideration in view of the issue of community and family honour and where the victim is very likely to be blamed and punished for her violation.

Based on this research the UK Muslim Women's Network graphically reported to the Crown Prosecution Service (CPS) 35 cases of appalling sexual abuse of Asian girls, mostly Muslim, by men from their own community, which featured the same order of sadistic, degrading sexual attacks and multiple rapes as those experienced by their white counterparts.

The physical abuse included: oral, anal and vaginal rape; role play; insertion of objects into the vagina; severe beatings; burning with cigarettes; tying down; enacting of rape such as ripping clothes off; and sexual activity via webcam. Sometimes the victims were drugged by alcohol and drugs to the extent that they were unaware of the scale of abuse, or the different ways in which they were being violated or by how many men. (Gohir, 2013, p 64)

The profile of the offenders was varied in terms of age, from young schoolboys to men in their sixties; however, the report states that two-thirds of offenders were from Pakistani backgrounds as were most of the child victims; with other offenders listed as Indian, Bangladeshi, Afghan and white.

In view of the evidence, it is hard to avoid the obvious conclusion that such calculated abuse fundamentally emerges from attitudes of gross misogynism and flagrant contempt for the victims, as well as any governing rules of law or religion – these are dysfunctions that cut across ethnic groups, class and caste. In the cases cited, underage girls, Asian and white, were made vulnerable (rather than simply *being* vulnerable) through systematic and experienced grooming, where their particular backgrounds and emotional need for love and attention, were cunningly exploited to the same vicious ends. The other conspicuous aspect in respect of the ethnicity of the perpetrators in these cases raises serious questions about underlying attitudes towards girls and women, which may somehow encourage or legitimise such behaviour. Bollywood films, for instance, are accused of celebrating predatory male behaviour in the commonplace storyline of rewarded male sexualised harassment of women (Gohir, 2013). Table 11 lists dominant oppressive patriarchal attitudes that tend to victimise girls and women.

Table 11: Oppressive patriarchal cultural practices and attitudes

• Women suffering in silence even when subjected to abuse for the sake of family honour
• The woman being blamed in family break-ups
• Divorced women carrying a greater stigma than divorced men
• A girl's body and sexuality controlled because she is held responsible for a family's honour
• Boys being valued more than girls from the celebration of their birth to adulthood
• Girls and women being expected to obey the males in the family usually father, brother or husband
• Girls and women being subjected to greater social restrictions
• Girls being subjected to forced and child marriages
• Girls and women being subjected to honour-based crimes
• Heaping shame on unmarried girls who lose their virginity
• Religious authorities are predominantly male
• Marital rape being considered normal
• In some instances, women not being allowed in mosques

Source: Adapted from Gohir (2013)

The UK Muslim Women's Network offers some key points for active awareness raising in ME communities, where denial and concealment of sexual exploitation of minors may be endemic. Furthermore for Muslim girls in particular, being withdrawn from sex education classes at school by their parents means that they are both deprived of learning about what constitutes sexual behaviour as well as information and assertiveness training on how to stay safe(r).

For frontline professional staff, criticisms are levied that services neglect the needs of BME communities. Moreover, professionals may be ignorant of the cultural dynamics and pressures victims may also be subjected to, thus adding to their vulnerability. One important caveat is that demonstrating cultural sensitivity on the part of social workers does not mean simple deferment to established and often gendered hierarchies of power within communities, unless this will materialise into established effective action to actively protect those at risk of sexual exploitation. Patriarchal systems of all types serve primarily patriarchy, not the female – and when girls and women are forced to carry the heavy social burdens of embodied virtue and shame, they are forced to conveniently play the part of society's scapegoats as well.

Accommodation of Muslim children

Child abuse and neglect is one of the foremost reasons for the accommodation of children in long-term care, be it residential, foster care or, for the fortunate minority, through adoption. There is a serious need for more research into the whole topic of accommodation and the subsequent adjustment process in relation to Asian children, which would generally include many, but obviously not all, Muslim children who require such services. Specific issues that pertain to Muslim children under these circumstances have still not received any dedicated investigation. However, it is generally acknowledged that the need for black, Asian and mixed-race foster and adoptive parents far outweighs supply. There has been much speculation about the reasons for these shortages, since social workers are keen to place children in families who share a common ethnic and cultural background. A pragmatic, often heard riposte is that this strategy of ethno-cultural placement relegates children to long-term residential care unnecessarily.

Intriguingly, some significant research data suggest that there are marked gender differences in how well boys and girls fare in long-term foster care with foster parents of a similar cultural background. These indicate that while ME girls, as might be expected, do well, counter-intuitively boys did not do as well and tended to deprioritise the topic of ethnicity over the everyday practicalities of getting on with life in their new family (Moffatt and Thoburn, 2001). The authors speculate whether the attitude of the boys might actually fit in better with white foster parents, who in general, being largely unaffected by them, were also likely to minimise 'race' politics. They also wondered if perhaps the behaviour of these boys was for some reason more threatening within ME families than it would seem in white families (Moffatt and Thoburn, 2001).

Case study 9: Accommodating the Afghani siblings

A referral of domestic violence was made to social services following concerns expressed about violent shouting that was frequently heard coming from the house rented by an Afghan family. It was found that the wife was being physically and psychologically abused by her very controlling husband and there were concerns that the children were also at risk. The wife, who was thought to be both isolated and depressed, was uncertain about whether to press charges against her husband, but it was agreed with professionals that he would leave the family home. However, it was found out later that the husband had demanded entry to see the couple's children, demands that the wife felt unable to refuse, and consequently he had complete access to the family home once again. The local authority called an emergency interdisciplinary strategy meeting where an Emergency Protection Order was sought and obtained because the mother was unable to guarantee the safety of the children or to stop the father entering the house. The children, a girl aged 13 and a boy aged 11, were subsequently removed to the care of a dog-owning[3] Kosovan Muslim foster family whose language, behaviour, meals, dress, toilette and general habits were completely different from those of the Afghani children to the extent that they had nothing in common. The boy was reported to be interacting quite well with the other children in the house, but the girl refused to leave her room, did not appear to want to integrate with the foster family, and instead stayed in constant touch with her mother by phone.

Religious commonalities clearly do not sufficiently compensate for cultural differences, however, a potentially more serious issue relates to suitability of care provision for unaccompanied children suffering from the trauma of experiencing war and atrocities, where increasingly social services are dealing with desperately needy and unprotected child refugees.

Case study 10: Fostering unaccompanied children

A group of Syrian refugees reached Britain after a long and hazardous journey – among them were a few children. One young boy, presumed to be Muslim, was unaccompanied by any family members. Social services responded by placing the child with a Muslim Bangladeshi foster family. The foster parents later reported finding it difficult to deal with the child as they could not easily communicate with him verbally or non-verbally: his behaviour and needs seemed very different from that which they were used to, while they also felt disturbed by his withdrawn behaviour, nightmares and bed-wetting.

Adoption and fostering

Frazer and Selwyn (2005) consider adoption from cultural and faith perspectives and consider both areas to be important issues for consideration by social workers. This is clearly an important point, bearing in mind that shared culture does not necessarily mean shared faith, and the converse is equally true.

Selwyn and Frazer (2005) argue that the population demographics of Britain explain why Muslim and Sikh families may be ultimately deterred from adoption, arguing that such families usually have a large number of young children to care for already. Moreover, Pakistani and Bangladeshi families often live in overcrowded homes, which lack basic amenities, and obviously this does not militate in favour of adoption in the view of either prospective parents or for placing agencies.

There are, however, two further very significant points to be made that are generally overlooked by non-Muslim academics when considering the topic of appropriate long-term placement of Muslim children in need. First, in many Muslim societies the adoption of Muslim children by non-Muslims is totally unacceptable, even in the case of national crises, such as the thousands of Indonesian children left orphaned and unprotected after the Southeast Asian Tsunami of 2004.

Second, it is not uncommon to be told that adoption for Muslims is *haram*, as there is no explicit guidance regarding it within the Qur'an. However, it has been said that it is open to discretion (Goonesekere, 1994), and consequently adoptions do take place in several Asian and Southeast Asian countries. Furthermore, some popular Islamic cyber sites point out that the Prophet Mohammed was an orphan himself and adopted orphans later in life. The rules for adoption under Islam are unusual to western societies, since the patriarchal prerogative appears to carry greater emphasis than the rights of the child to be parented (see Table 12). These stipulations strongly emphasise the outsider status of the adopted child in relation to lineage, property and marriage, and where a melding of identity between adopted child and family is not considered to be either desirable or acceptable. This has been stated in the following way: 'It is not possible for someone to assume parentage on the basis of a simple declaration; adoption then is considered an attempt to deny reality' (Gatrad and Sheikh, 2000, p 68).

Table 12: Adoption in Islam

• The adopted child retains the biological father's surname.
• The adopted child inherits from the biological family not the adoptive one.
• When the adopted child is grown the adoptive family are not considered blood relatives and therefore marriages can be contracted with one of them.
• If the adopted child is provided with property/wealth from the biological family, the adoptive parents must not intermingle that with their own.

Source: About.com: Islam (http://islam.about.com/cs/parenting/a/adoption.htm)

Furthermore, Goonesekere (1994) points out that adopted Muslim children are disadvantaged under Islamic law in relation to inheritance, citing a case in Sri Lanka where an adopted child's right to inherit was legally challenged.

The ambiguities surrounding adoption from the Islamic perspective, coupled with the legal anomalies across societies, are likely to hold implications for Muslim families in the west. The assumptions underpinning adoption by social work agencies are not necessarily mutually shared or understood by those ME families. Thus the problem of low uptake in the adoption of Muslim children may be far more fundamental than the otherwise important points raised regarding demographics and socioeconomics. If so, it could well be that appropriate long-term foster care is a more feasible and culturally acceptable proposition for many Muslim families, who are currently discouraged from formal adoption.

Notes

[1] The term *zina* refers to 'unlawful' sexuality and encompasses adultery, fornication, rape, prostitution and homosexuality.

[2] Bradford in the North of England boasts a high concentration of Asian families of Pakistani, Bangladeshi and Indian heritage.

[3] Dogs are considered to be *haram* for most Muslims who therefore rarely own them as pets.

SIX

Muslim families
and health

Medicine in historical Islam

Historically the Muslim world has enjoyed a very long and enlightened attitude towards health and healing, in which Persian and Hellenic medical knowledge provided a useful foundation for Muslim scholarship to develop into a rich repository of learning. For example, the celebrated centre of medical learning in Cairo held three large hospitals by the year 872 BCE. These were apparently built in a cruciform shape to hold separate wards. By 1284 in Cairo the Qalawun hospital set up by the Sultan of the same name was offering the following remarkably modern sounding healthcare:

> The mentally ill were kept apart from those with physical symptoms and men were housed separately from women. There were also separate units for patients with eye disorders, stomach complaints and those needing surgery. Hospital doctors by that stage had begun to specialise and the Qalawun records tell us that it employed physicians, surgeons and ophthalmologists, as well as administrators, nurses, accountants and orderlies. (Masood, 2009, p 88)

The great Islamic cities of Baghdad and Cordoba were also the sites of many hospitals, which boasted a system of interns as well as teaching and library facilities. They supplied rudimentary nursing care, held well-stocked pharmacies and even ran outpatient services (Udwadia, 2001). Rassool (2000) refers to how hospitals' wards were divided into those catering for specific maladies, such as infectious diseases and mental illness. Consequently, during the early medieval period, these centres of medical excellence were unparalleled throughout the civilised world, where in Europe the sick and destitute were reliant on the skills and charity of monks for succour and healing.

This impressive focus on medicine can be viewed as deriving from the Islamic emphasis on the interrelation between health, sickness and spiritual growth where illness is regarded as a testing ground for spiritual soundness, whereby the faithful are rewarded for enduring these trials with patience (Sheikh and Gatrad, 2000). However, as the Prophet Mohammed affirmed, the stricken should nevertheless seek help for their illness, since 'There is a cure for every malady save one – that of old age' (Sheikh and Gatrad, 2000, p 34).

Faith, culture and health

Today, in common with the US, the health status of British Muslims is difficult to quantify as statistical data are not gathered on faith groups. What is known is that there are higher rates of heart disease and diabetes among people of South Asian origin (Swerdlow et al, 2004). Filtered data on health from the UK National Census 2011 permits us to see that the percentage of Muslims reporting to be in 'bad or very bad' health stands at 5.5 per cent (MCB, 2015), which is similar to the national average of 5.6 per cent. Anomalies here relate to the much smaller population of Muslims compared to the rest of the UK and the very much younger average age of Muslims in the country compared to the national average, which should logically have raised the percentage in this group. Although the picture is slightly better in terms of disability compared to the national average, Muslim women aged 65 and over report significantly higher levels of impairment to their daily activities owing to disability than the national average (MCB, 2015). The link between poverty and poor health is also made apparent in these data sets. Whereas for the US, although Muslims benefit from higher socio-economic status, specific data on health in this group is, as yet, lacking (Laird et al, 2007).

Breaking down the UK statistics into details is difficult, particularly where owing to religious prohibitions some health issues such as alcohol and substance abuse may be carefully concealed within Muslim populations. Although research suggests that while smoking is considered a lesser offence among young Asian Muslims, it nonetheless flies in the face of 'religious obligations to guard one's health and steward one's finances'. This may lead to avoidance of revealing addictions (Bradby, 2007, p 664) – and thereby preventing the user from obtaining the help that they need.

Regardless of faith everyone is heir to the possibility of serious illness throughout their life, something that Islam fully acknowledges, and obviously, the health afflictions of Muslims are shared across ethnicity and creed. Some might argue that an emphasis on faith is far less relevant to our understanding of the needs of patients than that of cultural background. Furthermore, literature devoted to medical anthropology focuses primarily on cultural interpretations of health and disease as primary signifiers dictating behaviour and cognition, whereas other forms of analysis would focus on ethnicity and socio-economic status as offering more significant insights into health.

Faith, however, becomes particularly relevant to practitioners when these come into conflict with medical models, nursing and administrative protocols that make few or no allowances for individual needs. This could be in relation to understanding the needs for religious observance in Muslim stoma patients, whose involuntary production of faeces (or gas) during prayers is regarded as nullifying their observance – a deeply demoralising situation (Kuzu et al, 2001). Or, for instance, by assisting Muslim women to access breast screening services (Millon Underwood et al, 1999).

In this chapter we outline some of the health issues that social work practitioners may need to consider in work with Muslims (although some issues pertain equally to other groups), bearing in mind, once again, the need to avoid essentialising clients into an undifferentiated mass. Here, and in the next chapter, we draw some lifespan parameters around the topic of health, in so far as they are loosely framed by the boundaries of birth and death.

There are a number of faith-based organisations offering supplementary and culturally sensitive services in social and healthcare (Crisp, 2014; Warden et al, 2016). However, social workers in multidisciplinary, health-based teams are likely to share certain professional values with other professionals, in which nursing is increasingly taking a more transcultural approach, as well as recognising the need for spiritual sensitivity (Andrews, 2006; Rassool, 2000). In this way the reductive attitude of biomedicine is mediated by a focus that takes greater account of the personal background of patients and clients, together with the interwoven and complex factors of 'politics, economics and values' (Andrews, 2006, p 84). Transcultural nursing indicates transferring skills to the care of people from many diverse backgrounds. This approach is therefore compatible with both ecological social work perspectives of individuals and a culturally sensitive, person-centred approach.

The variety of health issues pertaining to Muslim individuals and families is obviously vast and cannot be contained within the scope of one relatively brief chapter. It is our aim therefore to discuss some of the more conspicuous or serious needs of Muslim patients in multidisciplinary health settings, while adding the qualification that this is an area that demands further research and investigation as a whole.

Reproduction

As has already been mentioned, Muslim families value children, and indeed reproduction is considered an essential rite of passage to the achievement of fully adult status. In many regions of the world, Muslim families have often been bigger than the European norm; and this has been linked to agrarian, subsidence-based societies, although even in wealthy, urbanised countries the trend towards larger families has been evident.

Part of the reason for this high fertility rate is based on faith, as well as cultural values and socio-economic realities. Additionally, where women are valued primarily in a biological role, and where there is a cultural preference for sons, there is likely to be a high ratio of children per union (bearing in mind also the additional factor of polygamy) (Obermeyer, 1994). However, this trend appears to be changing where the UN (Hughes, 2011) notes a welcome fall in the fertility rates in the Middle East, specifically Tunisia, Algeria, the UAE, Libya, Kuwait, Qatar and Morocco (Hughes, 2011) – all countries which boast high levels of either economic or cultural capital.

This notwithstanding, children are highly valued by Muslims. Although not every pregnancy will be welcome, the avoidance of conception varies widely across the Muslim world. Although there are those who believe that the use of contraceptives is unacceptable on the grounds of faith, some will resort to coitus interruptus (withdrawal) as being the one method that receives sanction under Islam, based on the words of the Prophet (Bahar et al, 2005). However, there will be many Muslims who quietly or overtly practise a variety of methods that are considered more reliable than this, but among many of the faithful and those in developing nations, coitus interruptus is likely to be the preferred, and often indeed sole, method of family planning.

In the global north high fertility rates in women have not been viewed in a positive way, even though the fertility rate in Europe is dropping so alarmingly in many countries such as Spain and Germany that the future economic and human resource shortfalls constitute a serious national threat (Kassam et al, 2015). Making up this population shortfall through immigration to encourage the birth of more children does not seem to have been incorporated in many politicians' speeches as a particularly positive solution to an approaching demographic crisis. It is therefore questionable if attitudes have moved on to the point where comments such as this are no longer made in antenatal settings:

> When an Asian woman comes in to have her fifth or sixth baby they are so rude to her, especially if she doesn't speak English. They say terrible things right to her face, like 'I'd do something to your husband if I could' or 'This one should be sterilised' and she often just smiles politely because she doesn't understand. (Schott and Henley, 1996, p 183)

Racist and Islamophobic attitudes connect with underlying fears that minority groups threaten majority populations through, here, perceived over-breeding, and evidently elicit hostile responses. This can be exacerbated if health professionals believe that minority families have larger than average families on sexist grounds, in which parents favour sons over daughters. Social workers have an important role to play in health-based settings to support particularly vulnerable women, while addressing some of these concerns and prejudices among health professionals, as these are likely to have a negative impact on the wellbeing and treatment of hospital patients.

Pregnancy and birth are periods in a woman's life when she will be increasingly exposed to contact with health professionals, many of whom will be men. For women, regardless of culture and faith, this is an anxiety-provoking time, particularly when subjected to medical procedures that can be worrying, uncomfortable or even degrading, as internal examinations are often felt to be by many women. For women who have experienced female genital mutilation, any strictly necessary (as opposed to just routine) examinations require the highest levels of sensitivity by staff, as they are likely to be deeply dreaded, as will be discussed further (Wardere, 2016).

Respect for modesty and dignity is often overlooked in busy antenatal settings, where it is easy for any woman to feel merely processed and dehumanised. Traditionally an unthinking obedience often seems to be expected by medical staff. It is not surprising therefore that some women from minority ethnic (ME) groups will not always cooperate fully with staff, leading to a hardening of existing prejudice towards an assumed state of benighted ignorance among such patients. This issue becomes all the more important in relation to foetal screening procedures, where the purposes should be carefully considered with patients. It is particularly important to weigh up the value of such procedures with couples, particularly if dealing with those whose religious convictions would not permit them to abort a malformed foetus in any event. This caveat is one that applies not only to Muslims, but also to other religious groups.

It is a common belief among Muslims that 'ensoulment' of the foetus occurs 120 days after conception, corresponding roughly with the 'quickening' or feeling of the foetal movements by the mother (Obermeyer, 1994; Gatrad and Sheikh, 2001). After this point termination (abortion) is considered inadmissible under Islam. However, if this would seriously endanger the life of the mother then termination may be acceptable (Yeprem, 2007), presumably given the practical issue that mother dying in childbirth normally meant little chance of survival of the infant. Gitsels-van der Wal et al (2015) state that for some Muslims pregnancy resulting from rape and illegitimacy may also constitute grounds for termination. Yet there seem to be divergent views on this point relating to which theological school of thought communities adhere to. According to the Hanifi tradition of Islamic interpretation (followed by Moroccan Muslims for instance) pregnancy can be terminated up to the first 120 days under certain conditions, whereas in the Mâlikî tradition (followed for instance by Turkish Muslims) terminations are not permitted at all (Gitsels-van der Wal et al, 2015). It should be said as well that for many Muslims termination may not be considered an option at any point, through personal belief or simply because it is not available in their society.

Given these restrictions, extending foetal screening to all pregnant women without considering the implications on an individual basis could be regarded as unhelpful, paternalistic and wasteful of resources. However, equally it should not be assumed that a screening will not be helpful to Muslim women, as some would opt for termination even at a later stage of pregnancy, while for others advance warning of any potential problems might be welcomed for those wishing to plan ahead. In each case, couples should be given the facts as well as the options open to them to make an informed decision by having access not only to medical and genetic advice, but also to counselling and spiritual support.

Even normal pregnancies for women from ME communities are unlikely to reach the post-birth period without some collision with health staff. One area for Muslim women revolves around fasting at Ramadan. Although certain sectors of Muslim society are exempted for a time from fasting due to frailty, illness or pregnancy, some women will choose to fast. Their reasons may be pious, or communal – in wishing to join the rest of the family; or they may be aware that the fast will be postponed until a less convenient time. Medical staff are often unsupportive of this idea, and although there is little medical evidence to show that this is actively harmful to women and their unborn babies, the medical advice is likely to be disapproving without considering any options that would help pregnant Muslim women deal with the Ramadan expectations more effectively (Fowler et al, 1990)

Childbirth is a particularly vulnerable time in a woman's life when the unfamiliar, the insensitive or the coercive is harmful to the birthing woman and her unborn baby, both psychologically and physiologically. The busy and impersonal environment of a hospital, compounded by potential language barriers and staff ignorance of faith practices, can make this a lonely and worrying time for many women. Concerns can relate to a lack of information, contact with male doctors, availability of *halal* food, together with the very different expectations that may be present regarding how much care and support a birthing woman will receive (Reitmanova and Gustafson, 2008). Some Muslim women will feel unable to attend antenatal classes owing to the presence of men (usually expectant fathers). Sheila Kitzinger, the famous birthing activist, describes visiting a London mansion to coach an inexperienced, pregnant Gulf aristocrat to provide her with the sole antenatal class she would receive (Kitzinger, 2005). Private antenatal classes are obviously not an affordable option for most Muslim mothers, who may then feel that they have to forgo them altogether.

It is not possible to make generalisations regarding good birthing practice for Muslim women, since this is so clearly tied to personal expectation, education and culture rather than faith alone. Nonetheless, some worrying early research data show that South Asian women, many of whom may be Muslim, are offered less pain relief in labour than white women (Schott and Henley, 1996). The authors go on to say that the reasons for this distinction are unclear but may be tied to language barriers and the belief among midwives that Asian women make an exaggerated fuss during labour. On the other hand, women across cultures often derive relief from being able to express pain without necessarily indicating a wish for pain relief, while some will go through the labour process virtually in silence. These different ways of managing pain are indicative of personal coping strategies, personal values and cultural conditioning, as well as how well women are supported by family and staff during labour.

In a number of cultures the placenta carries important symbolism and there are many different ways of dealing with it. However, for Muslims it is considered to be polluted (as is menstrual blood) and should be disposed of as soon as possible (Schott and Henley, 1996). Finally, these authors advise that Muslim women are not expected to say formal prayers, which involve bodily movements, during menstruation and 40 days after giving birth. They are also exempt from the 36th week of pregnancy due to the physical exertions required.

The newborn baby may become the subject of several important Islamic rituals that welcome her or him into the world. The first proper word that the baby should hear is that of *Adhan*, the call to prayer where the baby will hear the name of Allah, followed by the declaration of faith (Gatrad and Sheikh, 2000).

The authors go on to describe other rituals, such as the *tahneek*, where softened date (or honey) may be rubbed on the baby's upper palate preferably by a respected family member. A *taweez* is often tied around the infant's neck or wrist: this pouch contains a prayer designed to protect the baby and should only be removed during an emergency. Finally, if the baby is a boy he is likely to circumcised in the first few days after birth. 'Circumcision' of female infants can also occur, although this is often a much more serious event and is discussed later in the chapter.

Islam encourages women to breastfeed their babies up to the second year. Although this practice ties in well with World Health Organization recommendations, breastfeeding beyond a few months is still regarded as rather dubious and self-indulgent in the west, despite the benefits to the baby and mother. For Muslim mothers in addition to the obvious nutritional and emotional benefits breastfeeding additionally carries strong spiritual significance (Williamson and Sacranie, M, 2012).

Social work practitioners are unlikely to be involved in the birthing and postnatal processes normally; however, they do have an important role to play in relation to infertility issues. This, as is generally appreciated, is a deeply traumatic condition, where a huge sense of grief, bereavement, personal inadequacy and guilt can be experienced. More than being solely a personal tragedy this is one that also extends to the wider family, where a break in the generational chain can cause a significant and resounding sense of failure and loss.

In some communities where the status of women is linked to childbearing the inability to produce a child is likely to seriously jeopardise her standing in the family and community. Furthermore, in some Muslim countries the failure to produce a child may well lead to repudiation by the husband or being obliged to accept the minor role in a polygamous union.

The search for a solution that most couples will consider when a normal conception fails to occur carries important implications and restrictions within the Muslim world. As we have seen, fostering rather than adoption may be more acceptable for Muslims and assisted conception is only acceptable under certain conditions. Donor sperm is never acceptable since progeny should only be the product of the sacred union of husband and wife (Aboulgar, 2006). By contrast, provided that donor eggs are used within polygamous unions this may be a legitimate way forward; however, such resorts are not viable in the western world where polygamy is illegal. Thus the choices before a Muslim couple may be more restricted than for others in the same position. This may lead to a reduced chance of producing offspring and a greater risk of spousal rejection of wives, as well as that of domestic abuse in certain cases.

Genital mutilation

The term 'genital mutilation' is one that most people will immediately associate with females, as in reference to 'female genital mutilation' (FGM). This, however, could equally be applied to any practice that interferes with or amputates part of the genitals in either sex. Not all Muslims circumcise their sons, although the vast majority do, and this practice differs in terms of when it is done, for example just after birth or considerably later for Malay boys in Malaysia. Circumcision may be highly ritualised, where in Malaysia and Muslim-dominated areas of Thailand it is often a crowded, staged event in a mosque.

Male circumcision is stated to be a *hadith* owing to Prophet Mohammed's pronouncement on this issue, in common with Judaism, another Semitic religion. The reasoning often offered for the need for male circumcision is that it is an obligation for the faithful as part of their innate religious integrity (*fitrah*); and that furthermore this practice is connected to purity (*tahaarah*), *as* foreskins are said to retain drops of urine, which for religious purposes of prayer are considered unclean. Circumcision on the grounds of faith and not for medical need is a vexed issue for healthcare funded from the public purse, like the UK National Health Service (NHS). The issue of resourcing unnecessary medical procedures that are not without risk is compounded by the associated ethical issues. Consequently, some Jews are now revisiting circumcision of male children as being out-dated, traumatic and harmful. It also raises the question of whether baby boys are entitled to protection from sexual mutilation, since, it is argued, circumcision is not compatible with either human rights or the Hippocratic oath (Baer, 1997; Svoboda, 1997).

The Islamic mandates that prescribe the removal of foreskins on grounds of health and hygiene are commonly rehearsed. However, it is true to say that this is a highly controversial topic that has not received much serious consideration by Muslims, who continue to advocate the circumcision of males as obligatory. Abu-Salieh is one of the few Muslim writers who outwardly condemns male circumcision, commenting wryly:

> [I]nternational organizations have generally refused to involve themselves in the issue of male circumcision. It is likely, they are afraid of being considered anti-Semitic. This is notably the case with the World Health Organization, the United Nations Fund for Population Activities, UNICEF, and Amnesty International. These organizations, responsible for overseeing the protection of human rights, are always ready to criticize – and correctly so – female sexual mutilation but have become accomplices in the violation of the fundamental human right of male infants to an intact body. The fear of anti-Semitism paralyses them. (Abu-Salieh, 1997, pp 54–5)

Consequently, as Sheikh and Gatrad (2000, p 61) briefly comment, the attempts of 'Muslim apologists' to argue against the practice are unlikely to be successful. In the meantime, circumcision is promoted among sub-Saharan males as a cost-effective protective factor in the spread of HIV/AIDS (van Dam and Anastasi, 2000).

Female genital mutilation

If the circumcision of boys from faith communities is still contentious in many western countries, amputation of and interference with the genitals of girls and women is increasingly regarded as an outrage. The reason for this is that the misnomer 'female "circumcision"', now more correctly referred to as female genital mutilation (FGM), is frequently a far more traumatic, life-threatening event than male circumcision, with serious lifelong repercussions on the physical and mental health of females, very many of whom are Muslims.

The WHO has estimated that FGM has been practised on 200 million currently living girls and women across 30 countries (WHO, 2016). These include several African countries from the Atlantic to the Horn of Africa, as well as being found in Egypt, Israel, Yemen, Oman, the UAE, the OPt, Saudi Arabia, India, Pakistan, Indonesia, Malaysia and even Colombia (gov.UK, 2016a, p 9); while other communities who practice FGM include Afghans and Kurds. '(The) highest prevalence rates of 90% or more are found in Somalia, Sudan, Djibouti, Egypt, Guinea and Sierra Leone. In other countries such as Nigeria, Kenya, Togo and Senegal, the prevalence rates vary between 20% to 50%' (London Metropolitan Police, 2016).

FGM is not, however, confined to these regions alone but is also practised in ME communities in Europe, Australia, New Zealand, the US and Canada as well. Cultural practices tend to travel with migrating populations and consequently children from particular ME communities are often removed from the country of residence for a summer 'holiday' in the family's country of origin, only to return with genital mutilations (gov.UK, 2016b). The risk of FGM is high for those who originate from countries where FGM is practiced. In the UK this encompasses approximately 103,000 girls and women (Wardere, 2016). It is estimated by FORWARD (the leading UK research and community activist NGO, promoting African diaspora women's health and developments issues) that at least 60,000 more girls are at risk of FGM in the UK alone. Additionally, between September 2014 and January 2015, 2,600 new cases of FGM in British girls were discovered. Furthermore there is a grave suspicion among the authorities in the UK that 'cutters' are now being brought into the country on short visits by families for the purpose of group mutilation of British children (Wardere, 2016).

There are a number of forms of FGM practised with varying degrees of trauma attached, listed in Table 13.

Table 13: Types of female genital mutilation

Type 1	Clitoridectomy: Total or partial removal of the clitoris
Type 2	Excision: Removal of the clitoris and labia minora with or without removal of the labia majora
Type 3	Infibulation (otherwise known as Pharaonic circumcision): Amputation of the clitoris, the labia minora, parts of the labia majora and stitching both sides of the wound to cover the entire vulva and urethra, leaving a very small vaginal entry
Type 4	All other harmful interference of the genitals including pricking, piercing, incising, cauterising, scraping and stretching

Ras-Work (1997) notes various other 'refinements' of FGM where 'deinfibulation' is carried out to permit sexual intercourse and childbirth of women experiencing Type 3, as here the vaginal entry has been stitched to an unnaturally small opening. 'Reinfibulation' may then be performed following childbirth or if the husband is absent from home for long periods of time. The *gishiri* cut is performed by traditional midwives cutting into soft tissue to enlarge the vaginal opening during childbirth. Finally, the *angurya cut* is described as traditional surgery to remove the hymen loop on female infants in Nigeria (Ras-Work, 1997).

Feminist analysis points to female genital mutilation as a practice that is rooted in the control of women's sexuality. The repercussions of FGM destroy female physio–psycho–sexual integrity leading to lifelong problems connected to normal development, resulting in long-term damage to reproductive organs, bladder and bowels. Sexual dysfunction has been found to be present in 80 per cent of women with FGM due to physical and psychological harm (Wardere, 2016). Furthermore, owing to mutilation resulting in dense scar tissue in the vulva, childbirth is particularly hazardous to women who have undergone Type 2 and 3 FGM with highly escalated risk of stillborn births and maternal deaths.

The massive physical and psychological trauma of such crude, violent assaults on the female anatomy hardly bears thinking about, particularly when considering that these procedures are often inflicted on infants and small girls usually without any anaesthetic or medical knowledge, equipment or back-up whatsoever. Needless to say FGM kills a number of children owing to shock, blood loss and infection.

FGM and the Muslim connection

The origins of FGM are unclear although it is interesting to note that some form of circumcision has been found on ancient Egyptian female mummies, and is thought to mark a class distinction. Furthermore, it was apparently practised in the fifth century BCE, among the Phoenicians and Hittites, for example (Ras-Work, 1997). Since then it has been found across Africa and the Middle East and is also present to a lesser extent in Jordan and Syria (Minces, 1992) and in some South Asian and Southeast Asian Muslim communities (Dorkenoo et al,

2007). It has even been found among certain tribes in the Buraimi Oasis in the United Arab Emirates (Brooks, 1995). Boddy's (1989) anthropological study of a Sudanese Muslim tribe (practising Type 3 FGM) examines the social construction of 'circumcision' practices as an important rite of passage from child to adult status. She describes how for boys their genitals will be revealed, but for girls they will be covered, sheared and stitched to smoothness, distinguishing them as virtuous, fertile and esteemed in contrast to the status of prostitutes in the community.

The connection of FGM to Islam is hotly contested by a number of scholars who rightly point out that it is a pre-Islamic tradition and found among some animist and Christian communities as well. A typical situation can be found in Ethiopia where approximately 90 per cent of females, including Christians, Muslims and Jews, have experienced sexual mutilation. It is routinely accepted that this is an embedded cultural practice rather than being Islamic, where it is often further stated that it is not condoned in the Qur'an. FORWARD also seeks to educate the public that this is decidedly not an Islamic mandate (FORWARD, nd).

Nonetheless the existence of a connection between FGM and Islam is firmly believed by many people living in Muslim societies, such as Egypt. Theological justification for the practice often relies on a conversation claimed to have been held between Mohammed and a female practitioner of FGM, in which it is said that he did not prohibit the practice but advised her not to cut too deeply in order not to destroy all sexual pleasure (Abu-Salieh, 1997). Furthermore, circumcision (for males) is described as a *sunnah*: meaning that it conforms to tradition commensurate with Islam; however, in relation to women it is described as *makrumah*: meaning a religiously non-mandatory, but nevertheless religiously *meritorious*, action (Abu-Salieh, 1997).

Whether this is a factual or mythical paraphrasing of Mohammed's words, it is undoubtedly the case that many Muslims across the globe regard FGM as sanctioned under Islam. It is also a message that is now promulgated through social media creating contradictions and ambiguities about Islam's actual position on this. Thus in quite a few Muslim-dominated regions the practice continues as being essential for female Muslims as an identity marker and to ensure a respectable future within the community:

> A common strategy used by various agencies around the world to eradicate female circumcision has been to argue that the practice pre-dates Islam and therefore is cultural and not religious... However, this kind of argument does not acknowledge the complexity of contemporary identities and the way that practices may be appropriated into tradition and become authentic to that tradition. (Newland, 2006, p 396)

In the UK there are a growing number of specialist health resources for women with FGM, a condition which usually comes to light during routine health assessments and antenatal care. There is also a mushroom growth of NGO community education and support programmes working in this area. Formal social work intervention in FGM issues is likely to fall under child protection work as a form of child abuse. Yet it is something of a concern to see that apart from NGO community education and support programmes there is little research undertaken or commentary made on this particular subject in the social work literature.

Case study 11: Intersectionalities of gendered violence

Aladi, a Muslim single mother, originally from Nigeria, arrived in the UK aged around 17 years with her baby girl, later settling in Scotland. She came to the notice of the local authorities as a particularly vulnerable refugee with fragile mental health needs. Owing to Aladi's instability manifested in her erratic emotional state, general inability to cope as well as poor parenting skills, and a conspicuous lack of bonding attachment, baby Layla was quickly placed in foster care. Since arriving in Scotland Aladi has been hospitalised on several occasions owing to serious clinical depression and, at times, florid post-traumatic stress disorder.

Following short-term statutory social services intervention, Aladi is today supported by a psychiatrist, psychologist, community psychiatric nurse and her Muslim NGO social worker who works hard to try to engage her in therapy and coping skills. This is a very challenging social work case as Aladi's ability to engage effectively is variable, where at times she seems keen to work with her support worker but at others withdraws completely for weeks at a time, sinking deep into herself, lying in a darkened room, virtually incommunicable and unable to retain information in her memory.

Aladi's story epitomises one of terrible multiple loss and trauma since early childhood. Her parents died when she was a young child and she was then passed into the care of her mother's closest friend. However, her foster mother's partner began to sexually abuse Aladi and after suffering for some time she eventually confided the abuse to her aunt and foster-mother. Aladi was disbelieved and soon after was subjected to FGM, which she interprets as the punishment inflicted on her by her guardians for her supposed lying. Her life from then on became even more unsettled and she was sent from one hostel after another, until, at 11 years old, Aladi was sold to traffickers. As an enslaved child she was forced into a life of brutal prostitution resulting in a pregnancy and unwanted birth at around the age of 16. Aladi's parenting skills are highly compromised as she seems unable to love or to care for Layla properly. Consequently, Aladi's ability to build a better future for both herself and her child appears very uncertain.

Considering the scale of this global problem prosecutions for FGM are universally rare. The case of Egyptian 13-year-old girl Suhair al-Bataa who died following FGM (outlawed in Egypt in 2008) resulted in a prosecution of her doctor and father. Worryingly both were subsequently acquitted (BBC, 2014a). France's tough approach of education, public shaming and a ten-year prison tariff seems to be achieving some successes. Furthermore, because all French children are routinely medically scrutinised from top to toe it is difficult for families to conceal cases of FGM.[1]

It is estimated that there are 28,000 women living in Sweden who originate from countries practising FGM. Worryingly a significantly high number of this group have also subjected daughters born in Scandinavia to FGM (Litorp et al, 2008). FGM is also criminalised in Australia although the exact provision in law depends from State to State (for details see Australian Government, 2013). In the US FGM is also a crime under Federal law (for details see Cornell University Law School, nd), although a clearer view of the extent and the risk of FGM and support strategies there have yet to be developed (Goldberg et al, 2012). In the UK legislation the 1985 Prohibition of Female Circumcision Act was followed by the 2003 Female Genital Mutilation Act (Williams, 2007). This has now been amended under the Serious Crime Act, 2015 to include the following additional offences:

- failing to protect a girl from FGM
- extra-territorial jurisdiction over offences of FGM committed abroad by British nationals or residents
- lifelong anonymity for victims of FGM
- FGM protection orders to protect girls at risk
- a mandatory reporting duty for specified professionals to report a known case of FGM to the police.

The main explanation for the dearth of prosecutions even in nations increasingly well acquainted with the problem is that by criminalising FGM this covert practice has been driven underground making it even harder to investigate. Even where it is part of the culture, FGM is regarded as primarily women's private business (Wardere, 2016). Not surprisingly, the UK police force, for example, have found it incredibly difficult to persuade victims of FGM to bring charges against their families (Wardere, 2016), although this responsibility is now likely to be increasingly borne by the Crown Prosecution Service independent of the victim's attitude towards prosecution.

The undercover nature of FGM has generated an argument for the medicalisation of FGM, where it is claimed that since it is so entrenched culturally, at least this would ensure that this procedure would be carried out by health practitioners under sterile medical conditions. This idea is regarded as an ethical quagmire in carrying out mutilating surgery of no known health benefits and smacks of a defeatist 'if you can't beat them, you might as well join them'. Moreover, using a qualified physician clearly did not prevent the tragic and unnecessary death of Suhair al-Bataa.

It almost goes without saying that many social workers will struggle with the issue of FGM as violence against women and girls, but also in relation to a horribly devastating act performed on children of such tender age. Parents who are complicit in subjecting their daughters to FGM (and often this is the decision of older matriarchs in the extended family) do not regard this as a form of abuse, but as safeguarding their child's future by the standards of their own cultural norms. Social workers may in turn be duly anxious about challenging practices that are regarded as cultural and even faith-based.

Because anti-oppressive/anti-discriminatory, culturally sensitive practice is a fundamental of social work education most social workers internalise these values very early on in their education. Many practitioners therefore are highly concerned not to appear racist, ethnocentric or xenophobic. This in turn can create real dilemmas when working with ME communities where practices regarded as harmful in the host culture are fully engrained as the cultural norm in that community, and particularly where non-compliance to those norms has been seen to carry severe penalties. Wardere (2016) describes the agony she experienced as a six-year-old child violently held down while her genitals were sliced off with an old razor by the community 'cutter' during her unspeakable infibulation initiation and 'healing' period after. Yet she also makes it very clear how much her mother, who participates in this terrible ordeal, genuinely loved her. This paradox is likely to baffle many social workers, who are nonetheless obliged to treat the matter as a serious child protection case – where normally parental love and concern is not the motivation of serious violence towards children.

Education as prevention is one of the most important weapons in fighting FGM and this represents a vital challenge for social workers, researchers, advocates and teachers from ME communities in undertaking key educational work to explain the health consequences of FGM (which are often not understood as anything other than the consequently normalised, miserable trials of womanhood), and to explain the great opportunities open to girls other than conformity to normative biological-sexual constructions and complete marital dependency. (For more information on cultural interpretations of FGM and associated statutory legal framework in the UK, see HM Government, 2016).

Disability and Islam

Islamic principles in essence do not discriminate against people with disabilities, but instead view disability as manifesting different abilities (Waldman et al, 2010). Accordingly, Muslims are encouraged to extend care to those in need (El Naggar Gaad, 2001). An example of this can be found in Section 25 of the Constitution of the United Arab Emirates, where people with disabilities are regarded as being subject to care by primarily their families or other caregivers, as well as equal in status to others (Alghazo et al, 2003). Furthermore, historically, disability has sometimes been very successfully incorporated into mainstream society, as in the case of blind public reciters of the Qur'an, whose popularity was based on their ability to permeate the segregated worlds of men and women without offence (Abdel Haleem, 2001).

Nevertheless, although Islamic precepts are liberal and progressive in this regard, it is once again culture that largely dictates responses towards disability, including exposure to human right concepts and discourses of empowerment. It has long been asserted that families of Middle-Eastern origin tend to harbour negative attitudes towards disability in progeny (Sharifzadeh, 1998). This is similar to the attitudes that can be found in Lebanon and Jordan, while in Palestine disability has been viewed as a blight on family honour, and even as supernatural and maleficent (Ashencaen Crabtree, 2007a; 2007b).

In her study of women's experiences of disability in the Middle East, Abu-Habib (2007) noted that many girls are deprived of opportunities open to others, including that of basic education. Ironically, however, some had the advantage of experiencing greater freedom and autonomy than their non-disabled sisters owing to being seen as consequently less in need of (or deserving of) patriarchal guardianship. Notwithstanding this, women and girls with disabilities in the Middle East are often subjected to neglect, physical and sexual abuse (Ashencaen Crabtree and Williams, 2011). This is by no means unknown in the UK where some argue that in general 'child abuse and neglect are inextricably interwoven with disability' (Cohen and Warren, 1990, p 253).

The greatest majority of children with disabilities are born in developing regions, including countries in the Arab Gulf (Milaat et al, 2001). Many nations still struggle to extend education to all able-bodied children regardless of gender, let alone those with disabilities (Ashencaen Crabtree and Williams, 2009). The Education for All (EFA) Global Action Plan sponsored by UNESCO, UNICEF and the World Bank (UNESCO, 2009) has provided a spur to nations, given the influential power of these bodies, but despite an extension on the 2005 deadline to 2015, only one third of countries have achieved all six EFA goals (UNESCO, 2009; 2015).

The countries of the Gulf Cooperation Council (GCC), which include the Kingdom of Saudi Arabia, Kuwait, the UAE, Qatar, Bahrain and Oman, are clearly trying to make concerted strides towards inclusive education (Ashencaen Crabtree and Williams, 2009). This does not necessarily mean, however, that general prejudice towards those with disabilities is not present. In one study of Kuwaiti students jointly studying social work and education, 60 per cent viewed people with learning disabilities as inefficient and idle in the workplace, and around 52.5 per cent declared that they would feel embarrassed to receive a guest with learning disabilities in their home (Salih and Al-Kandari, 2007).

Nonetheless, social attitudes towards disability are changing in light of violent conflict in the Middle East where in reference to the OPt 'physical and cognitive disability among Palestinian youth has come to be viewed as a heroic stigmata denoting active resistance to occupying forces' (Ashencaen Crabtree and Williams, 2009, p 11).

Like Palestine (Atshan, 1997), in Afghanistan disability (in men presumably) is also associated with martyrdom of having sustained injuries in heroic defence of their country. An association that is reinforced at the highest levels given the title and jurisdiction of the 'Ministry of Martyrs and Disabled' (Trani et al, undated).

Care and care-giving

In the UK a few studies have been carried out on Pakistani and Bangladeshi families caring for a child or children with disabilities. Fazil et al (2002) notes the social and economic deprivation of participating families, in which, contrary to the stereotypes, there was little support from the extended family. Furthermore, it was found that mothers were burdened with the majority of care, and were sometimes regarded as culpable for the birth of a disabled offspring, and even subject to abuse. These findings are commensurate with similar observations of attitudes towards mothers in the Middle East, in which women tainted by these kinds of births may be rejected or displaced (Ashencaen Crabtree, 2007b). The issue of diaspora also mediates in the practical division of care-giving in Pakistani families, where potential family support may be geographically inaccessible (Goodley et al, 2015).

How disability may be viewed within the family and immediate community will also influence family perceptions of their disabled relative. In her unpublished doctoral study, Buckman (2011) observes how British Muslim carers often frame their duties within religious constructions. An interesting aspect of this study is that while health services are viewed positively, social services are viewed in the contrasting negative light of threatening the family sense of honour (*izzat*) (Buckman, 2011).

Case study 12: Complex needs and appropriate care

A routine domiciliary visit was made by a new social worker to follow up on services received by a young woman and her family, Asma, a cheerful, Pakistani girl of 17 with complex needs: physical and cognitive was that day being cared by her 19-year-old sister who received the visitor with marked antipathy, announcing bluntly that she did not like social workers. Intrigued by this reception the social worker listened to a litany of complaints where it was angrily claimed that Asma was most certainly being neglected in her periodic respite care as she recently came home with a soiled incontinence pad. Moreover, the family were sure she was not being fed properly at the resource either, as Asma took so long to be spoon fed that no one outside the family would have the patience to do a proper job. The question was posed to the social worker, how could anyone who did not love Asmi like her family did, and probably did not understand their culture either, possibly provide appropriate care for her?

In reference to another early study, Bywaters et al (2003) comment on the supranormal explanations given by parents to account for their child's disability. These parents regarded themselves as being punished by divine will, which the authors claim is not congruent with Islamic beliefs, as they understand them. However, supernatural entities such as *jinns* can be regarded as responsible for illnesses and misfortune, rather than attributed solely to the will of Allah (Atshan, 1997). Such views were identified in Ashencaen Crabtree's (2007b) study of family care-giving of children with disabilities in the UAE; however, this attitude was a minority one. Far more prevalent was the more positive message of affirmation of the child and the family's belief in the Islamic view of illness and disability as a test of piety set for the faithful.

Subversive strategies denoting pride were also detected in the narratives of participating Arab mothers in relation to their disabled child. The title of *Umm* meaning 'mother of' is adopted by many Arab mothers where commonly the eldest son's first name will be added, for example, 'Umm Yusuf'. It was therefore highly significant as a public statement when one mother adopted the appellation of her younger and disabled daughter (Ashencaen Crabtree, 2007a). Evidently when a religious view towards disability is held this is much more likely to lead to a positive attitude towards disability itself and to recognise the intrinsic value of people with disabilities.

An additional factor preventing parents from accessing health and social care services is that of shame, according to Bywaters et al (2003). This may be held in conjunction with a sense of powerlessness felt by families towards the idea that either they or professionals can alter circumstances or alleviate them in any meaningful way. In this vein, Fazil et al (2002) comment on the low uptake of services by Asian families that is related to a negative perception of what can be achieved: 'Finally, such attitudes are said to lead to low expectations of their children's future as adults and to reduced willingness by parents to encourage their children to achieve maximum independence' (Bywaters et al, 2003, p 503). The following case study illustrates some of these dilemmas.

Case study 13: A collision of values and beliefs

Jamal, a young Pakistani man with significant learning disabilities living with his caregiving family was referred to a local social work team for an assessment of need. The allocated social worker found that he spent most of his day doing little and usually sitting in the family's parked car outside the house for hours on end. Because the car was parked within the locked compound surrounding the house this was considered by Jamal's family to be an appropriately safe environment for him.

Having assessed Jamal's needs, day care was suggested, which the mother, as main carer, showed some interest in receiving. The client was duly placed in a resource suited to his assessed needs and soon the day care staff reported that he was beginning to make good progress: he was interacting well with staff and other service users, and particularly enjoyed the specialist music sessions at the centre. The family who had yet to visit the resource personally were duly told the good news.

One month after starting at day care Jamal was abruptly withdrawn from the centre by his family who claimed that all the stimulation he was receiving was having a bad effect on his character. They disclosed that their son was now less content to sit passively at home but was more excitable, and had started becoming noisy, using both verbal articulations as well as trying to recreate percussion rhythms with household items. All this the family found to be entirely unacceptable. Earnest attempts made to persuade them to return their son to the centre were rejected, as were invitations to visit the centre and see for themselves how well he was doing. With many misgivings the social worker had no choice but to accept the family decision, remove Jamal from the centre and close the case. After several tantrums it was reported that Jamal's behaviour at home returned to its former passive, inactive state.

This particular case highlights several important points. The family apparently did not regard any progress by their son as a real possibility; his personal development was permanently static, so far as they were concerned. The only wish made by the family was that Jamal was taken care of in a suitably protective environment for a few hours a week to give the family some respite. All attempts to educate the family into a greater understanding of what could be achieved for him was treated with much doubt. By contrast the social worker's argument that Jamal had the right to achieve his optimum development was effectively dismissed by the family. Unfortunately, since Jamal was not competent to express his own wishes on the subject, and his feelings could only be inferred from his behaviour (arguably a subjective evaluation), it was not ultimately possible to override the family's decision, since in other respects they were sufficiently observant of his basic needs. The caring role, from the family's point of view, was one restricted to prevention of harm solely, rather than maximising learning opportunities and normalising this young man's otherwise stunted human potential.

A sad and frustrating case, then, by social work standards, and one that connects with the concepts of social disability and disabling environments. It is also instructive as an example of the mismatch of values, attitudes and expectations as they were played out between the social worker and the client's family. It is worth being reminded, however, that although the professional position today is that every client is capable of personal growth, this was not always the case. The warehousing of people with disabilities was the norm until relatively recently.

Probably the faculty of speech and appropriate social behaviour, more than physical ability, is the common yardstick that most people globally have used to measure how far people with disabilities merit the care and courtesy extended to others. The following extract taken from a research interview with an Arab grandfather of a severely autistic child in the Gulf offers some further insights into this hypothesis. Here the participant conveys deep dissatisfaction that the early intervention service involved had yet to teach the child to speak: 'If people don't understand or talk they cannot greet people properly. Then people won't respect them. If he [grandson] doesn't live in this world [verbal communication], he will be like an animal' (Ashencaen Crabtree, 2007b, p 253).

This quote illustrates the guardian's lack of realism regarding his grandson's abilities. Second, and more to the point, it conveys a very real and understandable fear regarding the boundaries that were felt to mark the human (with all that that implies) from the non-human.

The controversial issue of consanguinity

In 2005 the BBC announced the startling findings that British Pakistanis were 13 times more likely to have offspring with genetic disorders than the general population, regardless that these births made up only 3 per cent of total numbers of children born in the UK (BBC News, 2005b). However, high levels of perinatal mortality and congenital malformations within the Pakistani communities had been noted for some time (Ahmad, 1994). Since then Baroness Flather, herself of Pakistani heritage, was reported as denouncing first cousin marriages as leading to high rates of disability (Swinford, 2015).

Connected to this, in many developing, impoverished countries infants born with disabilities have been far less likely to survive than those in more affluent regions. However, in the west the situation may be reversed. 'Deprivation, consanguinity and the general reluctance of Muslims to abort foetuses with congenital abnormalities are key reasons for the high levels of handicap found amongst the Muslim community' (Sheikh and Gatrad, 2000, p 67).

Accordingly, the experience of dealing with disabilities in the family on a long-term basis has been a new one for many first- and second-generation British Muslim families, but is by no means uncommon.

Consanguineous marriages and the question of a higher risk of birth defects have been a thorny, if somewhat taboo, topic in the UK for some time as apparently questioning a much respected cultural tradition in some ME communities. However, first-cousin marriages have been a common enough union in the UK historically, including the union of the great Evolutionary theorist, Charles Darwin to his cousin Emma, with whom he had a large family, of whom three children died in childhood, including one born with disabilities, ascribed later as probable Downs Syndrome (Bittles, 2009). Interestingly the second-born son, George Darwin, later devoted his scientific career to examining the potential influence of first cousin marriages on health concluding that there was less risk for resulting progeny than in fact was believed to be the case.

It is not only in the UK that concerns are being increasingly pronounced on the potential risk factors of consanguineous unions. A study of Bedouin groups in the Lebanon note the influence of religious affiliation, where Christian Bedouins have half the rate of first-cousin marriages compared to Muslim Bedouins; although this is also viewed as a long established, pre-Islamic tradition (Mansour et al, 2014). In Israel (somewhat ironically given its history) the state has been accused of promoting a eugenics-type programme of selection, where it is claimed that disabled citizens are both marginalised and rejected as failing to fit the national ideal of the physically 'strapping' settler (Raz, 2004; Weiss, 2002). Consequently increasingly falling rates of 'inbreeding' (Zlotogora et al, 2002, p 681) among Arab Muslims in Israel are deemed a great public health success (Na'amnih et al, 2015).

As Bittles (2009) notes, there is a tendency to assume that all birth defects in ME communities where first-cousin marriages are commonplace are the tragic consequence of this custom. Elevated rates of deafness in Bangladeshi and Saudi

Arabian families (Albanyan, 2016; Bittles, 2009) suggests that other factors than solely first-cousin marriages may be responsible, such as potentially environmental and diagnostic factors or a genetic defect in the wider population gene pool, which implicates non-consanguineous unions as well. For social workers therefore it is important to retain a critical awareness of these uncertainties and the potentially oppressive and racist discourse surrounding consanguinity.

Mental health issues

Much has been written on the topic of ethnicity and mental health issues and close consideration has been given to racial preponderance of psychiatric hospital admissions; less commonly on the uptake of mental health services among ME groups. In this book we will not revisit these areas in detail, as essentially this is a broad and complex area falling outside of our remit here.

Mental illness is an important issue for Muslim communities, which, as we have seen, have historically held an abiding interest in this topic in relation to humane care and healing (Rassool, 2000). Shahrom Hatta (2001) asserts that the legal aspects of forensic psychiatry have always been present in the care of people with 'mental illness' (recognising that this term is a modern medicalised one) in Islam. Thus the 'insane' person (*majnun*) suffered from abnormality in terms of emotion, cognition and behaviour. 'For more than thirteen hundred years, Muslim physicians have recorded the various ways of treating the insane; including prayers, social manipulation, music therapy and pharmaco-therapy' (Hatta, 2001, p 183).

Melancholia was one such abnormal state that received scholarly attention from these physicians (Hatta, 2001). Today we would refer to this state as clinical depression, an affective disorder that the World Health Organization classifies as one of the foremost conditions that affects people worldwide.

Keshavarzi and Haque (2013, p 238) offer an interesting discussion of the 'conceptualization of the human soul' composed of four areas: *naqs, aql, ruh* and and *qalb.*

This is compared to the Freudian philosophy of mind, where the *naqs* is seen as encompassing aspects of the psychoanalytic 'ego' as well as the 'id'. Figure 2 outlines the basic holistic model where each part holistically interacts with the other and where the main manifestation is manifested in terms of the symbolised 'heart' as embodied, enacted personality traits.

Among many Muslims worldwide the concept of possession is fully accepted, indeed the very word *majnun* means a person possessed by a *jinn* (Hatta, 2001). *Jinns* (better known to western audiences as *geniis*) are creatures of fire, who although invisible to us occupy human habitats and occasionally human bodies. Curiously, it is said that *jinns* may either be believers or non-believers, where it is the latter who will possess humans (Rashid et al, 2012). *Iblis*, the fallen angel (the Islamic counterpart of Lucifer), is thought to be 'the source of much mental, physical and psychosocial suffering' (Al-Krenawi and Graham, 1999, p 55) in his

Figure 2: Conceptualisation of the human soul

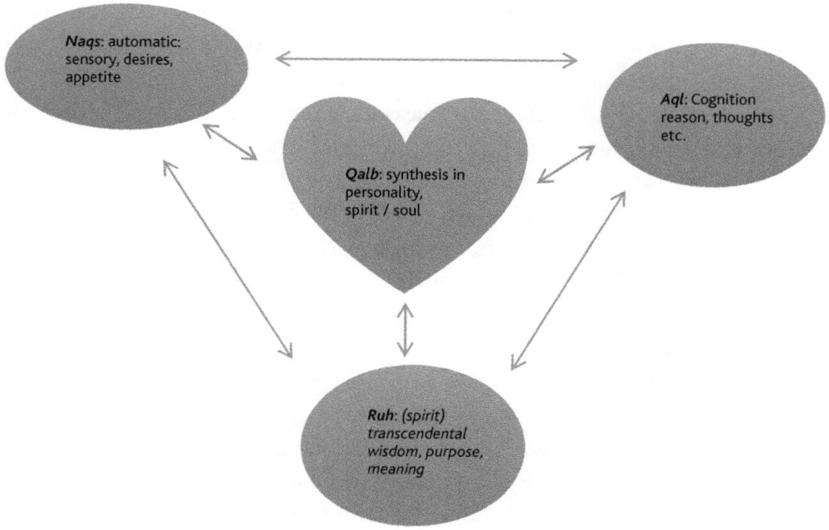

Source: Adapted from Keshavarzi and Haque (2013, pp 238–9)

new persona of *Shaitan* (Satan). Accordingly, postpartum psychosis, obsessive-compulsive disorder, substance abuse and many other dysfunctions and ailments can be attributed to *jinns* (Hanely and Brown, 2014; Al-Solaim and Loewenthal, 2011; Rashid et al, 2012).

Sometimes, therefore, the biomedical and psychoanalytical model that social workers understand and operate within may have little relevance to an individual whose frames of reference come from a very different perspective, as the following case study suggests.

Case study 14: The possessed Arab student

An Arab social work student was anticipating her forthcoming wedding that had been traditionally arranged by her parents. The ceremony took place during the academic semester, but following the honeymoon period she failed to return to class due to an unspecified but serious illness. Her western lecturer inquired after her frequently and eventually her classmates confided that this mysterious sickness was attributed to possession by a *jinn*, which had entered her body during the wedding. Every time her husband approached her for sexual congress she would show florid signs of demonic possession. No blame was attributed to either party by family or friends. It was merely accepted as an unfortunate event that would hopefully be cured in due course, eventually enabling her to return to normal functioning in relation to her duties as a newly married woman and student (Ashencaen Crabtree, 2008).

Similar to Christianity, for Muslims the Manichean struggle between good and evil battles for ascendancy between the physical and spiritual self; where the latter is propelled towards greater goodness and perfection, while the former manifests itself in 'cruelty, greed and aggression' (Abu-Ras et al, 2008, p 161).

The power of prayer is often emphasised as vital to healing in the Islamic framework and is effective in casting out *jinns*, and irrespectively, piety is generally understood to be very important in protecting one's health and general wellbeing. In this vein Al-Krenawi and Graham (1999, p 53) discuss the role of the Arab 'Koranic mental health' healer who, through combining prayer with traditional healing, is not dissimilar to other traditional Muslim healers: the Malay shaman – the *bomoh* – or the *bak* of Uzbekistan (Rasanayagam, 2006). The role of such individuals is usually to provide a culturally informed healing ceremony that is also regarded as compatible with the Muslim faith. This is despite the fact that shamanistic Muslim healers, as opposed to *imams* are often as much disapproved of in Islam, just as spiritualists are by Roman Catholics, being fundamentally rooted in paganism – albeit that both *bomohs* and *imams* are often treating the same bio-psycho-social conditions (Ashencaen Crabtree, 2012). Given the centrality of their religious authority *imams* therefore, are often called on as a resource for help and support in managing distress and confusion (Al-Krenawi, 2016).

As can be seen, therefore, Muslim cosmology is rich in supernatural entities, both benevolent and malign, whose agency is viewed as the means to either elevate human nature or divert it to degradation and ruin. For interdisciplinary practitioners, however, these frames of reference may seem to be yet further examples of delusion and psychosis where there is ignorance of cultural and cosmological variation. There are lessons for social work to learn from the journey psychiatry has undertaken in the past two decades towards accommodating religio-cultural interpretations, owing to a battery of strong critique emerging from within its own ranks (Fernando et al, 1998; Chakraborty, 1991).

South Asian communities and mental health

Based on a number of studies Ineichen (2012) notes that although British South Asians appear to experience equally good or even better rates of mental health than other groups, the picture is somewhat more complicated than would at first appear. The presentation of schizophrenia, for example, appears to differ from the general norm where paranoia and hallucinations do not seem to be a main characteristic of the illness. It is also suggested that South Asian families may be better at containing (or possibly concealing) florid mental health problems in relatives (Ineichen, 2012). Whether psychosis is manifested through a different set of cultural behaviours in South Asian people is open to further research, but depression and anxiety is nevertheless viewed as a common mental health issue.

Depression is subject to gender distinctions, where women are at the highest risk of mental illness globally (Wood Wetzel, 2000). This has been linked to the multiple forms of oppression whose impact falls more heavily on females throughout their lives, and includes all manner of abuses under the broad headings of sexism and patriarchy, sexual exploitation and violence, poverty and capitalist exploitation. It is therefore not particularly surprising to learn that, although British South Asians as a group are estimated to have the same or lower rates of depression and anxiety than the general population, depression has been estimated as twice as high among 'Asian and Oriental' women, compared to white British counterparts (Burr and Chapman, 2004). There is clearly a discrepancy operating here, in which the authors differentiate between depression that is *treated*, and that which remains medically undetected. The hypothesis tested is that women of South Asian origin tend to somatise their depression, in which mental distress is translated into physical symptoms. The findings suggest that while these participants are aware of their emotional distress, they are much more likely to seek medical help from GPs for headaches and flu, as *legitimate* reasons for seeking help, whereas depression is regarded as '"moaning, worrying" and being upset' (Burr and Chapman, 2004, p 444). This finding is supported in another study into the expression of mental illness where Muslim Asian women formed the majority of the participants (Fenton and Sadiq-Sangster, 1996). This too echoes an earlier study in which only one third of South Asian participants, primarily Pakistani, are male (Husain et al, 1997).

Writing from the UK Pilkington et al (2015) note that ME groups and in particular South Asians are less likely to access services for mental health problems than the rest of the population, despite higher levels of risk of mental illness for South Asian women. Equally although the South Asian migrant population has grown considerably in the US over the past decades, there is conspicuous under-utilisation of mental health services, irrespective of this ME community facing the collision of cultural values across generations (Inman et al, 2014).

Fenton and Sadiq (1996) lay out some of the factors eroding the mental health of the female Asian participants in their study, a very significant risk factor related to relationship problems, especially where the family is considered central to the wellbeing of its members. The extended Asian family is often regarded as a source of practical and emotional support to the extent that formal service providers may assume that their input is not necessary. However, such assumptions are by no means always correct in the case of the caregiving relatives with disabilities (Katbamna et al, 2004). Research findings into family care indicate that this is often given with devotion and can be a very enriching experience leading to personal growth in carers (Hastings and Taunt, 2002). At the same time, it is often demanding, socially isolating, physically and emotionally exhausting, and imposes heavy financial penalties on families as well (Read, 2003). These are all factors that once again have an impact on the mental health of carers/care-givers, cutting across ethnic and faith divides in the UK and usually falling to the lot of mothers. In line with this observation, a study by Husain et al (1997), suggests that it is mostly marital difficulties, burdens of care and housing problems that predominate as stressors in the lives of South Asian women.

Although most Asian families in the UK do not live in extended families, when this structure is in place this in itself can be another source of stress and anxiety. Sonuga-Barke and Mistry (2000) contribute their findings to a small but growing body of research literature regarding the psychological benefit to mothers and children in extended Hindu or Muslim families, which specifically include a resident grandmother. The results are interesting: while children were shown to fare well, as did grandmothers, the mental health of mothers, and particularly Pakistani Muslim mothers, suffered in consequence. The majority of mothers, with an emphasis of Muslims over Hindu mothers, experienced higher rates of depression and anxiety compared with counterparts living in nuclear families. The authors suggest that this may be due to the feelings of a loss of agency and control in situations where grandmothers are overly intrusive. However, it is also noted that Muslim mothers tended to be younger than the Hindu participants in the study, with the inference that they therefore lack authority and self-confidence (Sonuga-Barke and Mistry, 2000).

Patriarchal socio-sexual control within the family setting relating to *izzat* constitutes another major risk factor for mental health problems for women and girls, particularly in relation to domestic violence, which is separately associated with poor mental health outcomes for victims (Chew-Graham et al, 2002). As discussed in the previous chapter, abuse in all its variations clearly has serious consequences on both the mental and physical health of victims.

Perceived racial hostility has been another factor regarded as contributory to mental distress (Fenton and Sadiq, 1996; Fenton and Sadiq-Sangster, 1996). However, given the number of Islamist terrorist bombings since the 9/11 and 7/7 events, perceived Islamophobia has taken centre stage as a key source of deep anxiety for many Muslims, which in turn may constitute a trigger for mental health problems (Laird et al, 2007). Guru's study of the impact of counter-terrorism strategies on the families of suspected terrorists provides an insight into the trauma experienced on primarily women and children,

> The kids were frightened – crying…screaming. They even wet themselves standing. They were so scared when they saw their father on the floor…Even the older ones urinated themselves because they were so scared. I tried to reassure them that he would be back soon… but I could not stop them crying. (Guru, 2012a, p 1166)

Guru (2012a; 2012b) accordingly argues that social work needs to engage with the political, social and material realities facing Muslim families and cannot seek to operate in a sanitised vacuum.

Other areas of risk relate to poverty and deprivation, which have long been linked to mental health problems, and, as the demographic evidence shows, many Muslim Asian families in the UK are obliged to live under circumstances of privation, with few good employment prospects.

A further point worth considering relates to the issue of migration. In relation to the preponderance of African Caribbean men in psychiatric care, studies have considered the impact of cultural dislocation, the removal from supportive networks and the effects of racism on migrants (Rack, 1982; Acharyya, 1996; Barnes and Bowl, 2001). Similar dynamics exist in the west for other migrant groups who experience racism and assimilation problems, in which they too are often at risk of mental health problems (Noh et al, 1999). In Canada, migration appears to be a factor in mental health morbidities among the South Asian population, that once again particularly affects migrant women (Islam et al, 2014).

Addictions

Islam frowns upon behaviour likely to induce addiction; consequently alcohol, gambling and substance use are all forbidden to Muslims (Rashid et al, 2012; Lee et al, 2014). Addictions hold potential co-morbidity connections with mental health problems. For Muslims therefore the recourse, commonly taken by people of other religions, to seek faith-based help (in addition to or as a substitute for formal services) may feel inaccessible to Muslim addicts.

Case study 15: Substance abuse

Bilal, a 45-year-old man of North African descent came to the UK as a refugee, where he has been granted permanent leave. Approximately a decade ago Bilal was diagnosed with severe depression, which he manages by self-medicating, although he is also addicted to opiates and other illegal substances. Referred to the adult statutory safeguarding team following concerns of financial abuse and general self-neglect, he presented as withdrawn and under the influence of illegal substance. Nonetheless Bilal was pleased to hear that his social worker was a practising Muslim and would observe confidentiality about Bilal's religiously unacceptable addictions. In the social work assessment process it became evident that Bilal wanted to stop using heroin and other drugs because he felt too impure to visit his mother, other members of the family or attend the mosque. His social worker managed to gain Bilal's consent to refer him to the local drug and alcohol services. A complex plan of care was subsequently developed following the 12 Steps model of addiction treatment, involving submission to a higher being as well as identifying a mentor/sponsor. A Muslim doctor from the same denomination and an *imam* were eventually identified to work with Bilal as mentors. Although formal support was in place for Bilal to address all his needs, his view was that the more severe the harm the nearer he was to Allah's aid, which might come in his lifetime or even after his death, but needed to be awaited with pious patience. Bilal's reading of verses from the Holy Qur'an (Soora al Jinn (72);18) gave him the confidence he needed to be able to join Narcotics Anonymous.

Following a detoxification programme, Bilal moved to better lodgings and continued to engage with services. He is now an active member at the mosque, volunteering to help local language school students who attend it, praying regularly and being open about his experiences. The social worker concluded that Bilal was feeling empowered as the support plan was based around his religious beliefs and the outcome met his needs. He is currently drug free, busy with voluntary work and planning to visit his mother in Africa soon.

Finally, extreme distress may ultimately be enacted in suicide, which for Muslims, as in Christianity, is a mortal sin. It is therefore often regarded as a criminal act in some Muslim countries, and in general is treated as a taboo subject (Sarfraz and Castle, 2002; Pritchard and Amanullah, 2006). Suicide statistics globally may be camouflaged under the category of 'other violent accidents', which are duly much inflated compared with minimal figures for suicide (Pritchard and Amanullah, 2006, p 422). These authors warn practitioners against overlooking possible collusion between interpreters, the patient and family with the aim of minimising the extent of the mental distress, and hence the risk of stigmatised suicide. However, more recent British studies reveal that attempted suicide and suicide are high among both young and older South Asian women, while self-harm among these young women is higher than for young males (Ineichen, 2012).

Note
[1]   The prevention strategy in France is open to being framed as intrusive state-sponsored abuse to prevent a greater cultural abuse. Arguably each carries oppressive elements.

SEVEN

Ageing and end of life

Here we consider issues relating to Muslim elders across a number of overlapping domains in keeping with the holism of Islam. First, the current demographic trends in ageing are set out in respect of fiscal and care-related pressures placed on that provision. In the following section ageing is examined from within the Qur'anic frame of reference and in so doing provides the crucial religious context from which to discuss appropriate and sensitive care of elderly Muslims.

When considering Muslim communities, ageing and age-related issues, a dual perspective is required where first, it is important to view older Muslims as part to the general ageing population – as many age-related issues affect all groups of older people. Yet it is equally important to consider them as a sub-group of minority ethnic (ME) or racialised communities, because the interaction of age with social structures and systems is analysed and researched in terms of ethnicity and national origin, rather than faith affiliation. The long history of Muslim ME migration to the UK, taken in consideration with the development of national social policy for health and social care provision, provides useful insights into the issues and implications of providing religio-cultural appropriate care in western multicultural, multifaith societies.

Ageing trends in the UK

In common with most developed nations the population of the UK is ageing and projections suggest an increase in the median age as well as in the proportions of older people in the population (ONS, 2015). Alongside the increase in the number of older people, reflecting the ageing of the 'baby boomer' generation, people are also living longer – at least in the western hemisphere – with an increase in those over the age of 85 years. From the mid-1970s to 2014, the proportion of those aged over 65 has grown by 47 per cent, constituting 18 per cent of the total population. The population of those over 75 has increased by 89 per cent during the same period, constituting 8 per cent of the population (ONS, 2015).

Although the ME population of the UK continues to be younger than that of the white British population, and within that statistic Muslims have the youngest age profile, trends in ageing are expected to be similar, with an increase in the proportions of older people from ME backgrounds. Census data also shows that although the proportions of Muslim people aged 65 and over is relatively small compared to the Christian population, it still constitutes the largest group of older people when compared to other minority faiths (Buddhist, Hindu, Jewish, and Sikh).

Within the ageing Muslim population, as is the case with any other population cohort, there is great diversity in ethnic profiles, national origin and cultural practices. Although precise statistics of the breakdown of Muslim elderly are not available, it is likely that by far the majority are South Asian, mainly of Pakistani and Indian origin. By contrast it is expected that the profile of the UK Bangladeshi Muslim population will remain younger than that of the Pakistani and Indian groups.

By 2051, in England and Wales, there will be an estimated 3.8 million Black and minority ethnic older people aged 65 and over and 2.8 million aged 70 and over (Lievesley 2010, p 5). Similarly, by 2026, it is predicted that the group aged over 70 in ME communities will comprise more than 800,000 people increasing to 2.8 million by 2051. Thus as ageing populations increase and become more ethnically diverse, anticipating the health and care needs with a view to planning appropriate provision becomes increasingly important across nation states.

Consequently, the UK's ageing population is but part of a global population trend due to decreased mortality and declining fertility. Globally, the number of older persons (aged 60 or over) is expected to more than double, from 841 million people in 2013, to more than 2 billion in 2050. Moreover, senior citizens are projected to exceed the number of children for the first time in recorded history by 2047.

An aspect of ageing likely to be observed globally is the so-called 'feminisation of ageing', as women living in modern industrialised societies experience much improved maternal health and typically tend to live longer than men. In relation to longevity, however, the implications of high numbers of people living to a very old age relates to the increased likelihood of co-morbidities. Commensurately resourcing sufficient service provision to cope with these population changes will need to be significant.

Global implications for ageing populations

Globally, there has been a surge in interest in aging populations and the implications for social and economic development. A United Nations report on ageing cited a major concern in relation to old-age support ratios (number of working-age adults per older person in the population) which are already low in the more developed regions in the world, as well as some developing countries, and are expected to continue to fall in the coming decades.

Not only does this changing ratio have implications for the concept of family-based care but also for support provision for the elderly, especially in a period of global financial instability, which has placed pressure on the financing of support services. Consequently there are a host of age-related factors, which, while not specific to ethnicity or faith, may require specific and targeted responses.

Evidence suggests that health appears as the most important issue in relation to quality of life in ageing (Sidell, 1995). The direct health-related implications of an ageing population are numerous. Age-related decline and the presentation of co-morbidities may mean that older people experience frailty in addition to a complex set of illnesses and disability. Across ethnic groups health status is uneven and ethnic health inequalities are substantially greater in older age than in earlier life (JRF, 2013). For example, Bangladeshi and Pakistani populations in the UK suffer from higher rates of diabetes and cardiovascular disease than the rest of the population. Furthermore older Pakistani and Bangladeshi people are more likely to report limiting long-term illness than other groups; while across genders these groups are more likely to report poorest health in comparison to the white British group (JRF, 2013).

Ageing can have diverse effects on cognitive function. It is well established that memory declines with old age, but for those who suffer more pronounced cognitive dysfunction, typically a form of dementia, there are likely to be significant issues related to support and care (Kensinger, 2016). In the UK, an important implication of the ageing population generally, is the likely increase in the number of people with dementia from ME backgrounds (Moriarty, 2010). Government policy responses (DoH, 2009; 2010) have called for care services to take ethnicity into account in order to ensure that these groups achieve equal access to services. Nevertheless, although highlighting the need for specially tailored provision these policy documents do not explicitly refer to faith affiliation and service provision.

It is widely recognised that loneliness, social isolation and social exclusion are key risk factors for ill health and mortality in older people (Steptoe et al, 2012; WHO, 2002). As people become older, and less mobile due to illness, an increase in social isolation may result. By 'social isolation' we refer both to a diminishing social network and the lack of a useful role in society (Age UK and NHS England, 2015). The reduction in social networks through illness and death means that older people often miss out on peer interactions, an aspect directly associated with loneliness. Among some groups, there also may be reduced interaction with neighbours and family members (Findlay and Cartwright, 2002).

Research has recorded the importance placed by ME groups on being close to family and/or those from the same ethnic and linguistic backgrounds (Gill et al, 2014). Gender plays an influence where older women are more likely to enjoy better social networks than male counterparts, with the result that they may experience less social isolation (Manthorpe et al, 2010).

In addition, older Bangladeshi and Pakistani people regard living close to family, local shops and places of worship as important in reducing feelings of isolation (Age UK, nd). The absence of being able to share cultural beliefs and rituals with others, together with participation in religious activities, are all factors contributing to social isolation.

The concept of social isolation is a subjective experience and consequently related to individual and cultural perceptions of relationships and intimacy together with general functioning and social activity. Consequently, it may be experienced in almost any setting, apart from the obvious situation of living alone, and so includes the following situations:

- living in residential care;
- living with families whose members have become too busy to have quality time or quality interaction with the older person;
- feeling excluded from or not given opportunities to play their traditional role (British Columbia Ministry of Health, 2004).

The interaction of ethnicity and old age

There are a number of important social and family factors that interact with old age. While these may be true for all groups of older people they are particularly salient for ME older people. Living in poverty affects health outcomes as well as general wellbeing. Once again the UK provides a useful example as the most established western country receiving Muslim migrants. Here ME, and in particular Bangladeshi and Pakistani senior citizens, are more likely to experience poverty in old age, having usually been employed in lower paid jobs. Throughout their lives they may also have been more reliant on welfare benefits compared to individuals from other groups. The 'feminisation of poverty' phenomenon is also manifested in older British Bangladeshi and Pakistani women, who have experienced either low levels of employment activity or no paid employment at all.

Migration and settlement brings both new opportunities and disadvantages, where people can become distanced from important relationships in the wider family network, resulting in a loss of supportive social ties. Older parents, who have lived independently and then migrated to live with their children in old age (such as the US and Canada) may experience a loss of independence and a severing of their social networks that are not easily substituted in the disorientating and unfamiliar new cultural environment. Building new social networks in old age can be more difficult than in earlier life and for many ME migrants this is likely to be compounded by language barriers as well. Linking up to useful resources and services is also likely to be hampered by lack of knowledge of the local environment and culture, leading to heavy reliance on immediate family and loss of peer interaction (Cloutier-Fisher et al, 2006; Findlay and Cartwright, 2002).

Furthermore, it is by no means unlikely that vulnerable ageing individuals who have recently migrated may find it hard to adjust to norms and values that are in conflict with those in their country of origin. A deeper appreciation of Islamic precepts serves to illuminate for practitioners the sense of marginalisation that elderly Muslim migrants often experience in struggling to establish a foothold of orientation in cultures that may seem so brutally oblivious to the respect, honour and compassion owed to seniority.

Case study 16: Migration, cultural norms and mental health

An elderly Yemeni lady with moderate dementia was sent from the Yemen by relatives to live with her married nephew in London, since it was thought that formal health and social care services in this country would be more appropriate to meet her needs. Soon after her arrival the nephew contacted social services to request assistance as his aunt was proving to be more dependent than he and his wife had anticipated. On visiting the family, the social worker found the lady in question to be a frail individual with no English language abilities. The assessment suggested that the client was feeling very insecure by her relocation to an entirely new cultural setting, being a move that had not been of her choosing. Her ensuing wandering behaviour at home had resulted in the family locking her into her bedroom at night, which had greatly aggravated her anxiety. On consultation, the family stated that they wished to continue caring for her but were keen to opt for day care during the week.

Day care provision was arranged at a centre where there were a significant number of Asian clients, with whom it was hoped she would eventually make friends. Here she seemed subdued, but that was considered to be an understandable adjustment to her new setting. Unfortunately, after a few days the placement was jeopardised by a sudden deterioration in her mental health status, when she was found to be very distressed on arrival at the centre. The nephew confided that he and his wife were finding it very difficult to get his aunt onto transport in the morning due to her hysterical behaviour, but had no idea why she was so reluctant to go.

On investigation the social worker uncovered the reason for the client's distress. Although once at the day centre this lady was segregated from males in an all-female Asian clique, compatible with her cultural norms, no such division was in place on the transport used, where males and females were placed together according to logistics. This close proximity to unrelated men had created a huge conflict in the client, exacerbating her distress and, consequently, her dementia. Once her nephew's wife took over the role of driving her to the centre in the family car, she returned to her previous levels of functioning and no further incidents of psychotic-type behaviour were reported.

Models of care

There is global awareness that the ageing population presents something of a 'time bomb' in relation to the provision of health and social services; and that despite the advances made in prolonging lifespans increased longevity does not necessarily equate to a healthy life. This has led to an international push to conceptualise 'healthy' and 'active' ageing for the elderly in explicit terms. Policy and practice frameworks of healthy ageing promotes the combination of social participation and physical health in maintaining quality of life in ageing (Findlay and Cartwright, 2002) as articulated in this WHO statement, 'Among older adult populations, social integration and participation in society are regarded as important indicators of productive and healthy aging...and it has been suggested that social support has a strong protective effect on health' (British Columbia Ministry of Health, 2004).

Well in advance of national approaches, and recognising the population trends globally, the UN has focused on older people since 1982, when the UN General Assembly endorsed an International Plan of Action on Ageing. Nearly a decade later, it produced a document setting out 'principles for older persons' (UN, 1991). Referred to as the 'new paradigm', the principles identified were independence, participation, care, self-fulfilment and dignity – with the policy framework requiring action in three fundamental areas:

- *Health*: It should be ensured that older people enjoy quantity and quality of life, and are able to manage their own lives as they grow older.
- *Participation*: National policies and programmes should be designed to support the full participation of older people in socioeconomic, cultural and spiritual activities.
- *Security*: Older people are ensured of protection, dignity and care in the event that they are no longer able to support and protect themselves. Families and communities are supported in efforts to care for their older members.

A decade on and echoing the UN principles, the WHO published its own policy framework for older people promoting the notion of 'active ageing'. It is important to note that it also defined 'quality' in old age as, 'an individual's perception of his or her position in life in the context of the culture and value system where they live, and in relation to their goals, expectations, standards and concerns' (WHO, 2002, p 13).

Designed to inform discussion and support the development of action plans for older population groups worldwide, this interpretation fails to take into account the dislocating impact of migration, in terms of the need and ability to adapt to what may be regarded as alien cultures and value systems. Even much younger migrants can find acculturation very challenging as appears to be the case for many (mostly) Iraqi migrants to Finland, thousands of whom have since preferred to be repatriated (Forsell, 2016).

A number of policy documents on ageing have been produced by successive UK governments stating their commitment to 'healthy ageing'. Different government departments have produced policy documents with a specific focus. For example, the Department for Work and Pensions, following the removal of the default retirement age, has focused primarily on extending working lives by setting out a case that working longer can benefit individuals, the economy and society. This sits alongside a policy to improving digital inclusion of older population groups (DWP, 2014). Meanwhile the health service in conjunction with the national charity, Age UK, has a practical guide for 'ageing well' which includes guidance on looking after oneself in old age (Age UK and NHS England, 2014). An earlier document, the *National Service Framework for Older People* (NHS, 2001), mirrored the UN and WHO documents, by setting out eight standards, mainly focused on ill health and social care. In addition, it called for innovative practice in health and social care and more research on older people to recognise 'the diversity of human culture and conditions and take full account of ethnicity, gender, disability, age and sexual orientation' (NHS, 2001, p 143). In respect of provision of care, this document refers explicitly to race, ethnicity and religion, which is crucially embedded in culturally competent practice: 'Good assessment also requires that the needs and circumstances of older people from black and minority ethnic communities are assessed in ways that are not culturally biased and by staff who are able to make proper sense of how race, culture, religion and needs may impact on each other' (NHS, 2001, 2.31, p 31).

Policy changes to social care law for England via the English Care Act 2014 (separate legislation exists for Scotland and Wales) mandates that local authorities must ensure client/service user wellbeing as one of the core principles with an emphasis on enabling people to have more control of their own lives. With regards to older people, policy formulations have failed to take into account ethnicity and culture because ME populations were not considered large enough to warrant specific attention. Policy makers and practitioners have not paid sufficient attention to the segmentation of population groups within these trends and thus largely ignored the ethnic and faith dimensions of ageing, histories of migration, and associated social inequalities. Moreover, irrespective of ethnicity and minority status, some research suggests that health and social services have failed generally to keep up with this demographic change (Oliver et al, 2014). As advocacy organisations point out plausible policy agendas on ageing need to reflect ethnic, cultural and faith differences.

Health and social care systems

With an ageing population and compounded by the effects of economic 'austerity' in the UK economy, there is a substantial financial implication for the provision of care for older people, irrespective of ethnicity and faith. With two thirds of the primary care budget spent on the over 65s and 70 per cent of health and social care spend on people with long-term health conditions (many of whom are likely to be older), research by Oliver et al (2014, p 3) asserts that there is a need to '"shift the curve" from high-cost, reactive and bed-based care to care that is preventive, proactive and based closer to people's homes, focusing as much on wellness as on responding to illness'.

Social care provision falls under the aegis of local authorities, which in turn are experiencing enormous financial pressures and as a consequence are making decisions in relation to the services they provide. A recent estimate suggests that around 52 per cent of gross local authority adult social care spend was on people aged over 65 (HSCIC, 2015).

Part of this personalisation of social care has also meant that individuals are given control over their care by way of a system of personal budgets allocated to them following a social work assessment and implementation of direct payments. This means that the responsibility of spending and managing personal budgets lies with the individual and not with adult social services. This carries obvious implications in terms of ensuring that such responsibilities can actually be undertaken by individuals without risk of self-neglect or financial exploitation by others.

Alongside the personalisation agenda there has also been an increase in the 'out-sourcing' of care provision to a wide range of providers including national private sector organisations, specialist third sector services and small community focused organisations. Little, however, is known about faith-based care that may be provided by local places of worship. The social care sector would therefore benefit from mapping out that elderly care embedded within a faith context, in order to fully understand the complex tapestry of providers, commissioning at the local level, and the nature of statutory care in providing appropriate and culturally sensitive services. The range of changes taking place in health and social care practice do not take into account the differential experiences on ME and faith groups or existing evidence on care disparities. It is important that how Muslim elderly people are served in the context of both policy and demographic changes is an issue that has not been adequately addressed in practice.

The principles and values of need-based care, dignity in old age and strong community networks seem fairly aligned with Islamic values of respect, esteem, mercy and honour towards the elderly. However, putting social care values into practice so that Muslim elderly people are honoured and respected presents some significant challenges. Although social care practice has developed significantly over the past few decades, evidence suggests that older people from BME groups continue to receive poorer treatment from health and social care services (Moriarty, 2008). Moreover, Mir and Sheikh (2010) identified a lack of willingness among professionals to interact with faith issues of service users.

Challenges of appropriate care provision

A significant number of barriers identified occur at the intersection of cultural/faith-based practices and structures. The perspective of the practitioner is embedded within organisational culture and the structures within which these organisations function, while for individuals and families, gaining an understanding of their rights and entitlements in the face of need, is compounded by a complex health and social care structure which can be difficult to navigate. Poor receptiveness may be a reason for lower uptake of services in the UK, so that help is sought only when a situation or health condition becomes acute.

Interestingly, some of the barriers to accessing services experienced by older Muslims are similar to those experienced by other groups. Barriers identified by Moriarty (2008) include lack of information, language difficulties, and differing expectations about how services can help, as well as poor mental and physical health. Racism constitutes another barrier whether overt or inadvertent at individual and institutional levels along with professional assumptions that ME families will provide any necessary care of sick relatives, along with the general presumptions of a 'colour-blind' approach to service provision and assessment. The concept of culturally sensitive care remains problematic. Cultural assumptions made by service providers may thereby prevent sufficiently sensitive service provision (Chau and Yu, 2009); and although there is renewed focus on individual need, there can still be a failure to appreciate inter-ethnic and inter-faith differences (Williamson and Harrison, 2010).

There are three specific issues that concern the care of elderly Muslims in the UK. First, how cultural groups define the ageing process may differ. Associated with cultural constructions of dementia, and other age-related illnesses, there exists cultural stigma attached to mental health problems, which may deter people from engaging with services (Bowes and Wilkinson, 2003; Mackenzie et al, 2006). In addition, there is an important distinction to be made between care that is 'caring' and care that is task oriented (Gill et al, 2014). Personalisation therefore may also mean empathy, cordiality and warmth along with some acknowledgment of an older person as an 'elder'. Finally, perhaps, the biggest gulf that exists is in relation to residential care, which Abdullah (2016, p 388) refers to as 'stigmatised' and commensurately may be perceived within Muslim families and communities as 'abandoning' the elderly and breaking religious obligations with consequential 'loss of face'. Addressing the stigma that surrounds residential care is an important challenge for both residential care providers and Muslim communities generally.

Case study 17: The guilt-ridden son

Munira had six children, four sons and two daughters. Widowed and living on her own, her children were all married with some living in different cities. She eventually moved to live with her youngest son, his wife, both of whom worked, and two grandchildren. With increasing age-related ill-health she became less mobile and was dependent on her son to take her to the local mosque and to other social activities. With time contact with her family became more limited and due to the son's busy, time pressured lifestyle, her wider networks dissipated. When Munira was diagnosed with dementia, the son, although feeling guilty due to the duty he felt to take care of his mother, made the decision to place her in residential care. His guilt was also combined with having to deal with community pressure and to explain his actions. Soon after Munira passed away, the son accepted that he had performed his Islamic duties well by making sure that his mother received the best possible care even if he was not able to provide that care for her himself.

Second, a more critical and reflective stance is required by practitioners to challenge the unhelpful and persistent assumption that ME groups 'take care of their own' even though in the case of older Muslims they are likely to live with their families (Gill et al, 2014). In the context of Muslim families in the west, a better phrase might be 'they would like to take care of their own'. This would acknowledge that economic constraints, household composition and other socio-economic factors may make care-taking of the elderly difficult, while recognising cultural and religious expectation to look after the elderly with dignity and mercy. Furthermore, this reformulation creates an opening to reflect on and discuss the best combination of formal and informal care for both older people and their families. It is important that the discourse on care of Muslim elderly people also needs to be shifted at the community level.

The challenges this constitutes should not be underestimated given the heavy responsibility that Muslims are expected to shoulder for their ageing parents, where the sayings of the Prophet, the *hadith*, are explicit in relation to the treatment of the elderly generally and the associated rewards. 'If a young man honours an elderly person on account of his age, Allah appoints someone to honour him in his old age' (Al-Tirmidhi). A point further reinforced in Al-Tirmidhi: 'He is not one of us who does not show mercy to our young ones and esteem to our elderly.'

Mothers and motherhood are highly exalted in Islam and therefore by honouring one's parents with gratitude it equally honours Allah. 'And we have enjoined on man (to be dutiful and good) to his parents. His mother bore him in weakness and hardship upon weakness and hardship, and his weaning is in two years – give thanks to Me and to your parents' (31: 14). Similarly, one source of the *hadith* records the Prophet as saying, 'Stay with her [your mother], for Paradise is beneath her feet' (Sunan An-Nasa'i). Moreover, the Qur'an indicates that those who do not offer the respect and dignity that should be afforded to one's parents are, in the eyes of God, doomed, with an implication of punishment beyond this life. 'But he who says to his parents: "Fie upon you both!"…Verily! They are ever the losers' (46: 17–18).

These Qur'anic verses and *hadith* set out the Islamic context of elderly care and more specifically the care of parents. In practical terms what this has meant is that there has been an underdevelopment of services for and approaches to elderly care within Muslim communities. The responsibility of caring for older people has been consigned to the domain of family life and the intersection of these religious precepts have overlapped with patriarchal family models, whereby care for the elderly has become the responsibility of sons and daughters-in-law, with mothers holding particular agency and power.

Within the context of changing societies where women are more active in the labour market, and people are living longer, the responsibility of caring for the elderly has put strain on family resources and the ability to take care of older family members. In Muslim families in the UK, particularly (referring mainly to Bangladeshi and Pakistani families), the intergenerational, extended family model within which the elderly live in 'dignity' and have 'agency' is continuing to undergo change, which is influencing care-giving.

The social stigma attached to seeking help (and therefore admitting that children are unable to take care of their elderly family members) will only be diminished if mosque and community 'leaders' recognise the difficulties and challenges of only informal family care especially for those presenting with co-morbidity and declining cognitive function.

The third and final point is that good practice in the care of older people from ME groups is insufficiently developed; and there is evidence to suggest that cultural awareness training among social care staff is at best limited (Gill et al, 2014). Even within active ageing and personalisation frameworks where service users have the opportunity to specify the services they actually need, a standard response has been the ethnic matching of service user to carer provider. The salience of the different dimensions of ethnic matching including linguistic similarity, regional or national background, preparation of culturally appropriate food, gender, religion (for support with ritual ablution for prayer), as well as general cultural familiarity and understanding, are likely to be specific to each individual (Gill et al, 2014). A considered approach to ethnic matching can only take place with the active involvement of service users and their families.

Cultural competence in elderly care

Although the notion of cultural competence is familiar to practitioners and policy makers alike, it seems that more work needs to be carried out to incorporate such approaches into social care practice as it pertains to elderly Muslim people. The default position, which has been observed more widely is to rely on community-based specialist services to provide day activities and support for BME groups. Reliant on local authority funding, these community organisations are also affected by cuts to funding at the local level while pressure on their services is likely to increase due to the changing demographic profile.

As nations grapple with the economic and social challenges of an ageing population, and research recognises participation in religious activities as one way to tackle social isolation, faith has yet to be considered an important aspect of daily life in social care practice with diverse groups of older people, and especially elderly Muslims. Significantly, if the premise of legislation like the UK Care Act 2014 'to enable people to have more control over their lives' is to be achieved, innovative approaches and reflective practice as praxis (informed by and informing theory) needs to be embedded within principles of care to enable Muslim elderly people to have the provision they need, both in terms of culture and faith. An important starting point would be to embed principles on the care of elderly Muslims, and more generally BME older people within local ageing and wellbeing strategies, action plans and commissioning requirements.

Islamic constructions of ageing

So far we have considered the issue of ageing in terms of global demographic trends and offered an examination of UK national social policy and service provision for BME elders and their families. We now view the terrain from a very different perspective but one no less critical to our understanding of the process of ageing in Muslim communities. In this section we begin to offer a more detailed overview of the Islamic landscape of ageing as informed by sacred texts.

Upon such foundations of knowledge, of which we hope to provide a modest introduction here, greater understanding of faith and belief, as well as culturally responsive services may be built.

Given the contemporary policy construction of old age as a looming social problem of overwhelming armies of uneconomic decrepit elders consuming scarce resources, governments are eager to postpone this day of reckoning by raising the retirement age or abolishing it altogether. Even in the ideologically inspired welfare states of Northern Europe, the noble cradle-to-grave social contract is now under considerable threat given the population imbalance of tax-earner supply versus pensioner demand on resources. The new rhetoric promulgating 'healthy' and 'active' ageing echoing across many industrialised nations is primarily a response to these demographic shifts to ensure that citizens remain as physically well and as economically active for as long as possible. The benefits that may be accrued to individuals through these measures are a plus rather than a main purpose, which is to avoid potential dependence on state resources for too long prior to death.

How then is the issue of ageing socially constructed in predominantly Muslim societies and, what is more important, how is ageing viewed from Muslim perspectives? In this section we will explore these intriguing questions with a view to interrogating terms and ideologies, together with gaining insights into the Islamic understanding of the twilight and nightfall of human life.

Ageing in Muslim societies

Indonesia boasts the largest population of Muslims in the world at 209,120,000 people, which constituted 87.2 per cent of the overall population in 2011, but nonetheless ageing is not yet regarded as a particular social problem based on population trends. Nor is industrialised Malaysia classified as an ageing nation, although Malay Muslims form the largest group of ageing citizens in this multicultural society (Ong et al, 2009). By contrast, their tiny neighbour, the Islamic sultanate of Brunei, was predicted in 2000 to start feeling the effects of an ageing population by 2010 (Cleary et al, 2000). That said, the wealth of the country, in inverse proportion to its size, may be cushioning this little nation from the beginnings of this trend.

The picture across the Middle East is highly variable in regards to ageing and is also complicated by factors of war, political turbulence and differing poverty indicators (Ashencaen Crabtree and Parker, 2014). Oil-rich nations such as the United Arab Emirates and the Kingdom of Saudi Arabia bestow on nationals generous pensions and good social care services with access to cheap migrant domestic labour. Thus if families are unable to offer sufficient care of their elderly relatives, buying in services is an affordable and feasible alternative. This stands in contrast to Egypt, for instance, which has experienced enormous social upheaval and civil conflict in the past decade. Here ageing is compounded by problems of poverty and disability. Notably as well, the feminisation of old age is much less apparent in Egypt in terms of female–male longevity. Intriguingly it is reported that in Egypt the majority of elderly people, standing at 83.6 per cent, are male breadwinners with two dependents to support (Aboulhassan and Abdel-Ghany, 2012).

Islamic conceptualisation of old age

The Holy Qur'an is the foremost and uncontested authority on the entire issue of ageing for practising Muslims, where the believer may be guided by *suras* (Quranic sections or chapters) to help interpret the meaning of ageing as well as due propriety and conduct. However, paradoxically, Islamic texts say relatively little and at the same time quite a lot about older Muslims and mainly in the context of family life. The Qur'an thus intones a reciprocal family relationship bound by the duty and responsibility and respect. 'And that you be dutiful to your parents. If one of them or both of them attain old age in your life, say not to them a word of disrespect, nor shout at them but address them in terms of honour' (17: 23).

A highly unsentimental, unvarnished view of ageing is offered in the Holy Qur'an. This does not pander to any notions of age as a happy time of 'golden girls' ageing glamour and youthful self-indulgence, as promulgated by western advertising and general media output. For Muslims a return to second youth is not one of just more carefree leisure time but that of physical and mental decline into a child's dependence upon others. 'And lower unto them the wing of submission and humility through mercy, and say: "My Lord! Bestow on them Your Mercy as they did bring me up when I was small"' (17: 24).

The whole social construction of ageing in the global north, where it is seen as an inconvenience to be relentlessly challenged by cosmetic surgery, extended employment and aerobic exercise stands at odds with the unvarnished depredations of ageing that the Qur'an reveals to us (Moody, 1990; Sapp, 2008). Old age here is viewed as a time of inexorable decline, physically and mentally.

On the surface of it this may seem attuned to timeworn, if not actually venerable, stereotypes of ageing that have existed for centuries. Shakespeare famously describes the life of 'man' (people generically) as divided into segments of age with accompanying stages of dependence or independence attached (Moody, 1990). These are the seven 'parts' (or ages) that individuals play throughout their lives on the world's stage of daily roles:

> The sixth age shifts
> Into the lean and slippered pantaloon,
> With spectacles on nose and pouch on side;
> His youthful hose, well saved, a world too wide
> For his shrunk shank; and his big manly voice,
> Turning again toward childish treble, pipes
> And whistles in his sound. Last scene of all,
> That ends this strange eventful history,

Is second childishness and mere oblivion,
Sans teeth, sans eyes, sans taste, sans everything.
(*As You Like It*, Act II Scene VII)

Combining both bathos and pathos this construction of ageing both amuses and appals. Unsurprisingly this is a notion of old age that is often fearfully rejected, here summed up by the famously defiant lyrics of a well-known English rebel rock band: 'Hope I die before I get old!' (The Who, 'My Generation', 1965).

A rich body of interdisciplinary work is beginning to emerge in relation to faith and spirituality across the life span, which is rich in reference to life experiences, metaphor and symbolism in illuminating this phenomenon. Although this body of work largely refers to Christianity and Judaism, this holds great relevance for Islam as the part of the Abrahamic triumvirate (Ashencaen Crabtree and Parker, 2012). However, while ritual observation of prayer is noted to increase in old age for the two former religions (MacKinlay, 2001), this may not be true of Islam. For Muslims the observance of prayer times is part of the habitual patterns of daily life inculcated from a very young age; although debatably greater piety in general is not necessarily manifested solely through prayer. In the 1960s Firth (1963, p158) observed of British Asian communities that Muslim, Hindus and Sikhs age 'in the context of the whole lifespan' rather than in the Shakespearean discrete and distinct 'ages'.

Erickson's well-known psychosocial lifespan model builds on the legacy of these earlier Renaissance interpretations of ageing by similarly dividing human life into stages, although here in terms of human development, where each has its own particular challenges to overcome by the holistically maturing person.

Accordingly, for the ageing individual the task is to resolve the dilemma of 'integrity versus despair' (Papalia et al, 2003). This refers to the existential dread a person may feel about approaching death and mortal extinction, compared to the satisfaction and contentment of feeling that despite some inevitable disappointments and losses, it has overall been a life worth living (MacKinlay, 2001; Ashencaen Crabtree and Parker, 2014).

Winlock (1963) adds that in contrast to the general assumption that increasing loss defines old age, with the passing of the years the individual's identity becomes more consolidated. Our *intrinsic* self (although this too is a contested notion) becomes anchored more firmly in terms of our values, beliefs, loyalties and habits, precisely by not being tied solely to the ephemera of transitory and 'giddy youth' and those superficial attributes that are so valorised in contemporary society. In other words, with growing age and personal maturity (recognising that some people may always evidence one without the other), we can achieve that which Erickson describes as *ego integrity*. Good ageing for Goodman (1999, p 66) constitutes 'joyful conscious ripening'. In turn Anthony (1963) uses the analogy of the brilliant but extinguishable flame of youth, mellowing to the consoling radiance of the sage.

This notion of elders undertaking the role of sage and mentor is completely compatible with Islamic views of seniority, as well as seamlessly connecting with MacKinlay's (2001) concept of the 'last career' (as borrowed from Heinz, 1994), where the elderly person becomes a conduit of cultural, religious/ritual, symbolic meanings and values passed on to younger generations. Finally, Goodman (1999), in reference to the writings of Rabbi Schachter-Shalomi, explores a renewal of the cultivation of the sage's role in old age, as a return to the honouring of elders in society; and thus healing the injuries to the status and role of seniority through acute ageism that traps in turn so many in a toxic cycle across modern generations.

Al-Asr: The late afternoon of old age

For the reader the Quranic sura, 'Al Asr', offers the familiar metaphor of the length of human life as condensed to a single day. In the late afternoon of life, one experiences many losses, in terms of physical strength, fertility and beauty; potentially as well we may also suffer from mental impairments; and perhaps most painfully of all, almost certainly will experience the death of those we love at some point. The Qur'an therefore, like the Torah, offers no saccharine depiction of the ageing process but frankly acknowledges the ravages of time 'whosoever we give long life we turn back to the process of creation' (36: 68; Sapp, 2008, p 22).

In Islam, a lack of realism, and even a certain impropriety is inferred, attached to denials of the ageing process. Furthermore, however badly compromised health may become in old age it does not in any fashion undermine the reverence and respect that pious, filial Muslims should hold towards their parents, rather the reverse. Elderly parents are not to be ridiculed, scolded or even contradicted by their adult children who are charged with their care (Moody, 1990). Since for Muslims lifelong learning and education is a religious duty for both genders, this does not obviate the need for elders to relinquish patterns of a lifetime in terms of religious observance and knowledge-seeking (Firth, 1963). Instead the 'habit energy' of a long, disciplined life lays down the bedrock of integrity in terms of principles and the associated patterns of conduct and interaction with others (Winlock, 1963, p 81). Quite simply therefore, ageing is just the normal way of 'doing living' (Barnard, 2004, p 182).

Yet, one what might ask, to what end should such Muslim stoicism in old age be directed? The pragmatic attitude towards death in Islam may seem unrelentingly grim in focusing so heavily on ageing as fundamentally 'the process of "being towards death"' as MacKinlay (2001, p 135, following Au and Cobb, 1995) declares. To reach old age is a sign of divine grace for Muslims, as it is for many, and yet it is also viewed as the 'vilest' condition (Moody, 1990). This seems an impossible paradox to resolve unless we are able to decode the profound message and its fundamental meaning. In Islam the ultimate destination of human life *is* its goal, which the faithful anticipate with trust and hope in Allah's mercy.

Islamic constructions of seniority may to some readers seem grim and anomalous by comparison to the new neoliberal formulations of 'old age' as materially, socially, politically and maybe even sexually empowered. In Islam, by contrast, ageing is not valued for its denial of losses but in the full knowledge and anticipation of them, through which wisdom and grace is bestowed. The long journey towards the grave is one rich with transcendent promise. 'To see dying as no more than what we call the end of life is to miss life's most intoxicating spiritual ascent' (Winlock, 1963, p 78).

Although subject to many different interpretations the collective reality of human suffering is recognised across all the organised religions. Arguably the dominant contemporary religion of many westernised societies unites capitalism, materialism and hedonism into a new secular faith. Suffering in this new framework has no point or value – it is to be avoided or rejected as miserably meaningless and futile (Bycock, 1996). Not so for the Abrahamic religions where, although the nuances may differ, each view suffering as rich in spiritual meaning and divine purpose. Accordingly, for Muslims (and other faith groups), Paradise awaits, and thus the decline of health and strength towards final death is the covenant between Allah and the faithful. The inevitable stripping of strength and vitality towards frailty and dependence upon others liberates the individual from vanity and autonomy towards helplessness literally, symbolically and spiritually.

> The meaning of old age therefore is both to celebrate Allah's power and goodness; but also to emphasise that all creation is completely dependent upon that. The ageing process enables Muslims to engage more fully in meditation upon divine truths that are requisite for wisdom and transcendence. Acceptance of the destiny of mortals in returning to Allah is revealed with increasing clarity by the ageing process – and is the ultimate manifestation of the meaning of 'Islam': to submit. (Ashencaen Crabtree and Parker, 2014, p 200)

End of life and coping with death

Death and bereavement, once everyday community events, are now issues that have become topicalised, in being part of the academic, theoretical discourse. Furthermore, although death in infancy and young adulthood (particularly in relation to childbearing) is still commonplace in some developing nations, very few in the developed world will have had personal involvement in this kind of untimely death. The modern-day experience of death is often that of the demise of grandparents, who die quietly out of sight in hospitals and hospices rather than at home. Consequently, death has become a remote and unlikely contingent; and, as has often been pointed out, some people feel so awkwardly embarrassed in the face of someone's bereavement they feel powerless to respond appropriately.

In a multicultural, multifaith environment, medical and social care staff will need to deal with the realities of death across ethnic and religious divides; however, unfamiliarity with faith, ethnicity and culture can intensify feelings of ineptitude.

Across the Muslim *ummah* bereavement reactions naturally vary, as they do for all people, according to levels of intimacy to the deceased, individual temperament, family conditioning and cultural norms. For example, death in Ethiopia is generally accompanied by a shrill, heart-rending ululation, while Bedouin women fall into a keening lament that may continue for days (Abu-Lughod, 1993). It is claimed, however, that Muslims are prepared for the issue of death from an early age as it is mentioned many times in the Qur'an (Raad, 1998). Islam, regardless of cultural variation, lays down some very clear guidance regarding how the faithful should grieve, its duration and how the bereaved should be supported in a return to adjusted living.

To reiterate then, Islam carries an austere message regarding mortality, where death is treated as a prosaic and natural inevitability and when it is important to die as a true Muslim and to have disposed of one's worldly goods according to Islamic inheritance laws. In preparation Muslims are encouraged to acquaint themselves with death by encountering, witnessing and reflecting on it as inexorable and close by (Raad, 1998). Such teachings begin in early childhood, and visiting the dying and attending graves is encouraged to reinforce the message (Firth, 1963). In fact, it is striking how matter-of-fact even very young Muslims appear to be towards a topic that is considered to be frightening, distasteful and embarrassing – to the extent of being shunned in contemporary western society (Ashencaen Crabtree and Baba, 2001; Holloway, 2006), as the main author discovered in discussing Elisabeth Kübler-Ross's (1970) seminal work with Malaysian Muslim students.

> The discussion of denial, anger, bargaining and guilt has frequently been seen by some students to be irrelevant in discussing the needs of dying Muslim clients. Such clients, through virtue of their religion and culture, are usually seen to have transcended these base emotions. What may be a frequent process among other races cross-culturally would not be expected to present emotional and psychological difficulties for Muslims. (Ashencaen Crabtree and Baba, 2001, p 479)

Death for Muslims, as is the case in Judaism and Christianity, is regarded as only a transition from one state of existence to another, where Allah's judgement awaits (Sheikh, 1998). This unavoidable human destiny is also the ultimate human goal that will bring the faithful into the presence of the divine and immutable, by whom the span of each living mortal is decided. Thus death heralds a new, transcendent state of being, through the shedding of those mortal remains that of themselves are not viewed as an end to human existence.

Duties towards the dying and the dead must be observed in Islam, where the former are encouraged to die piously uttering prayers with their last breath (Sheikh, 1998). The body must be ritually prepared for the grave within a specified time (Ashencaen Crabtree et al, 2008; Raad, 1998). Post-mortems are to be actively avoided for a number of reasons. Kormaromy (2004) claims that this is because it disfigures the body (Gatrad and Sheikh, 2002b), and because the inherent motive of questioning the cause of death is impious. Sheikh (1998) argues that post-mortems are disliked, but not strictly forbidden, because they will delay burial; and because it has been suggested by the Prophet Muhammed that maybe the dead can still experience physical sensations (Ashencaen Crabtree et al, 2008; Sheikh and Gatrad, 2000). Additionally, organ donation among Muslims appears to be rare, where it straddles an area of uncertainty and ambiguity regarding its acceptability in Islam (Rasheed and Padela, 2013).

Finally, mourning may follow a prescribed path where the bereaved family will be very closely supported for 40 days when public mourning is ritually brought to a close (Raad, 1998). However, Abu Lughod (1993) notes that although Islam prescribes the form of funeral and mourning rituals, local customs may provide a culturally-informed shape to proceedings, such as the highly demonstrative group lamenting engaged in by some Bedouin Arab women. This is regarded as potentially subversive in appearing to be public defiance or protest against Allah's will, which for piety demands acceptance and, following Kormaromy's (2004) point, 'dampens speculation' about causation and culpability (Abu Lughod, 1993, p 193).

Most Muslims would prefer to die at home, although this is a preference that is not exclusive to Muslims but is in fact one shared by many others. In discussing a study of palliative care issues of Bangladeshi patients in Tower Hamlets, Odette Spruyt (1999) notes that the majority of such patients chose to be cared for and die at home, with many wishing to die in their country of origin. She comments that the existing research literature links death in hospital with people of lower socio-economic status than those who experience 'home deaths'. However, in the case of many minority groups, and Muslims in particular, such a correlation does not hold fast. These families are more likely to be influenced by traditions that view family care of the dying as both an extension of normal care and a sacred trust (Spruyt, 1999; Gatrad and Sheikh, 2002a).

Individuals facing the end of life whose needs cannot be met entirely in the home are likely to need every reassurance that their cultural, faith-based needs will be respected within the new caring environment. Working constructively with the patient and their family to define and meet those needs is likely to alleviate the great anxieties some will feel about moving to unfamiliar, potentially frightening new surroundings, at an extremely vulnerable stage in life. Factors that are likely to be highly significant are those that relate to prayers, diet, pain[1] relief and of what kind (for some faiths, such as in Buddhism, maintaining mental acuity is spiritually important up to the last conscious moments of life). In addition, that they will have access to an appropriate spiritual adviser and their family should be welcome to keep them company during their care and at whatever time of day or night; and finally, that their bodies will be treated according to time-honoured custom in due course. Such stipulations will require commitment by the relevant health authorities and the staff serving them; however, much suffering may be alleviated by this kind of sensitive, inclusive approach.

Even in the event of good planning, not all eventualities can be covered. Furthermore, despite any evident need, some families will find the move towards formal care very hard. For when end-of-life care cannot be administered at home family members may feel public shame and private guilt, which can greatly exacerbate natural grief reactions and lead to conflict with service providers.

Case study 18: Family perception of abandoned responsibilities

A 72-year-old Pakistani man with cardiac and renal failure was referred to the community palliative care team to discuss respite care in the hospice. His family, with whom this gentleman lived, were anxious about other relatives viewing his admission to the hospice as an abandonment of their responsibility of care, especially as the hospice was seen as a white, middle-class, Christian environment.

The eldest son agreed to stay with his father during his time at the hospice. On admission he explained how upset his father was to leave his wife and home. The hospice doctor raised the issue of the resuscitation policy; this shocked the son, as he had expected his father to be resuscitated without question. The patient soon suffered a cardiac arrest, was resuscitated and transferred back to hospital where he later died. The death occurred at the weekend and within 24 hours of admission, leading to the involvement of the coroner with a consequent delay in releasing the body for burial. This caused further grief and distress for the family, who felt that if the patient had not gone to the hospice these problems would not have arisen.
Source: Adapted from Jack et al (2001, p 380)

It should be pointed out that, while euthanasia is forbidden under Islam, the artificial prolongation of the lives of all terminally-ill Muslim patients is not thereby implied. Instead, the withdrawing of treatment in some cases where the prognosis is inevitably that of imminent death is considered religiously acceptable (Sarhill et al, 2001; Da Costa et al, 2002; Gatrad and Sheikh, 2002a). Nonetheless, Gatrad and Sheikh (2002a) advise that such decisions are more easily reached where a Muslim physician is available to deal with Muslim families and support them in their decision-making. In turn, families may require the additional advice of senior male members of the family and religious advisers.

Because the spiritual dimension of death is predominantly emphasised in Islam the dying person will be helped to pray for as long as they are able (having first received the necessary ablutions); as well as listening to recitations of the Qur'an (Gatrad and Sheikh, 2002a). Ideally, their bed should be placed facing Mecca, which in the UK lies towards a south-east direction (Sheikh and Gatrad, 2000). One issue that may cause concern to medical staff in relation to hospital policies is the number of visitors the dying person may receive. This may be far in excess of the numbers usually visiting the bedside of dying hospitalised patients, for this is a time when people will seek forgiveness from the dying person for any trespasses they may have committed in the past (Sheikh and Gatrad, 2000).

Islam stresses the importance of accepting the reality of death by the dying, as well as the bereaved, where ultimately the dead are viewed as embarking on a journey to their true home 'returning to the Highest Company' (Sheikh and Gatrad, 2000, p 101). It would not therefore be proper for a devout Muslim to rail against divine judgement, as indicated in Kübler-Ross's stages, although Abu-Lughod (1993) mentions the conflict between that which faith dictates and the urges of culture and maybe even that of instinct. Moreover, as Ashencaen Crabtree and Baba (2001) point out, this assumption is to fall into the fallacy of conflating *is* with *ought*, where many dying Muslims may well feel emotions that they are discouraged from expressing. Working across faiths, social workers may need to reflect on how to support the needs of clients, as well as those of families, particularly when these needs are not simultaneously congruent. This would apply to the situation of the individual's strongly felt, emotional needs and what is prescribed by faith and culture. This is especially important for Muslim clients when what is being felt at that moment is perhaps the need and space to openly grieve about impending and perhaps untimely death.

After death has occurred, there are some immediate tasks that need to be accomplished by the family and their followers, thus medical staff should accordingly liaise closely with them to avoid family distress. Most of the funeral preparations will take place at home and often families will use the services of a nearby Muslim funeral committee to arrange for death certificates and the funeral (Schott and Henley, 1996).

According to Yasien-Esmael and Rubin (2005, p 497) under *shari'a* law upon hearing of a bereavement one should utter thanks to God, reciting 'We are all to God and we shall return to him. God, I ask you to provide the appropriate recompense for me for this tragedy/accident and leave me only the good from what has occurred.' The corpse must be washed by one or two respectable and pious fellow Muslims of the same sex who can be entrusted with the office, for even in death the proprieties of gender segregation and physical proximity should be observed (Yasien-Esmael and Rubin, 2005). The body will be wrapped in a simple white shroud; Sheikh and Gatrad (2000) add that this shroud would ideally be the cloth that had been worn on the *hajj* pilgrimage in life.

Prayers will be said over the body at the mosque or at the gravesite, which will not be marked by engraved headstones but may carry some other marker. It is very important that the body is buried as quickly as possible, its face turned towards Mecca. Under Islam the burial should take place within 24 hours of death; connected, no doubt, to the historical sanitary concerns regarding the effects of a hot desert climate on corpses. Consequently, any delays will cause distress to families as being disrespectful to the deceased and bringing fears that decomposition will commence, for embalming is not permitted (Schott and Henley, 1996).

Funerals mark further gender distinctions, for women may be prohibited from attending funerals, even that of their own child. This relates to Islamic precepts regarding attitudes of acceptance and decorum, which women are not considered to be able to uphold due to the perception that they are more emotional than men. Prophet Mohammed made it very clear that grief should not be expressed with voluble weeping and lamentations (and it is particularly forbidden at the graveside), owing in part to the potential sentience of the deceased as well as potentially appearing blasphemous.

Islam emphasises the desirability of a rapid return to normality following loss, where bereavement is structured across a strict timeframe. According to Yasien-Esmael and Rubin (2005), official mourning (*hidad*) takes place three days after the announcement of the death, where patience and forbearance are the hallmarks of a pious demeanour. Unlike the often overwhelming ritual for Christian families, where although beset by grief, they are often expected to provide food and drink for attendees to the funeral, in Islam visitors instead bring the food to the home of the bereaved in order to ensure that they eat properly. After seven days mourning is concluded, ablutions and a cleaning of the house mark the return to normal life, although the death may be officially marked 40 days later and again on the anniversary (Yasien-Esmael and Rubin, 2005).

Bereaved Muslims experience relief through being able to take a proactive stand to assist their deceased relatives in the next life by praying for them and performing meritorious deeds on their behalf, such as going on a *hajj*. For in death there are stages for the dead to pass through, which the living can ease by such good deeds in their name. Table 14 outlines these stages.

The souls of the dead attain their place in the celestial hierarchy according to their deeds in life. The highest place, it is said, is allotted to the prophets, while the souls of martyrs are free to choose their place in Paradise; some may not even enter into heaven itself, and the souls of non-believers will simply rot in their graves (Yasien-Esmael and Rubin, 2005).

In terms of practice, ordinary bereavement counselling services are likely to be problematic in relation to assisting potential Muslim clients. They in turn may regard the idea of seeking professional help for grief as being essentially irreligious, and therefore likely to induce or exacerbate guilt. The response of some service providers will probably be that assistance with such needs are best left to the family concerned and to their religious adviser. Consequently, there remain further questions to be answered about what kind of social work practice

Table 14: The Islamic schema of existence

• Life before conception
• The lower world (life on earth)
• The intermediate realm
• Judgement Day
• The Garden and the Fire

Source: Sheikh and Gatrad (2000)

would be appropriate for dying Muslims and their families, apart from close liaison with the latter to ascertain their expressed wishes.

Certainly for some there will be unmet needs regarding prolonged, suppressed or complicated grief. However, what kind of support practitioners can offer will remain unclear until the research gap into this exacting area is at least partially bridged. This could usefully highlight any outstanding issues of concern relating to the psychological and emotional adjustment of the dying and bereaved individuals, especially those who require more support than can be found in the existing framework of religious, cultural, family and community expectations. Such services could conceivably be particularly beneficial to those whose loss relates to stigmatised or specifically difficult circumstances. HIV/AIDS, suicide, domestic violence or death under traumatic or notorious circumstances are those that immediately come to mind as likely to require professional help.

Nor should we forget the needs of those who are simply unable to come to terms with dying and death in conformity with faith-based and socially sanctioned values and conduct. For relatives, grief complications can arise when there is a lack of a body to arrange a funeral for. The neglect of the disposal of corpses without proper funerary rites can cause additional deep distress, as in the case of Malaysian Airlines passenger flight MH17 shot down by a missile in July 2014 over the Ukraine, leaving hundreds of bodies strewn on the ground to decompose for days, much to the distress of their relatives.

Note
[1] Pain is a highly subjective state and varies across gender and ethnicity. It is claimed that some patients (women and certain ethnic groups) suffering from chronic and even terminal illness often have their experience of pain discredited by medical staff, who assume that the level of pain felt is in fact lower than is being reported by the patient (Werth et al, 2002; Croissant, 2005).

EIGHT

Muslim communities, crime, victimisation and criminal justice

Basia Spalek with Tracey Davanna

Introduction

Criminal justice issues are discussed in this chapter in relation to Muslim communities, particularly drawing on research undertaken in the UK, but also involving a broader international dimension by including other countries, notably France, Germany and Australia. Muslim communities as the victims of crime, Muslims as perpetrators of crime and criminal justice responses to victimisation are areas that are explored here. An underlying theme to this chapter is that whereas, traditionally, identities in relation to ethnicity have generated substantial research and policy attention within a criminal justice context, in the post-9/11 era religion as an identity marker is taking on greater significance, with attention being placed particularly, although not exclusively, on Muslim communities.

Ethnicity and criminal justice

In the UK, equality and diversity issues within the criminal justice system have traditionally been considered through a predominantly secular framework in relation to ethnicity rather than religious identity. This means that 'racial'/ethnic groupings have been identified and used to guide service delivery and provision, and religion has tended to be overlooked. For example, agencies of the criminal justice system record suspects', offenders', victims' and employees' identities according to 'racial' and/or ethnic categories, not religious categories. Thus, statistics in relation to stop-and-searches conducted by police under counter-terrorism legislation use racial rather than religious categories. This means that although statistics may suggest an increase in the number of Asians stopped and searched, it is not possible to gauge the circumstances of such events in these statistics (Garland et al, 2006). While direct and institutional racism by the police, the courts and the penal system has been extensively documented (Hood, 1992; Kalunta-Crumpton, 1999; Bowling and Phillips, 2002; Shute et al, 2005), and policies have been implemented to tackle these issues, discrimination on the grounds of religion has rarely been addressed. Whereas the Home Office regularly publishes statistical information about minority ethnic (ME) groups under the publication *Race and the Criminal Justice System: Statistics under Section 95 of the*

Criminal Justice Act, no similar publications are to be found in relation to faith. The 2006 Equality Act has established a new single Equality and Human Rights Commission (EHRC) that brings together all six strands of discrimination – ethnicity, age, gender, disability, religion and sexual orientation – into one unified organisation. Interestingly, when exercising its powers relating to its community functions, the EHRC is required to have 'particular regard' to ethnicity, religion or belief, suggesting that faith identities will increasingly be monitored and used for policy development and analysis.

Notably, the Prison Service in England and Wales has been monitoring the religious identity of inmates for a number of years. Prison statistics show that Islam is currently the second fastest-growing religion in British prisons, and Muslims appear to be over-represented in prisons by over threefold. Prison statistics show that on 30 June 2015 14.5 per cent of the prison population was Muslim, 18 per cent Roman Catholic and 19 per cent Anglican (Home Office, 2015). Since Muslims comprise 4.8 per cent of the general population (ONS, 2011), they are clearly over-represented in prison, an issue returned to later in this chapter. In France, since the second half of the 1990s, it has been illegal to ask someone to declare their religious faith, and so there are no official data about the religious or ethnic identity of French prisoners (Beckford et al, 2005). These authors argue that, in contrast to England and Wales (where religious identity is categorised by the prison authorities), French prisons give rise to highly individualised expressions of Islam, and opportunities for collective prayer are scarce in French jails (Beckford et al, 2005).

Muslim communities and victimisation

When focusing on victimisation, it is important to consider Muslim communities as members of ethnic communities, as well as being members of a religious grouping. This is because Muslims might be at a higher risk of certain types of crime due to their ethnicity as well as their religious affiliation. At the same time, the ways in which the process of victimisation is experienced may be influenced by individuals' identities in relation to their ethnicity as well as their religion.

National crime surveys suggest that people belonging to ME groups experience high levels of victimisation. For example, findings from the British Crime Survey show that Pakistanis and Bangladeshis (who are likely to be Muslims) are significantly more likely than white people to be the victims of household crime. They are also significantly more likely to be the victims of racially motivated attacks than Indians, black or white people (Clancy et al, 2001, p 2). Findings from the British Crime Survey also indicate that more than one third of assaults directed against Asian and black people are considered to be racially motivated by respondents (Bowling and Phillips, 2002). The impact of racist crime is particularly severe. Findings from the 2000 British Crime Survey indicate that a much larger proportion of victims of racial incidents said that they had been very much affected by the incident (42 per cent) than victims of other sorts of incidents (19 per cent) (Clancy et al, 2001, p 37).

In relation to Muslims being victims of crime on the basis of their faith identity, data are accumulating that measure the extent of faith communities' victimisation. It has to be emphasised, however, that any measures of victimisation are likely to be significant underestimations because individuals often do not report their experiences to the authorities. Recent research on young Muslim ex-offenders in London found discrimination on the grounds of both ethnicity and religion, illustrating the complexity of victimisation (Davanna, 2016). A majority of participants in this small-scale study were black and had converted to Islam in their mid-teens. As a result, they narrated early-life discrimination predominantly based upon ethnicity. This included numerous stop-and-searches by police as well as regular vicious 'racial' taunting. Since converting to Islam, they narrated strong prejudice emanating from both the government and especially the media in what many argue is a process of securitisation of Muslims in Britain. For example, Mythen et al (2013, p 384) describe this as 'risk subjectification' with young Muslims identified by governing elites as a danger to British security and requiring greater security initiatives. Allen argues this process was intensified by discovering the 7/7 bombers were British born (2010, p 222). As a result, the media promoted the idea of the 'home-grown' bomber that exacerbated the concept of the 'us' verses 'them' narrative between Islam and the west utilised by many especially since the attacks in America on 11 September 2001 (Allen, 2010, p 222).

In response to the securitisation of Muslims, Davanna (2016) found that young Muslims are changing their behaviour to protect themselves from fear that they be identified as the 'enemy within'. Self-protective behaviour included avoiding buying newspapers altogether or searching topics such as Palestine or Syria on the internet. This is similar to earlier findings by Mythen et al into 'checking behaviour', defined as 'conscious performance of self-restraint' (2013, p 391). This included covering up visible markers of Islam such as beards and hats. Both of these studies illustrate that growing up in the shadow of the attacks of 11 September 2001 and 7 July 2005 has left significant scars on these young people. Governing elites' attitudes towards Muslims has created a sense of frustration as to where young Muslims belong compounding a feeling of victimisation. The following case study illustrates the complexities of identities and the importance of ethnic identity as well as religious identity.

Case study 19: Negotiating one's 'Black self' within the Islamic faith through the prison experience

Richard's narrative can help illustrate the complexities of identities in Britain today, such as the importance of recognising both religious and ethnic identity markers. Richard is a young Ghanaian man brought up in London since he was ten years old. His life in London often featured many stop-and-searches by the police – 'so many I can't count' – as well as frequent vicious racial abuse, leaving him bemused and, as a result, questioning his belonging: 'I remember people driving past screaming "black monkey!" It always happens, and I'm like, 'Do you hate my skin colour? Do you want to be black or something? I don't understand.'

When he went to prison, he was the only one of the participants in the study who did not turn to Islam. He describes life in prison as particularly tough due to the pressures of what he had left outside and the consequences of being in prison. Initially he spent his early prison sentence getting upset about his girlfriend as well as finding it hard to be 'caged', leading to confrontations with others. While not utilising religion, however, he spent his time in prison learning about his 'black self'. This appeared important to Richard for two reasons, teaching him to accept himself and, consequently, understand his position as a Muslim. 'The best experience for me wasn't being black but in knowing about my black self...So it's like me learning about Africa, it's making me learn more so I can appreciate my skin colour.'

Learning about his Black heritage allowed him to better understand himself by accepting his black skin. It also allowed him to place himself within the Muslim religion when learning the history of Islam in Africa, giving him a sense of belonging. This highlights the process that Richard went through in positioning himself as an individual within his chosen identities. As he states: 'That's one thing, to become a Muslim you have to know yourself. First, who are you, not just your name, who are you?'

Today, when hearing racist taunts, rather than responding angrily as he previously would, he chooses to dismiss them. What is important is that when challenged by other Muslims about the place of black people within the Islamic faith, his historical knowledge gained in prison is used to challenge and educate others, a role he has readily accepted.

The Home Office Citizenship Survey, which does include faith identities and looks at perceptions and experiences of prejudice and discrimination (though not experiences of criminal victimisation), reveals that Hindus, Muslims and Sikhs are substantially more likely to say that they feel very worried about being attacked due to their skin colour, ethnic origin or religion than Christians, those of other religions and those of no religion (DCLG, 2006, p 28). According to a Home Office report published in 2001, *Religious Discrimination in England and Wales*, while in theory it is difficult to disentangle discrimination based on religious grounds from discrimination based on ethnicity, in practice some of the persons who were questioned in this study did appear to be the targets of discrimination and violence as a result of their religious beliefs and practices (Weller et al, 2001). In a survey looking at the effects of the events of 9/11 on discrimination and implicit racism in five religious and seven ethnic groups, religion was found to be more important than ethnicity in indicating which groups were most likely to experience racism and discrimination. Further evidence of the need to study victimisation through religious discrimination came in a study carried out by the Equality and Human Rights Commission (Weller, 2011). It reported that strong evidence prevailed of the greater discrimination faced by Muslims over other religions. This was particularly true in the second part of the decade, coinciding with the time that the government promoted the existence of 'home-grown' terrorists following the 7/7 London attacks (Allen, 2010, p 222). As discussed earlier, this promoted a significant threat level emanating from within British Muslim 'communities', which allowed another layer of fear to be constructed towards Muslims.

Implicit religious discrimination refers to daily life situations in which covert religious prejudice, such as being treated rudely or not being taken seriously, can be experienced. White Britons also reported a rise in post-9/11 discrimination, and of those in the study who said that they faced religious discrimination, almost half were Muslim (Sheridan et al, 2003, p 19). It is important to note that since 2005/06 the British Crime Survey has been monitoring the faith identities of respondents and so statistics in relation to the crimes that faith communities experience are likely to become available here.

In a post-9/11 environment, religious hate crime is increasingly featuring in the policies and practices of agencies of the criminal justice system. In Britain, under the 2001 Anti-Terrorism Crime and Security Act, a religiously aggravated element to crime was introduced, which involves imposing higher penalties on offenders who are motivated by religious hatred. So far, there have been relatively few religiously aggravated prosecutions; nonetheless, the majority of victims who have been involved have been Muslim. Between 2005 and 2006, out of 43 cases of religiously aggravated crime, 18 incidents involved Muslims as victims, three involved Christians as victims, and one involved a Sikh victim, with 21 victims' religious identities being unknown or not stated (CPS, 2005, p 45). Of course, the number of hate crimes that are prosecuted is tiny in comparison to the number of hate crimes that are actually committed, particularly as most victims do not report their experiences to the police.

Muslim community groups, often working in partnership with local police services, play an important role in monitoring and documenting instances of hate crime. For example, the Forum Against Islamophobia and Racism (FAIR), the Islamic Human Rights Commission (IHRC) and the Muslim Council of Britain are three organisations that monitor hate crimes committed against Muslim communities. According to the IHRC, there was a rise in the number of anti-Muslim attacks during the holy month of Ramadan (IHRC, 2006). More recently, TellMAMA was set up, an organisation supporting victims of anti-Muslim hatred (http://tellmamauk.org). Hate crimes against Muslims rise in the aftermath of Islamist linked terrorism. This illustrates that cultural/religious events can influence the incidence of faith hate crimes. Other events, at both national and international levels, can also influence the number of religious hate crimes that are committed. For example, following the 7/7 bombings, the Metropolitan Police Service recorded a sharp increase in faith-related hate crimes, including verbal and physical assaults (EUMC, 2005). In some parts of Germany, violent attacks on fast-food outlets owned by Muslims are a regular occurrence, and mosques and other Muslim-owned establishments have also been attacked. Attacks on Muslim-owned establishments in France and other countries of the European Union have also been documented (for more details see EUMC, 2006).

In the UK, government figures released in 2013 from data collected over the preceding two years documented 'race' hate crimes as the most common with an average of 154,000 per year. Religious hate crime was the second most common, an average of 70,000 per year. However, of these only an estimated 40 per cent are reported to police. These figures again support the need to consider the victimisation of Muslims often from two perspectives, ethnicity and religion, given some individuals may face double discrimination. Much of the increase in race and religious hate crime is thought to be due to a rise in offences in the months immediately after the gratuitous murder of an off-duty army soldier, Lee Rigby, in May 2013, savagely murdered on the street by violent Islamists in London (Creese and Lader, 2014).

As well as monitoring and documenting instances of hate crime, Muslim groups offer help and support to the victims of crime. For example, in Britain, some Victim Support schemes have developed good links with locally-based Muslim charities so that the volunteers who run these charities have the opportunity to be trained on how to provide support to victims by Victim Support (Spalek, 2006). The former Muslim Women's Helpline provided support to Muslim women over a wide range of issues including divorce, domestic violence, arranged marriages, sexual abuse and incest. Mushkil Aasaan (Community Care for Asian Families in Crisis) develops religious and cultural primary care packages that service providers can purchase; and the An-Nisa Society offers numerous services, which include accredited training in Islamic Counselling. The Muslim Youth Helpline (MYH) is a national faith and culturally sensitive support service for Muslim youth in Britain, developed from a realisation that young Muslim men were not accessing support services from within their own communities or from mainstream service providers. The MYH offers long-term support to clients, including befriending and faith/culturally sensitive service provision (Malik et al, 2007). Muslim welfare organisations have found that the fact that they cater to individuals' religious and spiritual needs means that there is a large demand for their services from, for example, secular women's refuges, mental health services and schools (Ahmad and Sheriff, 2003).

Over the past four decades there has been much research exploring the process of victimisation, and of course it appears that victims of crime often experience substantial psychological, emotional, behavioural, financial and physical impacts (Spalek, 2006). A growing body of work increasingly acknowledges ethno-cultural variables when documenting victims' experiences and processes of recovery. For example, Neville et al (2004) refer to an earlier study comparing black and white women's experiences of sexual assault, and found that black women were generally less likely to disclose the incident. Furthermore, they were more likely to believe that black women are generally at higher risk of being sexually assaulted than white women. Commensurate with the discussion in Chapter Five, a study by Choudry (1996, p 1), exploring Pakistani women's experiences of domestic violence, revealed that the Pakistani women who took part in this project felt that they faced dishonour and rejection within their own community if their marriages failed. In addition, they felt that language difficulties and restrictions of their personal freedom outside the family home made it very difficult for women to seek help from external agencies.

Notably, studies suggest that religion can be an important form of support for victims of crime. For example, a study by Shorter-Gooden (2004) reveals that some African American women may participate in a congregation or spiritual community as part of their coping strategies against the debilitating consequences of racism and sexism. Turning specifically to Muslim communities, Spalek (2002) suggests that some Muslim women who experience victimisation may turn to prayer, meditation and their local *imam* as a way of helping them cope in the aftermath of crime. According to a study of South Asians living in Karachi and Haslingden, Yorkshire, there was a commonly shared sense of victimisation among the South Asian Muslims. Such feelings were linked to the concept of the *ummah*, so that religious oppression and Islamophobia constitute important aspects of Muslims' perceptions as oppressed minorities (Quraishi, 2005).

It is important to highlight that mainstream victim services are secular in nature, which means that people's religious and spiritual needs are not addressed. For example, support services for the victims of domestic and sexual violence generally lack an appreciation of the centrality of faith in some women's lives. Once again, as indicated in Chapter Five, this means that women who hold religious beliefs may choose to stay in their abusive relationships rather than to go to seek help from an organisation which might ignore women's religious requirements, or, additionally, which may negatively judge them for conforming to what are prejudiced assumptions about the controlling and patriarchal nature of religion (Ahmad and Sheriff, 2003). These kinds of circumstances indicate that non-judgemental, culturally competent, outreach social work services, in conjunction with spiritual support, are needed to combat the sense of isolation, helplessness and probably misplaced loyalty that victims of domestic violence may experience.

It is also important to highlight that in the current climate, Muslim minorities are experiencing increased attention from the police and security forces. Community groups are consequently raising concerns that institutional racism, as highlighted by the Macpherson Report (1999), has developed into institutional prejudice against Muslims. In the UK, a series of anti-terror laws have been implemented, including the 2000 Terrorism Act, the 2001 Anti-Terrorism, Crime and Security Act, the 2005 Prevention of Terrorism Act, and the 2006 Terrorism Act. These new anti-terror laws have been criticised by civil liberties organisations as being draconian, and making little, if any, impact on national security. These laws have also provoked criticism from Muslim communities, who feel that they are being unfairly targeted. For instance, the Preventing Extremism Together Working Group on security/policing, set up in the aftermath of the 7/7 London bombings and consisting of representatives of Muslim communities, has raised concerns about the possible breadth of new powers being introduced by the 2006 Terrorism Act, thus: 'Inciting, justifying or glorifying terrorism as currently formulated could lead to a significant chill factor in the Muslim community in expressing legitimate support for self-determination struggles around the world and in using legitimate concepts and terminology because of fear of being misunderstood and implicated for terrorism by the authorities' (Home Office, 2005, p 77).

Muslims are being asked by governments to help combat extremism from within their own communities. However, the disproportionate use of anti-terror laws against Muslims might serve to alienate those communities that are needed to work in partnership with the police for the purposes of counter-terrorism (gov.UK, 2015). As discussed in Chapter Five, the introduced PREVENT (preventing violent extremism) agenda into British society expects professionals across various settings to look out for signs of radicalisation and to report people deemed 'at risk'. According to Kundnani (2009), the PREVENT agenda has destabilised police/community relations by placing Muslims as the 'suspect other', and has undermined community cohesion, with there now being widespread mistrust and community pushback against this agenda. Recent research has clearly highlighted the mistrust that already exists between Muslims and the government (Mythen et al, 2013; Davanna, 2016). For example, Davanna found that young Muslims narrated a sense of belonging to particular parts of London and to England overall, while feeling frustrated and angered by the government's attitude towards them. This led some of the participants to suggest that governing elites' attitudes towards Muslims was one explanation for young people becoming radicalised, initiated by the pain they felt in struggling to feel a sense of acceptance.

Similar strategies are taking place on the Continent. Soon after 9/11 a new set of emergency measures were passed in Germany. The new laws created by these measures have lifted the privileges traditionally afforded to religious organisations in Germany (which used to be viewed as needing extra protection, permitting religious organisations to form with relative ease) and have led to databases being created holding the profiles of German Muslims as well as other members of potentially extremist groups. Muslim organisations have been put under surveillance and those accused of having associations with terrorism or holding dangerous ideologies have been banned. The police have carried out massive raids on mosques that have yet to yield results. These policies have had a negative impact on community–state relations between Muslim groups and the authorities, leading to the greater isolation and segregation of Muslim communities from mainstream society (Bakir and Harburg, 2007).

Furthermore, in Australia, a raft of anti-terrorism legislation has been passed at both state and federal level, which gives wide-ranging powers to the Australian Federal Police and the Australian Security and Intelligence Organisation. These include the power to detain suspects for up to 28 days, during which time it is an offence (carrying the maximum penalty of five years) for the detainee to notify anyone, including a family member, that they have been detained. There is also the power to conduct strip searches on detainees of 16 and 17 years of age (Spalek and Imtoual, 2007). Poynting and Mason (2006) argue that the pursuit of the 'war on terror' since 9/11 in Australia has seen an increasing intrusion of the state into cultural and religious matters for minorities, particularly for Muslim communities. Political leaders are found to be routinely commenting on religious matters: for example, what is acceptable in a sermon and what is deemed as 'extreme' or 'radical'. The Muslim Community Reference Group (MCRG) constitutes the major federal government initiative with regards to engagement with Muslim communities. The MCRG's Statement of Principles and its National Action Plan indicate that the main task of the MCRG lies in assisting the Commonwealth government to identify, isolate and detain Muslim community members who are seen as 'extremists' or 'potential terrorists'. The MCRG has been severely criticised for supporting a government agenda that has little to do with the lives of most Australian Muslims and for promoting an association between 'terrorist' and 'Muslim' (Spalek and Imtoual, 2007).

Muslim communities and crime

In the aftermath of a series of bombings and attempted bombings in the UK, as well as in other liberal democratic societies, there has been considerable discussion and concern within the media and political arenas about the possible pathways to radicalisation that young men in particular may take, and the sites at which radicalisation or extremist recruitment may occur. Within these discussions, populations deemed 'at risk' from radicalisation have been identified. These feature North African male immigrants, second- or third-generation Muslims, particularly Pakistani males, and those (predominantly black Caribbean and East African) males who have converted to Islam. Places recognised as 'at risk' include universities, mosques, Islamic bookshops, youth centres and prisons. It is important to stress, however, that sustained and detailed research exploring potential pathways to 'radicalisation' is rare, as is public information about Islamist terrorists (Pargeter, 2006).

It should also be noted, however, that in certain communities some Muslim men have policed women's behaviour and inflicted psychological and physical violence on women who transgress cultural norms and dress codes (Macey, 1999). As mentioned in Chapter One, it is also claimed that within some Muslim youth subcultures religion may be used to justify and/or absolve deviant or criminal acts. Justifications may include claims that the victims are not Muslim or that they belong to a different religious community. Moreover, perpetrators may resort to paying some of the proceeds from crime to Islamic causes or centres as a way of absolving themselves from guilt. The Muslim Boys Gang in London consists of Muslim converts who use their newly-created Muslim identities as a justification for committing crimes of violence (Spalek et al, 2008). Such gangs are coming to the attention of the media. Shiv Malik (2007) writing in the *Observer* notes in reference to the atrocious gang problem in Tower Hamlets that, of the 27 known gangs there, 26 are Bangladeshi, and comments that early racist oppression towards the Bangladeshi community appears to have bred a culture of brutalisation in turn.

These issues need to be placed within a broader context that takes into consideration not only religious factors but also other dimensions, such as culture, class, ethnicity and masculinity. This is because although religion may be used as an identity marker by individuals, and indeed, may be used to justify crime and forms of anti-social behaviour, other factors are also at play. These suggest that Islam in relation to crime and violence should be approached from a multidimensional perspective, particularly when considering that in the present era Islam can be misrepresented and vilified as a result of geopolitical power plays that take place in the international arena.

The significant decline of the manufacturing sector in Britain over the past 30 years, alongside the reduction of secure long-term employment and the rise of short-term, unstable employment, has had a particularly severe impact on young men. This is especially the case for those who are unskilled and who live in areas where factories were once based, these having been closed down, reduced in size or replaced by supermarkets and other retail outlets. Young (1999) argues that some young men attempt to cope with the social and economic climate that surrounds them by creating subcultures based on the construction of strong or aggressive masculinities, where physical strength and other masculine powers are valued. Almost inevitably, without sufficiently influential moral guidance from leaders, mentors or similar beneficial outlets, this may lead to such outcomes as crime and harassment.

In Chapter One we referred to the underprivileged socio-economic backgrounds experienced by many Muslim families, while in Chapter Two we discussed the low employment figures experienced by Muslims across Europe. To counteract this psychologically, the allegiance to a global community, as exemplified by the concept of *ummah*, may make oppressed groups feel less marginalised in society. This connection with a global Islamic identity, one which has a rich and powerful history, may serve to undo local stereotypes of Islam, which may be particularly negative. So it might be argued that young Muslim men who are experiencing social and economic deprivation are reacting to their social situations in ways that are very similar to other marginalised male youth. It is important, however, to stress that in working to place Muslim offenders' experiences within a broader social and economic context we do not bypass the issue of faith altogether. If religion is, at times, used by offenders as a cultural resource when attempting to legitimise criminal activities, it might be argued that agencies of the criminal justice system must engage with offenders' faith identities as well as other aspects of their identities, such as class, ethnic identities and other relevant properties.

It is also important to stress that participation in religious activities, as well as having religious beliefs, may in certain contexts serve to reduce an individual's propensity to commit crime. The mosque is a site at which various educational, social, recreational as well as religious activities take place (Al-Krenawi, 2016), much like Christian churches. In respect of this, Wardak (2000) argues that the greater the involvement by Muslim youths in their community's social and religious life, the less likely they are to engage in crime. Wardak (2000) maintains that Islam constitutes a framework around which order is maintained in this particular community in Edinburgh.

Muslim communities, prisons and rehabilitation

The over-representation of Muslims in jails in England and Wales, coupled with concerns about conversion to Islam in prisons and the issue of radicalisation, have meant that Muslims in prison are increasingly featuring in policy agendas. The social characteristics of the prison population suggest that religious conversion is going to be a feature of prison life. Studies on religious conversion suggest that personal problems that characterise life situations before religious conversion involve a number of factors. Kose (1996), in reference to Snow and Phillips (1980), refers to these as the *spiritual* (involving the meaninglessness of life, a lack of direction and poor self-image); the *interpersonal* (including marital problems and parental problems); the *material* (unemployment, school-related problems); and finally, *character* (including drugs, alcohol and uncontrollable temper). The social characteristics of prisoners resemble these, thus, the prison population is socially and economically disadvantaged, with 43 per cent of prisoners having no educational qualifications at all and 23 per cent of prisoners having been in local authority care – this figure rises to 38 per cent for prisoners aged under 21, compared with only 2 per cent of people who have been in local authority care from among the general population. A large proportion of prisoners have also engaged in hazardous activities, such as drug taking, prior to their incarceration. Of sentenced males, 63 per cent have engaged in heavy drinking and between a third and a half have used heroin. Of male prisoners, 10 per cent have been mental health patients at some point prior to their incarceration and 64 per cent of sentenced males have some form of personality disorder (Morgan, 2002, p 1139). It seems plausible to suggest therefore that many prisoners will have experienced situations conducive to religious conversion prior to their imprisonment.

Added to this, the prison context itself is favourable to conversion. Prisoner autobiographies reveal the brutalising aspects of everyday life in prison. The lack of control over one's daily routine, the regular exposure to verbal, physical or sexual abuse, directly and/or indirectly, or indeed the constant stress of the potential of being victimised, form the backdrop to prison life (see Carter, 1974; McVicar, 1982; Cook and Wilkinson, 1998). These conditions can profoundly affect prisoners and turning to a religion may be one way of coping with prison life.

A small-scale study of Muslim converts in jails in England reveals that converting to Islam in prison may serve to protect an inmate by providing them with a social network that may reduce their risk of being victimised. At the same time, Islam can help inmates to cope with imprisonment in other ways; for instance, by lowering their levels of aggression so that their interactions with other inmates are less stressed, and reducing their likelihood of committing crimes while incarcerated (Spalek and El-Hassan, 2007). Davanna (2016) found that all of the participants in her study, with the exception of one, utilised Islam in prison in ways that benefited their lives. Prayers helped to calm them, as well as providing a daily structure, while communicating with Allah allowed a supportive dialogue. Seeking forgiveness from Allah was sometimes the first building block to changing their behaviour, acting as a disciplinary tool in limiting physical confrontations in prison and changing their attitudes for the positive. Understanding and recognising Allah's support at this time ensured that, upon release, lifestyles were changed so that seeking work and staying out of prison became the priority. Even if they were prevented from praying as much as they had in prison, considerable reflection appeared to take place as to how to improve their behaviour and follow a positive pathway with the support of Islam.

Case study 20: Prison converts

Conversion to Islam appears to provide some prisoners with a sense of identity and belongingness that was largely missing in their lives prior to religious conversion. This is perhaps unsurprising, given that social theorists have argued that contemporary western society is at a stage of late modernity, where traditional social affiliations, based on family or social class, have been eroded, as evidenced by, for example, the reduction in union and party political membership and the rise in the numbers of people living alone (Bauman, 2004; Furedi, 1997; James, 1997).

> Prisoner A: 'I was out in the world, not knowing anything, who I was, yeah? And Islam sort of gives you the thing "you are a slave of Allah". And what you're here for on this Earth, partly why you are brotherhood, part of a believer, *ummah* is it?'

> Prisoner B: 'It's definitely a brotherhood in Islam...I did have a sense of belonging before but to belong to people that have the exact same beliefs as me that's more important. 'Cos obviously I know where I'm from, I mean I know my people in terms of my country but they don't all believe in the same things as me and they don't even believe the same thing as each other. But as Muslims we have an identity and we all believe in Allah, Mohammed.'

Islam was seen by the participants as being inclusive of all, regardless of ethnicity or nationality:

> Prisoner A: 'In the Qur'an that's what it says, it says – brotherhood. It doesn't matter what nation, it's a religion for the world, innit? That's one of the things I love about it because you go to the mosque and you see white, brown, black, you just see all the colours, that's unity, innit.'

In relation to religious conversion, in some cases, converts may feel that they have little religious, spiritual and practical support upon leaving prison, and this may lead them back to their lives of crime:

> *Interviewer*: 'Do you think that it will be more difficult to practice Islam on the outside of prison?'

> *Prisoner B*: 'Much more difficult. On the outside I have no foundation for Islam, I'm living in a non-Islamic household and my friends are non-Islamic. The ones that are, they're not practising Muslims, they don't go to the mosque every Friday, they talk about Islam but they don't practice the rules as such.'

Source: Spalek and El-Hassan (2007)

Prison authorities have developed interventions with violent extremists who are incarcerated. Policy and research attention has been placed upon examining which regime characteristics are effective with violently extreme prisoners; what style of facilitation constitutes effective intervention; and the significance of a faith–based programme of intervention with this group of offenders. These developments are in their infancy and so currently little research exists addressing these concerns. It is important to stress that currently criminal justice practitioners rarely discuss religious or spiritual issues with their clients. In light of the importance of religion as a cultural resource for some offenders, it might be argued that a key policy development should be to train practitioners to open up space for considering religious and spiritual issues. Empirical research and exploration of this issue is needed, particularly in terms of how this should be done.

At the same time, offender resettlement programmes are increasingly involving Muslim community groups. In relation to offenders who convert to Islam while in prison, evidence suggests that there are specific resettlement issues to consider when these prisoners are released into their local communities (Spalek and El-Hassan, 2007). An innovative prison support group is the Youth Community Support Agency (YCSA) found in Glasgow. This is a 'through–care' team whose role is to support young BME prisoners and their families from the first day of prison to often well beyond their release date. With a recidivism rate of 39 per cent (national average in Scotland is 53 per cent), their success can be linked to two features of their work. First, they act as a bridge between prison life and resettlement, providing the same key worker when the client is in prison to helping reintegrate them back into society after release. Second, in often sharing similar religious and ethnic features as their clients, there is an understanding of how the prisoners often feel that they had failed God/Allah and their families. While many of their clients stated that it was their key workers' listening skills that were most significant, many also vocalised how the key workers understood them and their cultural pressures. For example, clients often narrated parental conflict, with parents who were brought up in Pakistan failing to understand the pressures of life for a teenager in Glasgow. The key workers were able to bridge this understanding, recognising this from their own personal backgrounds. As a result, clients understood that they had somewhere supportive and non-judgemental to go should the need arise.

Therefore, the involvement of Muslim groups in planning releases is to be encouraged, as these may be able to address released prisoners' specific religious, spiritual, cultural and social needs. For example, resettlement programmes run by Muslim communities through the use of local mosques can help provide wide-ranging support to ex-offenders, such as practical help in finding accommodation and work. An additional source of assistance would be the provision of spiritual and religious assistance and guidance where this is requested. What is abundantly clear, however, is that in a post-9/11 context, religion as an identity marker can no longer be bypassed.

For this to take place, common units of analysis within the social sciences may have to be better utilised. For example, in using the term 'identity' as a given conclusion instead of challenging its justification in research, we may be missing out on what this term can actually elucidate. In a recent study, 'identity' was resisted by the majority of participants given that it was deemed to bypass any opportunity for agency on their part (Davanna, 2016). An examination of this found that what was vital to these young male Muslim ex-prisoners was that they have control over the *process* of forming identities. This could be heard in their narratives on why they turned to Islam. Participants were assertive in expressing the various reasons for this and it was important to them that such narratives were told, whether they were converts or birth-right Muslims. The former often turned from Christianity to Islam as it was deemed to provide more personal guidance and structure to life, directing them on to a positive pathway and away from criminality. For the latter, prison was often utilised as a means of reconnecting to Islam, reminding them of the support Allah offered when they were most at need. Agency was important here, indeed dominant to their narratives, in choosing to centralise Islam and use Allah as a means of staying out of trouble. This included choosing new, more positive friendships and using prayer to create calmness. While Mythen (2012) has referred to this attachment as 'anchor identity', the participants in this study utilised words such as 'ideology' and 'values' and even 'it's me', conveying its centrality to them as individuals. An examination of the *process* of identity was key to understanding the attitudes of these young people.

This study also found that in contextualising the concerns of young male Muslim ex-prisoners, narratives of location are vital to help shed light on discrimination. Among the London participants of this study, in contrast to those in Glasgow and Edinburgh, another motive for resisting 'identity' usage arose given it was deemed to be a means of exacerbating discrimination. In defining 'identity', the London-based participants' connected it to group formation that provided limited opportunity to express one's individuality and, what was most important, was a means of constructing a homogeneous stereotype. Resistance to this came in the belief that through the construction of a crude essentialist Muslim 'group', governing elites could profile individuals hidden within it. For example, one of them spoke of being grouped alongside individuals such as Abu Hamza, the radical preacher. While he argued they could both be perceived as Muslim, significant differences could be also be overlooked. The process of group identity failed to consider their differentiation.

This finding adds another dimension to the growing academic work exploring the social construction of security and demonisation of Muslims taking place in the UK predominantly, but not exclusively, since the attacks of 9/11 and 7/7 (Mythen, 2012; Allen, 2010; Pantazis and Pemberton, 2009). While these authors have helped explain the processes and impact of government policies and media representation on the lives of British Muslims, this study discussed in this chapter helps to illustrate another means by which young Muslims believe this is occurring. By examining their narratives, it allows us to place this within other concerns that have been stated about 'identity' usage, such as its overuse and taken-for-granted basis (Brubaker and Cooper, 2000). Recognising the importance of the *process* of identification allows the concerns of these young Muslims to be better understood. This study also helps illustrate the importance of the narratives of location and belonging, requiring further work on the impact of locations on victimisation.

NINE

Concluding remarks

Reflecting on the journey

Since the first edition of this book the geo-political context has shifted markedly with many seismic changes shaping 'glocal'[1] balances of power. This second edition, like the first, has been a culmination of an ambitious undertaking in attempting to offer a comprehensive introduction to social work and Islam for practitioners, students and academics. The scope of the book is therefore deliberately and of necessity wide. Our authorial intention, however, has been to grapple and problematise issues and in so doing to avoid the easier task of offering an anaemic and anodyne account that remains at a superficial level in arguing for the 'oughts' rather than tackling what 'is'.

The central purpose of the book has been an attempt to expand on many of the assumptions and stereotypes that underpin the way Islam and Muslims are perceived in a transitional and challenging post-9/11 culture. A further aim has been to highlight both the conspicuous and, sometimes, less evident needs of Muslim individuals, families and communities in familiar contexts as well as across less familiar international settings. Throughout the book we have attempted to avoid parochialism and short-term, localised policy shifts of limited duration, in order to obtain a deeper understanding of and traction with international policy trends, arguably of greater utility to social work as a global, multicultural and multifaith profession.

In this objective we have been aided by nothing short of a quiet revolution of academic interest in a topic area that was once considered highly obscure. Today there is a growing body of useful research literature on social work and Islam seeking to inform social work practice, much of which is distilled in this volume, in addition to our own research among and interdisciplinary practice with Muslim service users and client groups.

Revisiting the terrain

In revisiting the first edition of *Islam and Social Work* we have been struck by how much has changed globally, although at the local, national levels some aspects, particularly perhaps socio-economic and educational factors, insufficient change has been seen. However, what is apparent is that the perception of 'Islam' has undergone a number of reconstructions, where a 'political Islam', a 'violent Islam' and a 'religious Islam' can be discerned, all of which carry numerous implications, as well as potential and possibilities.

Political Islam encompasses the civic and social participation of Muslims within society and across ethnicity, gender and class. It has a crucial task to play in terms of issues relating to identity, citizenship, democratic values and the multicultural agenda, which is often seen as increasingly in jeopardy in Europe. Mutual antagonism across sectors of society tend to drown out the more subdued voices of moderate, law-abiding Muslim citizens, although their views are vital in modifying extremist views and mediating across divisions in society. Where advocacy, partnership and negotiation is weak, the repercussions will be felt by vulnerable and impressionable members of society, as the following indicates: 'For some youths, the measure of their faith is proportionate to their rejection of the west, as if they defined Islam by what it is not, rather than what it is' (Irfan Cole, 2004, p 119).

Commensurately, Islam as a terrorist scourge poses an international threat to democratic nations and those national groups trying to recreate new political social orders that are not premised on corruption and tyranny. In this respect 'violent Islam' is, as King Abdullah of Jordan observes, a clear threat to political Islam, in promoting a dangerously homogenising, extremist Islamist discourse that runs counter to building diverse, peaceful and egalitarian civic societies.

Finally, 'religious Islam' forms the last point of this unstable triangle. Owing to the marginalisation of many Islamic denominations through the rise of hegemonistic religious interpretations and in conjunction with ideological Islamist aggression, keeping the candle of Islam burning as a gentle religion of peace and tolerance is increasingly eclipsed by Islam as a notionally terrifying and chaotic conflagration of neo-medieval violence. Daesh's bloody crusade to establish a new 'caliphate' based on fanatically fundamental religious interpretations, exemplifies this implosion of religio-political ideologies.

Thus Islam's celebrated, seamless holism can be viewed as either a cradle of potential that seeks to enhance and affirm the social, civic and spiritual wellbeing of all citizens in modern societies – or as a crucible of destruction in peddling values and beliefs that demonise and damn all but a very few. Although certainly demonising of the 'other' is by no means the prerogative and vice of Muslims, many of whom who would claim with much justification, that they above all are on the receiving end of such prejudice.

As we stated in Chapter Two, since the first edition, 'Islam' and 'the west' have moved further towards positioning themselves as huge monoliths of oppositional power locked in continual historical combat. This flies in the face of historical evidence, any conception of civil society and plain common sense. We live and work with Muslims, we teach and are taught by Muslims, we care for and are cared by Muslims, many of us are Muslims – more than this, we all belong to one human family, and for those readers of faith, we are all simply God's fallible and often frighteningly foolish, children – whatever one's name or understanding is of that overarching, omniscient, omnipotent, universal power.

Acknowledging faith

The 'post-secular' age (Crisp, 2010) demands that as practitioners we engage fully with the spiritual and religious meanings of not only service users/clients but also of those with whom we work – our colleagues – and perhaps even more critically to our personal and professional self-development, that of the transcendent which lies within ourselves. Beckett and Maynard (2005) suggest that Neil Thompson's original PCS model (personal/psychological, cultural/commonalities and structural/social) (Thompson, 1993) remains a useful vehicle to explore more fully the role of faith in the lives of clients. However, they also note the inherent tension of religion in that it may lead to resilience, as well as to inflexibility; to cohesion, as well as to exclusion and exclusiveness. As we have also seen, religious interpretations can be used to uphold damaging cultural norms and attitudes that oppress vulnerable groups within faith communities.

Taking due account of faith is essential in social work intervention with clients, which spiritually and functionally provides a critical resource of strength and solace to draw from. Faith thereby is an asset that should be valued and used by practitioners in developing their strengths-based practice. To fail to fully address faith and spirituality where that is important to individuals, or to view it as a mere 'bolt-on' to a social work assessment of need that focuses primarily on all other aspects of the psychosocial and physical, is not merely negligent and ignorant, it is nothing less than oppressive practice.

Future directions

Over the years many of the gaps in practice knowledge that we highlighted in the first edition are beginning to be excavated. The implications and impact of poor health and low socio-economic status for many first- and second-generation immigrant Muslims, along with ageing factors, obviously requires further elucidation and theorisation. The abuse of girls and young women in local communities is an extremely worrying situation that demands further attention. While questions of citizenship, multiculturalism, social inclusion and identity increasingly bedevil social commentators, politicians and the general public that must be opened for debate.

What emerges strongly from a theorised understanding of Islam, however, is the compatibility of social work with Islamic principles and evolving concepts. Thus the rise of research and discursive literature in this area is greatly to be welcomed in informing the profession. In 2008 we concluded the first edition by anticipating that the expertise of a new and larger generation of Muslim social workers would be able to make a very important contribution to social work. We repeat now that it is no exaggeration to say that their knowledge and professional collaboration have never before been so urgently needed.

Note
1   'Glocal' refers to the impact and influences of global and local phenomena upon each
    other.

References

Abdel Haleem, M.A.S. (2001) 'The blind and the Qur'an', *Journal of Qur'anic Studies/Majallat al-Dirasat al-Qur'anya*, 3(2): 123–5.

Abdullah, S. (2016) 'Kinship care and older persons: An Islamic perspective', *International Social Work*, 59(3): 381–92.

Aboulgar, M. (2006) 'Ethical aspects and regulation of assisted reproduction in the Arabic-speaking world', *Ethics, Law and Moral Philosophy of Reproductive Biomedicine*, 2(1): 143–6.

Aboulhassan, N.M. and Abdel-Ghany, T.M. (2012) 'The impact of urbanization and globalization in social welfare policies in Egypt: A critical analysis', in S. Ashencaen Crabtree, J. Parker and A. Azman (eds) *The Cup, the Gun and the Crescent: Social welfare and Civil Unrest in Muslim Societies*, London: Whiting and Birch, pp 246–65.

Abrams, L.S. and Moio, J.A. (2009) 'Critical Race Theory and the Cultural Competence dilemma in social work education', *Journal of Social Work Education*, 45(2): 245–61.

Abu Baker, K. and Dwairy, M. (2003) 'Cultural norms versus state law in treating incest: A suggested model for Arab families', *Child Abuse and Neglect*, 27(1): 109–23.

Abu-Habib, L. (ed) (2007) (ed) *Gender and Disability: Women's experiences in the Middle East*, Oxford: Oxfam Publication.

Abu-Lughod, L. (1993) 'Islam and the gendered discourses of death', *International Journal of Middle East Studies*, 25: 187–205.

Abu-Lughod, L. (2011) 'Seductions of the "honor crime"', *Differences*, 22: 17–63.

Abumalham, M. (1996) 'The Muslim presence in Spain: Policy and society', in W.A.R. Shadid and P.S. van Koningsveld (eds) *Muslims in the Margin*, Kampen: Kok Pharos Publishing House, pp 80–92.

Abu-Ras, W., Gheith, A. and Cournos. F. (2008) 'The imam's role in mental health promotion: A study of 22 mosques in New York City's Muslim community', *Journal of Muslim Mental Health*, 3: 155.

Abu-Salieh, S.A.A. (1997) 'Jehovah, His cousins, Allah, and sexual mutilations', in G.C. Denniston and M. Fayre Milos (eds) *Sexual Mutilations: A Human Tragedy*, New York: Plenum Press, pp 41–62.

Acharyya, S. (1996) 'Practicing cultural psychiatry: the doctor's dilemma', in T. Heller et al (eds) *Mental Health Matters*, London: The Open University/Macmillan Press, pp 339–45.

Adams, M. (2009) 'Muslims in Canada: Findings from the 2007 Environics Survey', *Horizons*, 10(2).

Afshar, H. (1996) 'Islam and feminism: An analysis of political strategies', in M. Yamani (ed) *Feminism and Islam*, New York: New York University Press.

Afshar, H., Aitken, R. and Franks, M. (2005) 'Feminisms, Islamophobia and Identities', *Political Studies*, 53: 262–83.

Afzal, A. (2014) '"Being gay has been a curse for me"', *Journal of Language and Sexuality*, 3(1): 60–86.

Age UK (nd) *Loneliness and Isolation Evidence Review*, www.ageuk.org.uk/documents/en-gb/forprofessionals/evidence_review_loneliness_and_isolation.pdf?dtrk=true.

Age UK and NHS England (2015) *A Practical Guide to Healthy Ageing*, www.england.nhs.uk/wp-content/uploads/2015/09/hlthy-ageing-brochr.pdf.

Agnew, A. (2012) 'An examination of ideological and practical approaches to small business development and social welfare policy in Palestine', in S. Ashencaen Crabtree, J. Parker and A. Azman (eds) *The Cup, The Gun and the Crescent: Social Welfare and Civil Unrest in Muslim societies*, London: Whiting and Birch, pp 120–33.

Ahmad, B. (1990) *Black Perspectives in Social Work*, Birmingham: Ventura.

Ahmad, F. and Sheriff, S. (2003) 'Muslim women of Europe: Welfare needs and responses', *Social Work in Europe*, 8(1): 30–55.

Ahmad, W.I.U. (1994) 'Reflections on the consanguinity and birth outcome debate', *Journal of Public Health Medicine*, 16(4): 423–28.

Ahmed, T. (2005) 'Muslim "Marginal man"', *Policy*, 21(1): 35–41.

Ait Sabbah, F. (1986) *La Femme dans l'Inconscient Musulman*, Paris: Albin Michel.

Ajala, I. (2014) 'Muslims in France and Great Britain: Issues of secularization, identities and loyalties post 9/11', *Journal of Muslim Minority Affairs*, 34(2): 123–33.

Al-Abduljawad, K.A. and Zakzouk, S. (2003) 'The prevalence of sensorineural hearing loss in Saudi children', *International Congress Series*, 1240: 199–204.

Albanyan, M. (2016) 'The benefit of cochlear implants upon the educational progress and placements of deaf pupils at primary school in Saudi Arabia', Unpublished doctoral thesis, University of York, UK.

Alcott, L. (1991) 'The problem of speaking for others', *Cultural Critique*, 1991–92, Winter: 2–31.

Alghazo, E.M., Dodeen, H. and Algaryouti, I. (2003) 'Attitudes of pre-service teachers towards persons with disabilities: Predictions for the success of inclusion', *College Student Journal*, D37(4): 515–22.

Al-Khateeb, S.A.H. (1998) 'Muslim women's perceptions of equality: Case study of Saudi women', *Mediterranean Quarterly*, 9(2): 110–31.

Al-Krenawi, A. (2012) 'Islam, human rights and social work in a changing world', in S. Ashencaen Crabtree, J. Parker and A. Azman (eds) *The Cup, The Gun and the Crescent: Social Welfare and Civil Unrest in Muslim societies*, London: Whiting and Birch, pp 19–33.

Al-Krenawi, A. (2016) 'The role of the mosque and its relevance to social work', *International Social Work*, 59(3): 359–67.

Al-Krenawi, A. and Graham, J.R. (1999) 'Social work and Koranic mental health healers', *International Social Work*, 42(1): 53–65.

Al-Krenawi, A. and Graham, J.R. (2000) 'Islamic theology and prayer', *International Social Work*, 43(3): 289–304.

Al-Krenawi, A. and Graham, J.R. (2001) 'The cultural mediator: Bridging the gap between a non-western community and professional social work practice', *British Journal of Social Work*, 31: 665–85.

Al-Krenawi, A. and Graham, J.R. (2003) 'Principles of social work practice in the Muslim Arab world', *Arab Studies Quarterly*, 25(4): 75–92.

Al-Krenawi, A. and Graham, J.R. (2007) 'Social work intervention with Bedouin-Arab children in the context of blood vengeance', *Child Welfare*, LXXVIII(2): 283–96.

Al-Krenawi, A. and Jackson, S.O. (2014) 'Arab American marriage: Culture, tradition, religion and the social worker', *Journal of Human Behavior in the Social Environment*, 24(2): 115–37.

Al-Krenawi, A., Graham, J.R. and Slonim-Nevo, V. (2002) 'Mental health aspects of Arab-Israeli adolescents from polygamous versus monogamous families', *The Journal of Social Psychology*, 142(4): 446–60.

Al-Shamsi, M.S.A. and Fulcher, L.C. (2005) 'The impact of polygamy on United Arab Emirates' first wives and their children', *International Journal of Child and Family Welfare*, 8(1): 46–55.

Al-Solaim, L. and Loewenthal, K.M. (2011) 'Religion and obsessive-compulsive disorder (OCD) among young Muslim women in Saudi Arabia', *Mental Health, Religion and Culture*, 14(2): 169–82.

Allen, C. (2010) 'Fear and loathing: the political discourse in relation to Muslims and Islam in the contemporary British setting', *Politics and Religion*, 4(2), Autumn.

Ammar, N.H. (2000) 'Simplistic stereotyping and complex reality of Arab-American immigrant identity: Consequences and future strategies in policing wife battery', *Islam and Christian–Muslim Relations*, 11(1): 51–69.

Amnesty International (2015) *Rohingya People: The Most Persecuted Refugees in the World*, www.amnesty.org.au/refugees/comments/35290/.

Andrews, M. (2006) 'The globalization of transcultural nursing theory and research', in M.M. Leininger and M.R. McFarland (eds) *Culture, Care, Diversity and Universality: A Worldwide Nursing Theory*, Boston, MA: Jones and Bartlett Publishers, pp 83–6.

Anitha, S. and Gill, A. (2009) 'Coercion, consent and the forced marriage debate in the UK', *Feminist Legal Studies*, 17: 165–84.

Anthony, M. (1963) 'The spirituality of old age', A. Jewell (ed) *Spirituality and Ageing*, London: Jessica Kingsley Publishers, pp 30–8.

Anwar, E. (2006) *Gender and Self in Islam*, London and New York: Routledge.

Archer, L. (2003) *Race, Masculinity and Schooling: Muslim Boys and Education*, Maidenhead: Open University Press.

Arkoun, M. (1994) *Rethinking Islam*, Oxford: Westview Press.

Asch, R.G. (2015) 'Eyes wide shut – Germany, the immigration crisis and Merkel's winter of discontent', *Open Democracy*, www.opendemocracy.net/can-europe-make-it/ronald-g-asch/eyes-wide-shut-germany-immigration-crisis-and-merkel-s-winter-of-di.

Ashencaen Crabtree, S. (1999) 'Teaching anti-discriminatory practice in Malaysia', *Social Work Education International Journal*, 18(3): 247–55.

Ashencaen Crabtree, S. (2007a) 'Maternal perceptions of care-giving of children with developmental disabilities in the United Arab Emirates', *Journal of Applied Research in Intellectual Disabilities*, 20: 247–55.

Ashencaen Crabtree, S. (2007b) 'Family responses to the social inclusion of children with developmental disabilities in the United Arab Emirates', *Disability and Society*, 22(1): 49–62.

Ashencaen Crabtree, S. (2007c) 'Culture, gender and the influence of social change amongst Emirati families in the United Arab Emirates', *Journal of Comparative Family Studies*, 38(4): 573–85.

Ashencaen Crabtree, S. (2008) 'Dilemmas in international social work education in the United Arab Emirates: Islam, localization and social need', *Social Work Education*, 27(5): 536–48.

Ashencaen Crabtree, S. (2012) *A Rainforest Asylum: The Enduring Legacy of Colonial Psychiatric Care in Malaysia*, London: Whiting & Birch.

Ashencaen Crabtree, S. (2013) 'Research ethics approval processes and the moral enterprise of ethnography', *Ethics and Social Welfare*, doi: 10.1080/17496535.2012.703683.

Ashencaen Crabtree, S. (2014) 'Islamophobia and the Manichean constructions of the "Other": A contemporary European problem', in S. Ashencaen Crabtree, (ed) *Diversity and the Processes of Marginalisation and Otherness: A European perspective*, London: Whiting and Birch.

Ashencaen Crabtree, S. (2015) '"The alternative Jerusalem tour" – after Jericho', March, http://blogs.bournemouth.ac.uk/research/?p=41446&preview=true.

Ashencaen Crabtree, S. (forthcoming) 'Social work with Muslim communities: Treading a critical path over the crescent moon', in B. Crisp (ed) *Routledge Handbook of Religion, Spirituality and Social Work*, London: Routledge.

Ashencaen Crabtree, S. and Baba, I. (2001) 'Islamic perspectives in social work education', *Social Work Education*, 20(4): 469–81.

Ashencaen Crabtree, S. and Husain, F. (2012) 'Within, without: Dialogical perspectives on feminism and Islam', *Religion and Gender*, 2(1): 128–49.

Ashencaen Crabtree, S. and Parker, J. (2014) 'Religion, Islam and active ageing', in M.L. Gómez Jiménez and J. Parker (eds) *Active Ageing? Perspectives from Europe on a Much Vaunted Topic*, London: Whiting and Birch.

Ashencaen Crabtree, S. and Williams, R. (2009) 'Inclusive education and children with disabilities in the Gulf Cooperation Council Member States', in A.E. Mazawi and R.G. Sultana (eds) *World Yearbook of Education 2010: Education and the Arab 'World' Political Projects, Struggles and Geometries of Power*, Abingdon: Routledge, pp 196–213.

Ashencaen Crabtree, S. and Williams, R. (2011) 'Ethical implications for research into inclusive education in Arab societies: Reflections on the politicisation of the personalised research experience', *International Social Work*, doi: 10.1177/0020872811416486.

Ashencaen Crabtree, S. and Wong, H. (2012) '"Ah Cha"! The racial discrimination of Pakistani minority communities in Hong Kong: An analysis of multiple, intersecting oppressions', *British Journal of Social Work*, doi: 10.1093/bjsw/bcs026.

Ashencaen Crabtree, S., Husain, F. and Spalek, B. (2008) *Islam amd social work: Debating values and transforming practice*, Bristol: Policy Press.

Ashencaen Crabtree, S., Parker, J., Azman, A. and Carlo, D.P. (2012) 'Epiphanies and learning in a postcolonial Malaysia context: A preliminary evaluation of international social work placements', *International Social Work,* Advance Access, doi: 10.1177/0020872812448491

Ashencaen Crabtree, S., Parker, J., Azman, A. and Masu'd, F. (2014) 'A sociological examination of international placement learning by British social work students in children's services in Malaysia', *Journal of Comparative Research in Anthropology and Sociology (Compaso)*, 5(1): 133–54.

Ashencaen Crabtree, S., Parker, J., Azman, A., Masu'd, F. and Carlo, D.P. (2015) 'Typologies of student experiences and constructed meanings of learning in international placements', *Asia Pacific Journal of Social Work and Development*, 25(1): 42–53, doi: 10.1080/02185385.2014.1003393.

Australian Government (2013) *Review of Australia's Female Genital Mutilation Legal Framework*, Final Report, Barton, ACT: Attorney-General's Department, www.ag.gov.au/publications/documents/reviewofaustraliasfemalegenitalmutilationlegalframework/review%20of%20australias%20female%20genital%20mutilation%20legal%20framework.pdf.

Baba, I., Ashencaen Crabtree, S. and Parker, J. (2011) 'Future indicative, past imperfect: A cross cultural comparison of social work education in Malaysia and England', in S. Stanley (ed) *Social Work Education in Countries of the East: Issues and Challenges,* New York: Nova, pp 276–301.

Baer, Z. (1997) 'Are baby boys entitled to the same protection as baby girls regarding genital mutilation', in G.C. Denniston and M. Fayre Milos (eds) *Sexual Mutilations: A Human Tragedy*, New York: Plenum Press, pp 197–204.

Bahar, Z., Okçay, H., Özbiçakçi, S., Beaer, A., Üstün, B. and Öztürk, M. (2005) 'The effects of Islam and traditional practices on women's health and reproduction', *Nursing Ethics*, 12(6): 557–70.

Bakir, S. and Harburg, B. (2007) '"Die Geister, die ich rief!" [The ghosts that I awoke]: German anti-terror law and religious extremism', preliminary report, Humanity in Action, Bochum, Germany: Ruhr University, www.humanityinaction.org/docs/Bakir_and_Harburg_Final%5B1%5D.doc.

Bangstad, S. and Bunzi, M. (2010) 'Anthropologists are talking about Islamophobia and anti-semitism in the New Europe', *Ethnos: Journal of Anthropology*, 75(2): 213–28.

Banks, S. (2006) *Ethics and Values in Social Work*, Basingstoke: BASW/Palgrave Macmillan.

Barise, A. (2003) 'Towards indigenization of social work in the United Arab Emirates', in Advancing Indigenous Social Work, conference proceedings, Kuching: Universiti Malaysia Sarawak, 20-21 October.

Barise, A. (2005) 'Social work with Muslims: Insights from the teachings of Islam', *Critical Social Work*, 6(2), http://www1.uwindsor.ca/criticalsocialwork/social-work-with-muslims-insights-from-the-teachings-of-islam.

Barn, R. and Sidhu, K. (2004) 'Understanding the interconnections between ethnicity, gender, social class and health: Experiences of minority ethnic women in Britain', *Social Work in Health Care*, 39(1/2): 11–27.

Barnard, K. (2004) Ageist theology: Some Pickwickian prolegomena', in A. Jewell (ed) *Spirituality and Ageing*, London: Jessica Kingsley Publishers, pp 130–96.

Barnes, M. and Bowl, R. (2001) *Taking Over the Asylum*, Basingstoke: Palgrave.

Bartoli, A. (2013) *Anti-racism in Social Work Practice*, St Albans: Critical Publishing.

Basharat, T. (2006) 'Hijab as an instrument of taking women off the sex economy', *Guidance and Counselling*, 21(4): 201–9.

Bauman, Z. (2004) *Identity: Conversations with Benedetto Vecchi*, Cambridge: Polity Press.

BBC News (2005a) 'Bomber attacked UK Muslim leaders', 16 November, http://news.bbc.co.uk/1/hi/uk/4440772.stm.

BBC News (2005b) 'The risk of cousin marriage', 16 November, www.bbc.co.uk/news/world-middle-east–30134078.

BBC News (2006) 'One in 10 "backs honour killings"', 4 September, http://news.bbc.co.uk/2/hi/uk_news/5311244.stm.

BBC News (2008) 'Sharia law in the UK is "unavoidable"', 7 February, http://news.bbc.co.uk/1/hi/uk/7232661.stm.

BBC News (2012) 'Rochdale grooming trial – 9 men jailed', 9 May, www.bbc.co.uk/news/uk-england-17993003.

BBC News (2014a) 'FGM in Egypt: Doctor and father cleared in landmark trial', 20 November, www.bbc.co.uk/news/world-middle-east-30134078.

BBC News (2014b) 'Last British troops leave Helmand', 27 October, www.bbc.co.uk/news/business-29784195.

BBC News (2015a) 'Syrian archaeologist "killed in Palmyra" by IS militants', 19 August, www.bbc.co.uk/news/world-middle-east-33984006.

BBC News (2015b) 'Palmyra – What the world has lost', 5 October, www.theguardian.com/science/ng-interactive/2015/oct/05/palmyra-what-the-world-has-lost.

BBC News (2015c) 'UK military deaths in Afghanistan: Full list', 12 October, www.bbc.co.uk/news/uk-10629358.

BBC News (2016) 'Muslim women's segregation in communities must end – Cameron', 18 January, www.bbc.co.uk/news/uk-35338413.

Becher, H. and Husain, F. (2003) *South Asian Muslims and Hindus in Britain: Developments in Family Support*, London: National Family and Parenting Institute (NFPI).

Beckett, C. and Maynard, A. (2005) *Values and Ethics in Social Work*, London: Sage Publications.

Beckford, J., Joly, D. and Khosrokhavar, F. (2005) *Muslims in Prison: Challenge and Change in Britain and France*, Basingstoke: Palgrave.

Bedell, G. (2004) 'Death before dishonour', *Observer*, 21 November.

Bell, D. (2007) 'In the name of the law', *The Guardian*, 14 June.

Bendixen, M. (2016) 'Denmark's selfish stance does nothing to help the global refugee crisis', *The Guardian*, 27 January.

Bhatti-Sinclair, K. (1994) 'Asian women and violence from male partners', in C. Lupton and T. Gillespie (eds) *Working with Violence*, Basingstoke: Macmillan, pp 75–95.

Bhatti-Sinclair, K. (2011) *Anti-racist Practice in Social Work*, Houndmills, Basingstoke: Palgrave Macmillan.

Bittles, A.H. (2009) 'Commentary: The background and outcomes of the first-marriage controversy in Great Britain', *International Journal of Epidemiology*, 38: 1453–8.

Blackwood, E. (1995) 'Senior women, model mothers and dutiful wives: Managing gender contradictions in a Minangkabau village', in A. Ong and M.G. Peletz (eds) *Bewitching Women, Pious Men: Gender and Body Politics in Southeast Asia*, Berkeley, CA: University of California, pp 124–58.

Blair, T. (2006) 'Our nation's future', Speech delivered at 10 Downing Street, 3 December.

Boddy, J. (1989) *Wombs and Alien Spirits: Women, Men and the Zar Cult in Northern Sudan*, Madison, WI: University of Wisconsin Press.

Bouhdiba, A. (1997) 'The child and the mother in Arab-Muslim society', *Psychological Dimensions of Near Eastern Studies*, 1997: 126–41.

Bowers, C.A. and Flinders, D.J. (1990) *Responsive Teaching*, New York: Teachers College Press, Columbia University.

Bowes, A. and Wilkinson, H. (2003) 'We didn't know it would get that bad': South Asian experiences of dementia and the service response', *Health and Social Care in the Community*, 11(5): 387–96.

Bowling, B. and Phillips, C. (2002) *Racism, Crime and Justice*, Harlow: Longman.

Bradby, H. (2007) 'Watch out for the aunties! Young British Asians' accounts of identity and substance use', *Sociology of Health and Illness*, 29(5): 656–72.

Brazile, D. (2015) 'Republicans playing a dangerous game', *CNN*, 10 December, http://edition.cnn.com/2015/12/10/opinions/opinion-roundup-donald-trump/index.html.

British Columbia Ministry of Health (2004) *Social Isolation Among Seniors: An Emerging Issue*, www.health.gov.bc.ca/library/publications/year/2004/Social_Isolation_Among_Seniors.pdf.

Brooks, G. (1995) *Nine Parts of Desire: The Hidden World of Islamic Women*, New York: Anchor Books and Doubleday.

Brubaker, R. and Cooper, F. (2000) '"Beyond identity"', *Theory and Society*, 29: 1–47.

Bucci, L. (2012) 'An overview of the legal and cultural issues for migrant Muslim women of the European union: A focus on domestic violence and Italy', *Crime, Law and Social Change*, 58: 75–92.

Buckman, S.K.N. (2011) *Performing Allah's work: Experiences of Muslim family carers in Britain*, Unpublished PhD, University of Nottingham.

Burr, E.G. (2005) 'Learning to teach Islam as a non-Muslim in the Twin Cities', *Teaching Theology and Religion*, 8(3): 155–63.

Burr, J. and Chapman, T. (2004) 'Contextualising experiences of depression in women from South Asian communities: A discursive approach', *Sociology of Health and Illness*, 26(4): 433–52.

Butalia, U. (2003) 'When culture kills', *New Internationalist*, December: 5.

Bycock, I. (1996) 'The nature of suffering the nature of opportunity at the end of life', *Clinics in Geriatric Medicine*,12(2): 237–52

Bywaters, P., Ali, Z., Fazil, Q., Wallace, L.M. and Singh, G. (2003) 'Attitudes towards disability amongst Pakistani and Bangladeshi parents of disabled children in the UK: Considerations for service providers and the disability movement', *Heath and Social Care in the Community*, 11(6): 502–9.

Calvo, R., Rojas, V. and Waters, M.C. (2014) 'The effects of universal source delivery in the integration of Moroccan immigrants in Spain: A case study from an anti-oppressive perspective', *British Journal of Social Work*, 44(1): 123–39.

Campinha-Bacote, J. (1999) 'A model and instrument for addressing cultural competence in health care', *Journal of Nurse Education*, 38(5): 203–7.

Carter, R. (1974) *'Hurricane': The 16th Round*, Ontario: Penguin.

CEOP (Child Exploitation and Online Protection) Centre (2011) *Out of Mind, Out of Sight: Breaking Down the Barriers to Understanding Child Sexual Exploitation*, London: CEOP.

Chakraborty, A. (1991) 'Culture, colonialism and psychiatry', *Lancet*, 337(8751): 1204–8.

Chand, A. (2000) 'The over-representation of Black children in the child protection system: Possible causes, consequences and solutions', *Child and Family Social Work*, 5(1): 67–77.

Chand, A. and Thoburn, J. (2006) 'Research review: Child protection referrals and minority ethnic children and families', *Child and Family Social Work*, 11: 368–77.

Charlsey, K. and Liversage, A. (2013) 'Transforming polygamy, migration, transcultural multiple marriages in Muslim minorities', *Global Networks*, 13(1): 60–78.

Chau, R. and Yu, S. (2009) 'Culturally sensitive approaches to health and social care: Uniformity and diversity in the Chinese community in the UK', *International Social Work*, 52: 773–84.

Chew-Graham, C., Bashir, C., Chantler, K. and Burman, E. (2002) 'South Asian women, psychological distress and self-harm: lessons for primary care trusts', *Health and Social Care in the Community*, 10(5): 339–47.

Chilcot, Sir John (2016) 'Sir John's public statement', 6 July, www.iraqinquiry. org.uk/the-inquiry/sir-john-chilcots-public-statement/.

Children and Young People Now (2003) 0–19 Update, www.childrennow.co.uk/ home/index.cfm.

Choudhury, T. (2005) 'Overview', in *Muslims in the UK: Policies for Engaged Citizens*, Budapest: Open Society Institute, pp 10–41.

Choudry, S. (1996) 'Pakistani women's experience of domestic violence in Great Britain', *Home Office Research Findings*, 43, London: HMSO, pp 1–4.

Cila, J. and Lalonde, R.N. (2014) 'Personal openness towards interfaith dating and marriage among Muslim young adults: The role of religiosity, cultural identity, and family connectedness', *Group Processes and Intergroup Relations*, 17(3): 357–70.

Clancy, A., Hough, M., Aust, R. and Kershaw, C. (2001) *Crime, Policing and Justice: The Experiences of Ethnic Minorities*, London: Home Office.

Cleary, M., Maricar, H.A. and Phillips, D.R. (2000) 'Ageing, Islam and care for older persons in Brunei Darussalam', in D.R. Phillips (ed) *Ageing in the Asia-Pacific Region*, London: Routledge, pp 322–33.

Cloutier-Fisher, D., Kobayashi, K. M., Hogg-Jackson, T. and Roth, M. (2006) *Making Meaningful Connection: A Profile of Social Isolation Among Older Adults in Small Town and Small City, British Columbia*, Report for the BC Ministry of Health, Victoria: Centre on Aging, University of Victoria.

Cockburn, P. (2014) *The Rise of the Islamic State: ISIS and the new Sunni Revolution*, London: Verso.

Coffey, A. (2014) *Real Voices: Child Exploitation in Greater Manchester*, http:// anncoffeymp.com/wp-content/uploads/2014/10/Real-Voices-Final.pdf.

Cohen, S. and Warren, R.D. (1990) 'The intersection of disability and child abuse in England and the United States', *Child Welfare*, 69(3): 253–63.

Connolly, K. (2016) 'Cologne inquiry into "coordinated" New Year sex attacks', *The Guardian*, 5 January, www.theguardian.com/world/2016/jan/05/germany-crisis-cologne-new-years-eve-sex-attacks.

Cook, F. and Wilkinson, M. (1998) *Hard Cell*, Liverpool: Bluecoat Press.

Cornell University Law School (nd) *Code no 116: Female Genital Mutilation*, www.law.cornell.edu/uscode/text/18/116.

Council on Foreign Relations (2011) 'Muslims in the USA', www.cfr.org/ united-states/muslims-united-states/p25927.

CPS (Crown Prosecution Service) (2005) *Racist Incident Annual Monitoring Report 2004–2005*, London: CPS.

Crabtree, S. (Ashencaen) (2006) 'A comparative analysis of social work responses to child abuse in the United Arab Emirates', *International Journal of Child and Family Welfare*, 9(4): 228–37.

Crampton, R. (2005) 'It's terrifying and shocking, said Ali, 19, then strode smartly away', *Times Online*, www.timesonline.co.uk/tol/news/uk/article541717.ece.

Creese, B. and Lader, D. (2014) *Hate Crimes, England and Wales, 2013/14, Home Office Statistical Bulletin 2014*, www.report-it.org.uk/files/home_office_hate_crime_data_201314.pdf.

Crisp, B.R. (2010) *Spirituality and Social Work*, Abingdon: Ashgate.

Crisp, B. (2014) *Social Work and Faith-based Organizations*, Abingdon: Routledge.

Croissant, J.L. (2005) 'Pain and culture', in S. Restivo (ed) *Science, Technology and Society: An Encyclopaedia*, Oxford: Oxford University Press, pp 363–7.

Da Costa, D.E., Ghazal, H. and Al Khusaiby, S. (2002) 'Do Not Resuscitate orders and ethical decisions in a neonatal intensive care unit in a Muslim community', *Archives Disease in Childhood: Fetal and Neonatal Edition*, 86: 115–19.

Danso, R. (2014/2015) 'An integrated framework of critical cultural competence and anti-oppressive practice for social justice social work research', *Qualitative Social Work*, 4(4): 572–88.

Davanna, T. (2016) 'Attitudes and identities of Muslim ex-prisoners', Unpublished PhD.

DCLG (Department for Communities and Local Government) (2006) *2005 Citizenship Survey Race and Faith Topic Report*, London: DCLG.

Dean, H. and Khan, Z. (1997) 'Muslim perspectives on welfare', *Journal of Social Policy*, 26(2): 193–209.

DoH (Department of Health) (2009) *The Dementia Strategy*, issued by the last Labour government but taken forward by the Coalition government, DoH, 2010.

DoH (Department of Health) (2010) *A Vision for Adult Social Care: Capable Communities and Active Citizens*, London: DoH.

DWP (Department for Work and Pensions) (2014) *Fulfilling Working Lives – A Framework for Action*, www.gov.uk/government/uploads/system/uploads/attachment_data/file/458861/fuller-working-lives.pdf.

Der Spiegel (2016) 'Chaos and violence: How New Year Eve in Cologne has changed Germany', *Spiegel Online International*, 8 January, www.spiegel.de/international/germany/cologne-attacks-trigger-raw-debate-on-immigration-in-germany-a-1071175.html.

Derin, S. (2005–06) 'The tradition of *suhl* among the Sufis: With special reference to Ibn Arabi and Yunus Emre', *Journal of Academic Studies*, 27(27): 1–12.

Dhami, S. and Sheikh, A. (2000) 'The family: Predicament and promise', in A. Sheikh and A.R. Gatrad (eds) *Caring for Muslim Patients*, Abingdon: Radcliffe Medical Press, pp 43–56.

Dias, D. and Proudman, C. (2014) 'Let's stop talking about honour killing, there is no honour in murder', *The Guardian*, 23 June, www.theguardian.com/commentisfree/2014/jun/23/stop-honour-killing-murder-women-oppresive-patriarchy.

Dienemann, J., Boyle, E., Baker, D., Resnick, W., Wiederhorn, N. and Campbell, J. (2000) 'Intimate partner abuse among women diagnosed with depression', *Issues in Mental Health Nursing*, 21: 499–513.

Doi, A.R.I. (1992) *Women in Shari'ah*, Kuala Lumpur: A.S. Noordeen.

Dominelli, L. (1994) *Anti-Racist Social Work*, Houndmills, Basingstoke: Macmillan Press/BASW.

Dominelli, L. (1996) 'Deprofessionalizing social work: Anti-oppressive practice, competencies and postmodernism', *British Journal of Social Work*, 26: 153–75.

Dorfman, R.A. (1996) *Clinical Social Work*, New York: Brunner/Mazel.

Dorkenoo, E., Morison, L. and MacFarlane, A. (2007) *A Statistical Study to Estimate the Prevalence of Female Genital Mutilation in England and Wales: Summary Report*, London: FORWARD (Foundation for Women's Health, Research and Development).

Douki, S., Nacef, F., Belhadj, A., Bousaker, A. and Ghachem, R. (2003) 'Violence against women in Arab and Islamic countries', *Archives of Women's Mental Health*, 6: 165–71.

DuBois, B. and Miley, K.K. (2005) *Social Work: An Empowering Profession*, Boston, MA: Pearson Education Ltd.

Dwairy, M. (2004) 'Culturally sensitive education: Adapting self-orientated assertiveness training to collective minorities', *Journal of Social Issues*, 60(2): 423–36.

El Naggar Gaad, E. (2001) 'Educating children with Down's syndrome in the United Arab Emirates', *British Journal of Special Education*, 28(4): 195–203.

Elgot, J. (2016) '"Absurd" visa rules on income force UK citizens into exile, court told', *The Guardian*, 22 February, www.theguardian.com/uk-news/2016/feb/22/absurd-minimum-income-visa-rules-forcing-uk-citizens-into-exile-court-told.

Elliott, L. and Treanor, J. (2016) 'French PM Manuel Valls says refugee crisis is destabilising Europe', *The Guardian*, 22 Jan, www.theguardian.com/world/2016/jan/22/french-pm-manuel-valls-says-refugee-crisis-is-destabilising-europe.

Ely, P. and Denney, D. (1987) *Social Work in a Multi-Racial Society*, Aldershot: Ashgate.

EOC (Equal Opportunities Commission) (2007) *Moving On Up: The Way Forward*, London: The Stationery Office.

Errington, S. (1990) 'Recasting sex, gender, and power: A theoretical and regional overview', in J. Monnig Atkinson and S. Errington (eds) *Power and Difference: Gender in Island Southeast Asia*, Stanford, CA: Stanford University Press, pp 1–58.

Eskind Moses, M. and Russ, M.B. (2014) 'Forced marriage', *Tennessee Bar Journal*, September: 32–34.

Esposito, J.L. (2002) *What Everyone Needs to Know About Islam*, New York: Oxford University Press.

EUMC (European Monitoring Centre on Racism and Xenophobia) (2005) *The Impact of 7 July 2005 London Bomb Attacks on Muslim Communities in the EU*, Vienna: EUMC.

EUMC (2006) *Muslims in the European Union: Discrimination and Islamophobia*, Vienna: EUMC.

Ewald, F. (1991) 'Insurance and risk', in G. Burchell, C. Gordon and P. Miller (eds) *The Foucault Effect: Studies in Governmentality*, London: Harvester Wheatsheaf, pp 197–210.

Faizi, N. (2001) 'Domestic violence in the Muslim community', *Journal of Women and the Law*, 10(2): 15–22.

Fathi, M. and Hakak, Y (forthcoming) 'Muslim parenting in the west: A review', *Sociology Compass*.

Fazil, Q., Bywaters, P., Ali, Z., Wallace, L. and Singh, G. (2002) 'Disadvantage and discrimination compounded: The experience of Pakistani and Bangladeshi parents of disabled children in the UK', *Disability and Society*, 17(3): 237–53.

Fenton, S. and Sadiq, A. (1996) 'Asian women speak out', in T. Heller, J. Reynolds, R. Gomm, R. Muston and S. Pattison (eds) *Mental Health Matters*, Basingstoke: Macmillan/Open University Press, pp 252–9.

Fenton, S. and Sadiq-Sangster, A. (1996) 'Culture, relativism and the expression of mental distress: South Asian women in Britain', *Sociology of Health and Illness*, 18(1): 66–85.

Fernando, S., Ndegwa, D. and Wilson, M. (1998) *Forensic Psychiatry, Race and Culture*, London and New York: Routledge.

Fikree, F.F. (2005) 'Attitudes of Pakistani men to domestic violence: A study from Karachi, Pakistan', *The Journal of Men's Health and Gender*, 2(1): 49–58.

Fikree, F.F. and Bhatti, L.I. (1999) 'Domestic violence and health of Pakistani women', *International Journal of Gynaecological Obstetrics*, 62(2): 195–201.

Findlay, R. and Cartwright, C. (2002). *Social Isolation and Older People: A literature review*, Brisbane: Australasian Centre on Ageing, University of Queensland.

Firth, S. (1963) 'Spirituality and ageing in British Hindus, Sikhs and Muslims', in A. Jewell (ed) *Spirituality and Ageing*, London: Jessica Kingsley Publishers, pp 158–74.

Fleischman, F., Phablet, K and Klein, O. (2011) 'Religious identification and politicization in the face of discrimination: Support for political Islam and political action among the Turkish and Moroccan second generation in Europe', *British Journal of Social Psychology*, 50(4): 628–48.

Fook, J. (1996) 'The reflective researcher: Developing a reflective approach to practice', in J. Fook (ed) *The Reflective Researcher*, Australia: Allen and Unwin, pp 1–8.

Forsell, T. (2016) 'Thousands of Iraqi refugees leave Finland voluntarily', *Reuters*, Feb 12, www.reuters.com/article/us-europe-migrants-finland-idUSKCN0VL0UE.

FORWARD (nd) *Female Genital Mutilation*, www.forwarduk.org.uk/wp-content/uploads/2014/12/FGM-Islam-Leaflet.pdf.

Fowler, H., Griffin, E. and Luesley, D. (1990) 'Antenatal attendance and fasting of pregnant Muslims during Ramadan', *British Journal of Obstetrics and Gynaecology*, 97: 861–2.

Frazer, L. and Selwyn, J. (2005) 'Why are we waiting? The demography of adoption for children of black, Asian and black mixed parentage in England', *Child and Family Social Work*, 10: 135–47.

Frost, D. (2012) 'Islamophobia: Examining causal links between the state and "race hate" from "below"', *International Journal of Sociology*, 28(11/12): 546–63.

Fuller, G.E. and Lesser, I.O. (1995) *A Sense of Siege*, Boulder, CO: Westview Press.

Furedi, F. (1997) *Culture of Fear: Risk-Taking and the Morality of Low Expectation*, London: Cassell.

Furness, S. and Gilligan, P. (2010) *Religion, Belief and Social Work: Making a Difference*, Bristol: Policy Press.

Gardener, M. (2007) '"Old" and "new": Contemporary British Antisemitism', *Engage*, 5, www.engageonline.org.uk/journal/index.php?journal_id=16&article_id=65.

Garland, J., Spalek, B. and Chakraborti, N. (2006) 'Hearing lost voices: Issues in researching hidden minority ethnic communities', *The British Journal of Criminology*, 46: 423–37.

Garr, M. and Marans, G. (2001) 'Ultra-orthodox women in Israel: A pilot project in social work education', *Social Work Education*, 20(4): 459–68.

Gatrad, A.R. and Sheikh, A. (2000) 'Birth customs: meanings and significance', in A. Sheikh and A.R. Gatrad (eds) *Caring for Muslim Patients*, Oxford: Radcliffe Medical Press, pp 57–72.

Gatrad, A.R. and Sheikh, A. (2001) 'Medical ethics and Islam: Principles and practice', *Archives of Disease in Childhood*, 84: 72–5.

Gatrad, A.R. and Sheikh, A. (2002a) 'Palliative care for Muslims and issues before death', *International Journal of Palliative Nursing*, 8(11): 526–31.

Gatrad, A.R. and Sheikh, A. (2002b) 'Palliative care for Muslims and issues after death', *International Journal of Palliative Nursing*, 8(12): 594–7.

Gill, A.K. and Van Engeland, A. (2014) 'Criminalization or "multiculturalism without culture"? Comparing British and French approaches to tackling forced marriage', *Journal of Social Welfare and Family Law*, 36(3): 241–59.

Gill, V., Husain, F., Vowden, K., Aznar, C. and Blake, M. (2014) *Exploring Satisfaction with Adult Social Care Services Amongst Pakistani, Bangladeshi and White British People*, London: NatCen Social Research.

Gilligan, P. and Akhtar, S. (2005) 'Child sexual abuse among Asian communities: Developing materials to raise awareness in Bradford', *Practice*, 17(4): 267–84.

Gitsels-van der Wal, J.T., Martin, L., Manniën, J., Verhoeven, P., Hutton, E.K. and Reinders, H.S. (2015) 'A qualitative study on how Muslim women of Moroccan descent approach antenatal anomaly screening', *Midwifery*, 31: 43–9.

Gohir, S. (2013) *Unheard Voices: The sexual exploitation of Asian girls and young women*, Birmingham: Muslim Women's Network.

Goldberg, H., Stupp, P., Okoroh, E., Besera, E., Goodman, D. and Daniel, I. (2012) 'Female genital mutilation/cutting in the United States: Updates estimates of women and girls at risk', *Public Health Reports*, 13: 1–8.

Goodley, D., Runswick-Cole, K. and Mahmoud, U. (2015) 'Disablism and diaspora: British Pakistani families and disabled children', *Review of Disability Studies*, 9(12–13): 63–78.

Goodman, J. (1999) Harvesting a lifetime, in A. Jewell (ed), *Spirituality and Ageing*. London: Jessica Kingsley Publishers, pp 65–70.

Goonesekere, S. (1994) 'The best interests of the child: A South Asian perspective', *International Journal of Law, Policy and the Family*, 8(1): 117–49.

Gough, D. and Lynch, M.A. (2002) 'Culture and child protection', *Child Abuse Review*, 11: 341–4.

gov.UK (2015) '2010–2015 government policy: Counter terrorism', www.gov.uk/government/publications/2010-to–2015-government-policy-counter-terrorism/2010-to–2015-government-policy-counter-terrorism.

gov.UK (2016a) 'Forced Marriage', www.gov.uk/stop-forced-marriage.

gov.UK (2016b) *Multi-agency Statutory Guidance on Female Genital Mutilation*, www.gov.uk/government/publications/multi-agency-statutory-guidance-on-female-genital-mutilation.

Gowricharn, R. and Mungra, B. (1996) 'The politics of integration in the Netherlands', in W.A.R. Shadid and P.S. van Koningsveld (eds) *Muslims in the Margin*, Kampen: Kok Pharos Publishing House, pp 114–29.

Graham, J.R., Bradshaw, C. and Trew, J.L. (2010) 'Cultural considerations for social service agencies working with Muslim clients', *Social Work*, 55(4): 337–46.

Graham, M. (2007) *Black Issues in Social Work and Social Care*, Bristol: Policy Press.

Graham, M. (2009) *Black Issues in Social Work and Social Care*, Bristol: Policy Press.

Green, J.A. (1999) *Cultural Awareness in the Human Services: A Multi-ethnic Approach*, Needham Heights, MA: Allyn and Bacon.

Guru, S. (2012a) 'Under siege: Families of counter-terrorism', *British Journal of Social Work*, 42: 1151–73.

Guru, S. (2012b) 'Reflections on Research: Families affected by counter-terrorism in the UK', *Journal of International Social Work*, 55(5): 689–703.

Haj-Yahia, M.M. (2003) 'Beliefs about wife beating among Arab men from Israel: The influence of their patriarchal ideology', *Journal of Family Violence*, 18(4): 193–206.

Hall, M. (2004) 'Ageing in Manitoba', *Social Isolation and Seniors in Winnipeg*, Winnipeg, Manitoba, www.health.gov.bc.ca/library/publications/year/2004/Social_isolation_workshop_report.pdf.

Halstead, M.J. and Lewicka, K. (1998) 'Should homosexuality be taught as an acceptable alternative lifestyle? A Muslim perspective', *Cambridge Journal of Education*, 28(1): 18–22.

Hamzah, M. (1996) 'In search of the female voice', *The Star* (Malaysia), 5 September.

Hanely, J. and Brown, A. (2014) 'Cultural variations in interpretation of postnatal illness: Jinn possession among Muslim commmunities', *Community Mental Health Journal*, 50: 348–53.

Hartsock, N. (1990) 'Postmodernism and political change: Issues for feminist theory', *Cultural Critique*, 14: 15–33.

Hasan, M. (2015) 'Aung San Suu Kyi's inexcusable silence', *Aljazeera*, 24 May www.aljazeera.com/indepth/opinion/2015/05/aung-san-suu-kyi-inexcusable-silence-150524085430576.html.

Hassan, R. (1993) 'The interface between Islam and psychiatric practice in Malaysia: A personal viewpoint', *Malaysian Journal of Psychiatry*, 1: 93–101.

Hassouneh-Phillips, D. (2001) 'Polygamy and wife abuse: A qualitative study of Muslim women in America', *Health Care for Women International*, 22(8): 735–48.

Hastings, R.P. and Taunt, H.M. (2002) 'Positive perceptions of families of children with developmental disabilities', *American Journal on Mental Retardation*, 107(2): 116–27.

Hatta, S. (2001) 'Islamic issues in forensic psychiatry and the instinct theory: The Malaysian scenario', in A. Haque (ed) *Mental Health in Malaysia*, Kuala Lumpur: University of Malaya Press, pp 181–96.

Haw K.F. with Shah, S. and Hanifa, M. (1998) *Educating Muslim Girls: Shifting Discourses*, Buckingham: Open University Press.

HBVAN (Honour based Violence Awareness Network) (nd) Statistics and Data, http://hbv-awareness.com.

Heath, A. and Li, Y. (2014) 'Reducing poverty in the UK: A collection of evidence reviews', *Joseph Rowntree Foundation*, www.jrf.org.uk/sites/default/files/jrf/migrated/files/Reducing-poverty-reviews-FULL_0.pdf.

Heinz, D. (1994) 'Finishing the story: Aging, spirituality and the work of culture', *Journal of Religious Gerontology*, 9(1): 3–19.

Hendriks, P, Lensvelt-Mulders, G and van E, H. (2015) 'New voices in social work: An explorative study of female Turkish and Moroccan-Dutch professionals in social work in the Netherlands', *Social Work Education*, 34(7): 1005–20.

Henkel, H. (2004) 'Rethinking the *dâr ak-harb*: Social change and changing perceptions of the West in Turkish Islam', *Journal of Ethnic and Migration Studies*, 30(5): 961–77.

Hill Collins, P. (1998) 'Intersections of race, class, gender and nation: Some implications for black family studies', *Journal of Comparative Family Studies*, 29: 27–36.

HM Government (2011) *CONTEST: The United Kingdom's Strategy for Countering Terrorism UK*, www.gov.uk/government/uploads/system/uploads/attachment_data/file/97995/strategy-contest.pdf.

HM Government (2016) *Multi-agency Statutory Guidance on Female Genital Mutilation*, www.gov.uk/government/uploads/system/uploads/attachment_data/file/512906/Multi_Agency_Statutory_Guidance_on_FGM__-_FINAL.pdf.

Hodge, D.R. (2005) 'Social work and the house of Islam: Orientating practitioners to the beliefs and values of Muslims in the United States', *Social Work*, 50(2): 162–73.

Hodge, D.R. (2006) 'A template for spiritual assessment: A review of the JCAHO requirements and guidelines for implementation', *Social Work*, 51(94): 317–26.

Hodge, D.R. and Nadir, S. (2008) 'Moving towards culturally competent practice with Muslims: Modifying cognitive therapy with Islamic tenets, *Social Work*, 53(1): 31–41.

Hollinsworth, D. (2013) 'Forget cultural competence: Ask for an autobiography', *Social Work* Education, 32(8), 1048–60.

Holloway, M. (2006) 'Death the great leveller? Towards a transcultural spirituality of dying and bereavement', *Transcultural Spirituality and Nursing Practice*, doi: 10.1111/j1365–2702.2006.01662.x, pp 833–39.

Holloway, M. and Moss, B. (2010) *Spirituality and Social Work*, Basingstoke: Palgrave Macmillan.

Home Office (2006) 'Offender Management Caseload Statistics', *Home Office Statistical Bulletin*, www.homeoffice.gov.uk/rds/pdfs06/hosb1806.pdfdate.

Home Office (2015) *'Preventing Extremism together' Working Groups*, August–October, London: The Stationery Office, http://webarchive.nationalarchives.gov.uk/20120919132719/http://www.communities.gov.uk/documents/communities/pdf/152164.pdf.

Hood, R. (1992) *Race and Sentencing*, Oxford: Clarendon Press.

Hopkins, N. and Kahani-Hopkins, V. (2006) 'Minority group members' theories of intergroup contact: A case study of British Muslims' conceptualizations of Islamophobia and social change', *British Journal of Social Psychology*, 45: 245–64.

Horevitz, E., Lawson, J. and Chow, J.C-C. (2013) 'Examining cultural competence in health care: Implications for social work', *Health and Social Work*, 38(3): 135–44.

Hourani, A. (1991) *A History of the Arab Peoples*, London: Faber and Faber.

Howell, W.S. (1982) *The Empathic Communicator*, Minnesota, MN: Wadsworth Publishing Co.

Hoyle, C., Bradford, A. and Frenett, R. (2015) *Becoming Mulan? Female Western Migrants to ISIS*, London: Institute for Strategic Dialogue.

HSCIC (Health and Social Care Information Centre) (2015) *Personal Social Services: Expenditure and Unit Costs England 2014–15*, Final release, www.hscic.gov.uk/catalogue/PUB19165/pss-exp-eng-14-15-fin-rep.pdf.

Hughes, C.L. (2011) 'The "amazing" fertility decline: Islam, economics and reproductive decision making among working-class Moroccan women', *Medical Anthropology Quarterly*, 25(4): 417–35.

Hugman, R. (2005) *New Approaches in Ethics for the Caring Professions*, Basingstoke: Palgrave Macmillan.

Hugman, R. (2009) 'But is it social work? Some reflections on mistaken identities', *British Journal of Social Work*, 39: 1138–53.

Human Rights Watch (2015) 'Thailand: Mass graves of Rohingya found in trafficking camp', www.hrw.org/news/2015/05/01/thailand-mass-graves-rohingya-found-trafficking-camp.

Hume, T. (2014) 'Aung San Suu Kyi's "silence" on the Rohingya: Has "the lady" lost her voice?' CNN, 1 June, http://edition.cnn.com/2014/04/15/world/asia/myanmar-aung-san-suu-kyi-rohingya-disappointment/.

Humphries, B. (2003) 'What *else* counts as evidence in evidence-based social work?', *Social Work Education*, 22(1): 81–91.

Humphries, C., Sandeep, A. and Baldwin, N. (1999) 'Discrimination in child protection work: Recurring themes in work with Asian families', *Child and Family Social Work*, 4(4): 283–91.

Husain, F. (2007) 'Educational underachievement and social disadvantage: A consultation with teachers', Unpublished, internal discussion paper, London: Save the Children.

Husain, N., Creed, F. and Tomenson, B. (1997) 'Adverse social circumstances and depression in people of Pakistani origin in the UK', *British Journal of Psychiatry*, 171: 434–8.

Hussain, Y. and Bagguley, P. (2012) 'Securitized citizens: Islamophobia, racism and the 7/7 London bombings', *Sociological Review*, 60: 715–34.

Ibrahim, N. and Abdalla M. (2010) 'A critical examination of Qur'an 4:34 and its relevance to intimate partner violence in Muslim families', *Journal of Muslim Mental Health*, 5: 327–49.

IFSW (International Federation of Social Work) (2016) 'Global definition of social work', http://ifsw.org/get-involved/global-definition-of-social-work/.

IHRC (Islamic Human Rights Commission) (2006) 'Islamophobia rampant in Ramadan in UK', press release, www.ihrc.org.uk/show.php?id=2147.

Ineichen, B. (2012) 'Mental illness and suicide in British Asian adults', *Mental Health, Religion and Culture*, 15(3): 235–50.

Inman, A.G., Devdas, L., Spektor, V. and Pendse, A. (2014) 'Psychological research on South Asian Americans: A three-decade content analysis', *Asian American Journal of Psychology*, 5(4): 365–72.

Irfan, S. and Cowburn, M. (2004) 'Disciplining, chastisement and physical child abuse: Perceptions and attitudes of the British Pakistani community', *Journal of Muslim Affairs*, 24(1): 89–98.

Irfan Cole, M. (2004) 'Education and Islam: a new strategy', in B. van Driel (ed) *Confronting Islamophobia in Educational Practice*, Stoke-on-Trent: Trentham Books, pp 111–28.

Islam, F., Khanlou, N. and Tamim, H. (2014) 'South Asian populations in Canada: Migration and Mental Health', *BMC Psychiatry*, 14: 154, doi: 10.1186/1471-244X-14-154.

Ixer, G. (1999) 'There's no such thing as reflection', *British Journal of Social Work*, 29: 513–27.

Ixer, G. (2013) 'Fifty years of professional regulation in social work education', in J. Parker and M. Doel (eds) *Professional Social Work*, London: Sage/Learning Matters, pp 188–206.

Jack, C.M., Penny, L. and Nazar, W. (2001) 'Effective palliative care for minority ethnic groups: the role of a liaison worker', *International Journal of Palliative Nursing*, 7(8): 375–80.

James, O. (1997) *Britain on the Couch*, London: Century.

Jani, J.S., Pierce, D., Ortiz, L. and Sowbel, L. (2011) 'Access to intersectionality, content to competence: Demonstrating social work education diversity standards', *Journal of Social Work Education*, 47(2): 283–301.

Jaspal, R. and Cinnirella, M. (2010) 'Coping with potentially incompatible identitites: Accounts of religious, ethnic, and sexual identities from British Pakistani men who identify as Muslim and gay', *British Journal of Social Psychology*, 49: 849–70.

Jawad, H.A. (1998) *The Right of Women in Islam*, Basingstoke: Macmillan Press.

Jawad, R. (2012) *Religion and Faith-Based Welfare*, Bristol: Policy Press.

Jay, A. (2014) *Independent Inquiry into Child Sexual Exploitation in Rotherham 1997–2013*, Rotherham Metropolitan Borough Council, www.rotherham.gov.uk/downloads/file/1407/independent_inquiry_cse_in_rotherham.

Jeffery, P. (1998) 'Agency, activism and agendas', in P. Jeffery and A. Basu (eds) *Appropriating Gender*, London: Routledge, pp 221–4.

Jejeebhoy, S.J. (1998) 'Wife-beating in rural India: A husband's right? Evidence from survey data', *Economic and Political Weekly*, 33: 855–62.

Jejeebhoy, S.J. and Cook, S. (1997) 'State accountability for wife-beating: The Indian challenge', *The Lancet*, March, Women's Health Supplement: Sl, 110–12.

Johnson, L.C. and Yanca, S.J. (2004) *Social Work Practice*, Boston, MA: Pearson.

Jordan, J., Mañas, F.M. and Horsburgh, N. (2008) 'Strengths and weaknesses of grassroot Jihadist Networks: The Madrid Bombings', *Studies in Conflict & Terrorism*, 31: 17–29.

JRF (Joseph Rowntree Foundation) (2013) 'Which ethnic groups have the poorest health?' *Ethnic health inequalities 1991 to 2011*, www.ethnicity.ac.uk/medialibrary/briefingsupdated/which-ethnic-groups-have-the-poorest-health.pdf.

Kalunta-Crumpton, A. (1999) *Race and Drug Trials*, Aldershot: Avebury.

Karmi, G. (1996) 'Women, Islam and patriarchalism', in M. Yamani (ed) *Feminism and Islam*, New York: New York University Press, pp 69–86.

Kassam, A., Scammell R., Connolly, K., Orange Malmö, Willsher, K. and Ratcliffe, R. (2015) 'Europe needs many more babies to avert a population disaster', *Observer*, 25 August, www.theguardian.com/world/2015/aug/23/baby-crisis-europe-brink-depopulation-disaster.

Katbamna, S., Waqar, A., Bhakta, P., Baker, R. and Parker, G. (2004) 'Do they look after their own? Informal support for South Asian carers', *Health and Social Care in the Community*, 12(5): 398–406.

Keating, F. (2000) 'Anti-racist perspectives: What are the gains for social work?' *Social Work Education*, 19(1): 77–87.

Kenan, G. and Burck, L. (2002) 'Trends in patrilineal parallel first cousin marriages among Israeli Arabs: 1949–1995', *Annals of Human Biology*, 29(4): 398–413.

Kensinger, E. (2016) 'Cognition in ageing and age-related disease', *Science Direct*, www2.bc.edu/elizabeth-kensinger/Kensinger_Corkin_EncycoNeurosci.pdf.

Keshavarzi, H. and Haque, A. (2013) 'Outlining a psychotherapy model for enhancing Muslim mental health within an Islamic context', *The International Journal for the Psychology of Religion*, 23: 230–49.

Khabaristan Times (2016) 'Council of Islamic Ideology declares women's existence un-Islamic', 26 May, https://khabaristantimes.com/national/council-of-islamic-ideology-declares-womens-existence-un-islamic/.

Khan, Z.H., Watson, P.J. and Habib, F. (2005) 'Muslim attitudes towards religion, religious orientation and empathy among Pakistanis', *Mental Health, Religion and Culture*, 8(1): 49–61.

Kitzinger, S. (2005) 'Sheila Kinzinger's Letter from Europe: Moslem values and childbirth', *Birth*, 32(1): 69–71.

Kleinman, A. (1988) *The Illness Narratives: Suffering, Healing and the Human Condition*, USA: Library of Congress.

Kling, Z. (1995) 'The Malay family: Beliefs and realities', *Journal of Comparative Family Studies*, XXVI(1): 43–66.

Koenig, M.A., Ahmed, S., Hossein, M.B. and Mozumder, K.A. (2003) 'Women's status and domestic violence in rural Bangladesh', *Demography*, 40(2): 269–88.

Koramoa, J., Lynch, M.A. and Kinnair, D. (2002) 'A continuum of child-rearing: responding to traditional practices', *Child Abuse Review*, 11: 415–21.

Kormaromy, C. (2004) 'Cultural diversity in death and dying', *Nursing Management*, 11: 32–5.

Kort, A. (2005) 'Dar al-cyber Islam: Women, domestic violence and the Islamic reformation on the world wide web', *Journal of Muslim Minority Affairs*, 25(3): 363–82.

Kose, A. (1996) *Conversion to Islam: A Study of Native British Converts*, London: Kegan Paul International.

Kreamelmeyer, K. (2011) 'Islamophobia in post 9–11 America', *Journal of International Diversity*, 4: 42–48.

Kübler-Ross, E. (1970) *On Death and Dying*, London and New York: Tavistock/Routledge.

Kundnani, A. (2009) *Spooked! How Not to Prevent Violent Extremism*, London: Institute of Race Relations.

Kuzu, M.A., Topçu, Ö., Keriman, U., Ulukent, S., Ekrem, Ü., Elhan, A. and Demirci, S. (2001) 'Effect of sphincter-sacrificing surgery for rectal carcinoma on quality of life in Muslim patients', conference proceedings, *The American Society of Colon and Rectal Surgeons*, 2–7 June, San Diego, CA: 1359–66.

Laird, L.D., Amer, M.M, Barnett, E.D. and Barnes, L.L. (2007) 'Muslim patients and health disparities in the UK and the US', *Archives of Diseases in Childhood*, 92(10): 922–6.

Laird, S. (2008) *Anti-Oppressive Social Work: A Guide for Developing Cultural Competence*, London: Sage.

Lee, G.P., Ghandour, L.A., Takache, A.H. and Martins, S.S. (2014) 'Investigating the association between strategic and pathological gambling behaviors and substance use in youth: Could religious faith play a differential role?', *The American Journal on Addictions*, 23: 280–7.

Lerner, G. (1986) *The Creation of Patriarchy*, Oxford: Oxford University Press.

Levi-Strauss, C. (1967) *Les Structures Élementaires de la Parenté* [*The Elementary Structures of Kinship*], Paris: La Haye.

LGBT Foundation (2016) *Gay Muslims in the UK*, http://lgbt.foundation/news/gay-muslims-in-the-uk/.

Lievesley, N. (2010) *The Future Ageing of the Ethnic Minority Population of England and Wales*, http://envejecimiento.csic.es/documentos/documentos/runnymede-futureageing-01.pdf.

Lindsey, J. (2012) 'Developing professional development and practice through professional supervision programmes in the Occupied Palestinian Territories', in S. Ashencaen Crabtree, J. Parker and A. Azman (eds) *The Cup, The Gun and the Crescent: Social Welfare and Civil Unrest in Muslim societies*. London: Whiting and Birch, pp 151–68.

Ling, H. K. (2007) *Indigenising Social Work: Research and Practice in Sarawak*, Selangor: SIRD.

Litorp, H., Franck, M. and Almroth, L. (2008) 'Female genital mutilation among antenatal and contraceptive advice attendees in Sweden', *Acta Obstreticia et Gynaecologia*, 87: 716–22.

London Metropolitan Police (2016) 'Female genital mutilation', http://content.met.police.uk/Article/Female-genital-mutiliation/1400009693144/1400009693144

Lorente, J.R. (2010) 'Discrepancies around the use of the term "Islamophobia"', *Human Architecture: Journal of the Sociology of Self-Knowledge*, VIII(2): 115–28.

Lyon, W. (1995) 'Islam and Islamic women in Britain', *Women: A Cultural Review*, 6(2): 46–56.

Lyons, K., Manion, K. and Carlsen, M. (2006) *International Perspectives on Social Work*, Basingstoke: Palgrave Macmillan.

Lyons, L. (1999) 'Re-telling "us": Displacing the white feminist subject as knower', Conference paper, 'Workshop on Southeast Asian women', Melbourne: Monash University.

McAskill, E. (2007) 'US Muslims more assimilated than British', *The Guardian*, 23 May.

McCloud, A.B. (1995) *African American Islam*, New York: Routledge.

McFarlane, J., Nava, A., Gilroy, H. and Maddox, J. (2016) 'Child brides, forced marriage, and partner violence in America: Tip of an iceberg', *Obstretrics and Gynecology*, 127(4): 706–13.

Mackenzie, C.S., Gekoski, W.L. and Knox, V.J. (2006) 'Age, gender, and the underutilization of mental health services: The influence of help-seeking attitudes', *Ageing and Mental Health*, 10(6): 574–82.

MacKinlay, E. (2001) *The Spiritual Dimension of Ageing*, London: Jessica Kingsley Publishers.

McNeill, T. (2006) 'Evidence-based practice in an age of relativism: Toward a model for practice', *Social Work*, 52(2): 147–56.

McVeigh, K. (2007) 'Murder victim told police four times she feared her family: Each time in vain', *Guardian Unlimited*, 12 June, www.guardian.co.uk/crime/article/0,,2100800,00.html.

McVicar, J. (1982) 'Violence in prisons', in P. Marsh and A. Campbell (eds) *Aggression and Violence*, Oxford: Basil Blackwell, pp 200–14.

Mahamud-Hassan, N. (2004) 'It doesn't happen in our society', *Index on Censorship*, 33(1): 38–41.

Malik, K. (2005) 'The myth of Islamophobia', *Prospect*, www.kenanmalik.com/essays/prospect_islamophobia.html.

Malik, R., Shaikh, A. and Suleyman, M. (2007) *Providing Faith and Culturally Sensitive Support Services to Young British Muslims*, Leicester: National Youth Agency.

Malik, S. (2007) 'Support artistic truth, Prince Charles – go to see Brick Lane', *Observer*, 30 September.

Mallon, G.P. (2005) 'Practice with families where sexual orientation is an issue: Lesbian and gay individuals and their families', in E.P. Congress and M.J. González (eds) *Multicultural Perspectives in Working with Families, Second Edition*, New York: Springer Publishing Company Inc., pp 199–227.

Mama, R.S. (2001) 'Preparing social work students to work in culturally diverse settings', *Social Work Education*, 20(3): 373–82.

Mansour, N., Chatty, D., El-Kak, F. and Yassin, N. (2014) 'They aren't all first cousins: Bedouin marriage and health policies in Lebanon', *Ethnicity and Health*, 19(5): 529–47.

Mansson McGinty, A. (2006) *Becoming Muslim*, New York: Palgrave Macmillan.

Manthorpe, J., Moriarty, J., Stevens, M., Sharif, N. and Hussein, S. (2010) *Supporting Black and Minority Ethnic Older People's Mental Well-being: Accounts of Social Care Practice*, London: Social Care Institute for Excellence.

Marranci, G. (2004) 'Multiculturalism, Islam and the clash of civilizations theory: Rethinking Islamophobia', *Culture and Religion*, 5(1): 105–17.

Mason, R. (2015) 'Nigel Farage accuses Muslims of "split loyalties"', *The Guardian*, 16 November, www.theguardian.com/politics/2015/nov/16/nigel-farage-accuse-british-muslims-conflicting-loyalties.

Mason, R. (2016) 'Jeremy Corbyn invites Donald Trump to a London mosque', *The Guardian*, 17 January, www.theguardian.com/politics/2016/jan/17/jeremy-corbyn-invites-donald-trump-to-visit-london-mosque.

Mason, R. and Sherwood, H. (2016) 'Migrant spouses who fail English test may have to leave UK, says Cameron', *The Guardian*, 18 January, www.theguardian.com/uk-news/2016/jan/18/pm-migrant-spouses-who-fail-english-test-may-have-to-leave-uk.

Masood, E. (2009) *Science and Islam: A History*, London: Icon Books.

Maududi, S.A. (1986) *Purdah and the Status of Woman in Islam*, Lahore: Islamic Publications Ltd.

MCB (Muslim Council of Great Britain) (2015) *British Muslims in Numbers: A Demographic, Socio-economic and Health Profile of Muslims in Britain Drawing on the 2011 Census*, London: MCB.

Mehdi, R. (1997) 'The offence of rape in the Islamic law of Pakistan', *Women Living Under Muslim Laws*, Dossier 18, Grabels: Women Living Under Muslim Laws (WLUML) Publications, www.wluml.org/english/pubsfulltxt.shtml?cmd%5B87%5D=i–87-2675.

Mernissi, F. (1975) *Beyond the Veil*, Cambridge, MA: Schenkman Publishing Company.

Mernissi, F. (1983) *Sexe, Ideologie, Islam*, Paris: Tierce.

Mernissi, F. (1991) *Women and Islam: An Historical and Theological Enquiry*, Oxford: Blackwell.

Mernissi, F. (2001) *Scheherezade Goes West*, New York: Washington Square Press.

Merry, M. (2005) 'Should educators accommodate intolerance? Mark Halstead, homosexuality and the Islamic case', *Journal of Moral Education*, 34(1): 19–36.

Midgely, J. (1981) *Professional Imperialism: Social Work in the Third World*, London: Heinemann.

Milaat, W.A., Ghabrah, T.M., Al-Bar, H.M.S., Abalkhail, B.A. and Kordy, M.N. (2001) 'Population-based survey of childhood disability in Eastern Jeddah using the ten questions tool', *Disability and Rehabilitation*, 23(5): 199–203.

Millon Underwood, S., Shaikha, L. and Bakr, D. (1999) 'Veiled yet vulnerable', *Cancer Practice*, 7(6): 285–90.

Minces, J. (1992) *The House of Obedience*, London: Zed Press.

Minh-ha, Trinh T. (1989) *Woman, Native, Other*, Bloomington, IN: Indiana University Press.

Mir, G. and Sheikh, A. (2010). '"Fasting and prayer don't concern the doctors… they don't even know what it is": Communication, decision-making and perceived social relations of Pakistani Muslim patients with long-term illnesses', *Ethnicity and Health,* 15(4), 327–42.

Mir-Hosseini, Z. (1996) 'Stretching the limits: A feminist reading of the Shari'a in post-Khomeini Iran', in M. Yamani (ed) *Feminism and Islam*, New York: New York University Press, pp 285–319.

Mlcek, S. (2014) 'Are we doing enough to develop cross-cultural competencies for social work?', *British Journal of Social Work*, 44: 1984–2003.

MM (MuslimMatters.org) (2014) *Gay and Muslim*, http://muslimmatters.org/2014/11/13/gay-muslim/.

Moallem, M. (2008) 'Muslim women and the politics of representation', *Journal of Feminist Studies in Religion,* 24(1): 106–10.

Moffatt, P.G. and Thoburn, J. (2001) 'Outcomes of permanent family placement for children of minority ethnic origin', *Child and Family Social Work*, 6: 13–21.

Moghissi, H. (1999) *Feminism and Islamic Fundamentalism*, London: Zed Books.

Mohammad, R. (2005) 'Negotiating spaces of the home, the education system and the labor market', in G.W. Falah and C. Nagel (eds) *Geographies of Muslim Women*, New York and London: The Guilford Press, pp 178–202.

Mohan, B. (2002) 'The future of social work education: Curriculum conundrums in an age of uncertainty', *Electronic Journal of Social Work*, 1(1): 1–10.

Monnig Atkinson, J. (1990) 'How gender makes a difference in Wana society', in J. Monnig Atkinson and S. Errington (eds) *Power and Difference: Gender in Island Southeast Asia*, Stanford, CA: Stanford University Press, pp 59–63.

Moody, H.R. (1990) 'The Islamic vision of aging and death', *Generations*, 14(4): 15–19.

Moriarty, J. (2008) *The Health and Social Care Experiences of Black and Minority Ethnic Older People*, Better Health Briefing Paper 9, London: Race Equality Foundation, www.kcl.ac.uk/sspp/policy-institute/scwru/pubs/2008/moriarty2008health.pdf.

Moriarty, J. (2010) 'Competing with myths: Migrant labour in social care', in M. Ruhs and B. Anderson (eds) *A Need for Migrant Labour? Labour Shortages, Immigration and Public Policy*, Oxford: Oxford University Press.

Morgan, R. (2002) 'Imprisonment: A brief history, the contemporary scene and likely prospects', *The Oxford Handbook of Criminology*, 3rd edn, Oxford: Oxford University Press.

Morrison, W. (1995) *Theoretical Criminology: From Modernity to Post-modernism*, London: Cavendish Publishing Limited.

Moxley Rouse, C. (2004) *Engaged Surrender: African American Women and Islam*, Berkeley, CA: University of California Press.

Munford, R. and Saunders, J. (2011) 'Embracing the diversity of practice: Indigeneous knowledge and mainstream social work practice', *Journal of Social Work Practice*, 25(1): pp 63–77.

Munir, A.B.B. (1993) 'Child protection: principles and applications', *Child Abuse Review*, 2(2): 119–26.

Mythen, G. (2012) 'No-one speaks for us: Security policy, suspected communities and the problem of Voice', *Critical Studies on Terrorism*, 5(3): 409–24.

Mythen, G., Walklate, S. and Khan, F. '(2013) '"Why should we have to prove we're alright?": Counter-terrorism, risk and partial securities', *Sociology*, 47(2): 383–98.

Na'amnih, W., Romano-Zalekha, Kahaba, A., Pollack Rubin, L., Bilenko, N., Jaber, L., Honovich, M. and Shohat, T. (2015) 'Continuous decrease of consanguineous marriages among Arabs in Israel', *American Journal of Human Biology*, 27: 94–6.

Nasser, K., Dabbous, Y. and Baba, D. (2013) 'From strangers to spouses: Early relational dialectics in arranged marriages among Muslim families in Lebanon', *Journal of Comparative Family Studies*, 44(3): 387–406.

Neville, H., Oh, E., Spanierman, L., Heppner, M. and Clark, M. (2004) 'General and culturally specific factors influencing black and white rape survivors' self-esteem', *Psychology of Women Quarterly*, 28: 83–94.

Newland, L. (2006) 'Female circumcision: Muslim identities and zero tolerance policies in rural West Java', *Women's Studies International Forum*, 29(4): 394–404.

NHS (National Health Service) (2001) *National Service Framework for Older People*, Department of Health, www.gov.uk/government/uploads/system/uploads/attachment_data/file/198033/National_Service_Framework_for_Older_People.pdf.

Nielsen, J.S. (1999) *Towards a European Islam*, Basingstoke: Macmillan Press.

Noh, S., Kaspar, V., Hou, F. and Rummens, J. (1999) 'Perceived racial discrimination, depression and coping: A study of Southeast Asian refugees in Canada', *Journal of Health and Social Behavior*, 40: 193–207.

O'Malley, P. (1992) 'Risk, power and crime prevention', *Economy and Society*, 21(3): 253–75.

Obermeyer, C.M. (1994) 'Religious doctrine, state ideology and reproductive options in Islam', in G. Sen and R.C. Snow (eds) *Power and Decision: The Social Control of Reproduction*, Boston, MA: Harvard University Press, pp 59–75.

Oliver, D., Foot, C. and Humphries, R. (2014) *Making our Health and Care Systems Fit for an Ageing Population*, London: The King's Fund.

Ong, A. (1995) 'State versus Islam: Malay families, women's bodies and the body politic in Malaysia', in A. Ong and M.G. Peletz (eds) *Bewitching Women, Pious Men: Gender and Body Politics in Southeast Asia*, Berkeley, CA: University of California, pp 159–94.

Ong, F.S., Phillips, D.R. and Hamid, T.A. (2009) 'Ageing in Malaysia: Progress and prospects', in T.-H. Fu and R. Hughes (eds) *Ageing in East Asia*, London: Routledge, pp 138–60.

Ong, P., Sim, F., Tengku, D. and Hamid, A. (2009) 'Social protection in Malaysia – Current state and challenges towards practical and sustainable social protection in East Asia: a compassionate community', in M.G. Asher, S. Oum, and F. Parulian (eds) *East Asia – Current State and Challenges*, ERIA Research Project Report No. 9.

ONS (Office for National Statistics) (2002) *Social Focus in Brief; Ethnicity 2002*, London: ONS.

ONS (2011) 'Religion in England and Wales 2011', www.ons.gov.uk/peoplepopulationandcommunity/culturalidentity/religion/articles/religioninenglandandwales2011/2012-12-11.

ONS (2015) 'Ageing of the UK population', http://webarchive.nationalarchives.gov.uk/20160105160709/http:/www.ons.gov.uk/ons/rel/pop-estimate/population-estimates-for-uk--england-and-wales--scotland-and-northern-ireland/mid-2014/sty-ageing-of-the-uk-population.html.

Ortega, R.M. and Faller, C. (2011) 'Training child welfare workers from an intersectional cultural humility perspective: A paradigm shift', *Child Welfare*, 90(5): 27–49.

Paloma, V., García-Ramírez, M. and Camacho, C. (2014) 'Well-being and social justice among Morrocan migrants in Southern Spain', *American Journal of Community Psychology*, 54(1): 1–11.

Pantazis, C. and Pemberton, S. (2009) 'From the "old" to the "new" suspect community', *British Journal of Crimonology,* 49(5): 646–66.

Papadopoulos, I. (ed) (2006) *Transcultural Health and Social Care: A Development of Culturally Competent Practitioners*, Edinburgh: Churchill Livingstone.

Papalia, D.E., Wendkos Olds, S. and Duskin Fieldman, R., 2003, *Human Development*, 9th edn, Boston, MA: McGraw-Hill.

Pargeter, A. (2006) 'North African immigrants in Europe and political violence', *Studies in Conflict and Terrorism*, 29(8): 731–47.

Parker, J. (2010) *Effective Practice Learning in Social Work*, 2nd edn, Exeter: Learning Matters.

Parker, J. and Bradley, G. (2014) *Social Work Practice*, 4th edn, Sage: Learning Matters.

Parker, J. and Doel, M. (2013) 'Professional social work and the professional social work identity', in J. Parker and M. Doel (eds) *Professional Social Work*, London: Sage/Learning Matters, pp 1–18.

Parker, J., Ashencaen Crabtree, S., Baba, I., Carlo, D.P. and Azman, A. (2012) 'Liminality and learning: International placements as a rite of passage', *Asia Pacific Journal of Social Work and Development*, 22(3): 146–58.

Parker, J., Ashencaen Crabtree, S., Reeks, E., Marsh, D and Vasif, C. (forthcoming) "River! that in silence windest". The place of religion and spirituality in social work assessment: Sociological reflections and practical implications', in C. Spatscheck, S. Ashencaen Crabtree and J. Parker (eds) *Methods and Methodologies of Social Work: Reflecting professional intervention*, Erasmus SocNet, Vol III, London: Whiting and Birch.

Patel, N., Humphries, B. and Naik, D. (1998) 'The 3 Rs in social work: religion, "race" and racism in Europe', in C. Williams, H. Soydan and M.R.D. Johnson (eds) *Social Work and Minorities*, London: Routledge, pp 182–208.

Payne, M. (2005) *The Origins of Social Work*, Basingstoke: Palgrave Macmillan.

Peach, C. (2006) 'Muslims in the 2001 Census of England and Wales: Gender and economic disadvantage', *Ethnic and Racial Studies*, 29(4): 629–55.

Peletz, M.G. (1995) 'Neither reasonable nor responsible: Contrasting representations of masculinity in a Malay society', in A. Ong and M.G. Peletz (eds) *Bewitching Women, Pious Men: Gender and Body Politics in Southeast Asia*, Berkeley, CA: University of California, pp 176–23.

Perria, S. (2015) 'Why is Aung San Suu Kyi silent on the plight of the Rohingya?', *The Guardian*, 19 May, www.theguardian.com/world/2015/may/19/why-is-aung-san-suu-kyi-silent-on-the-plight-of-the-rohingya-people.

Pilkington, A., Msetfi, R.M. and Watson, R. (2015) 'Factors affecting intention to access psychological services amongst British Muslims of South Asian origin', *Mental Health, Religion and Culture*, 15(1): 1–22.

Platt, L. (2002) *Parallel Lives? Poverty Among Ethnic Minority Groups in Britain*, London: Child Poverty Action Group.

Poynting, S. and Mason, V. (2006) '"Tolerance, freedom, justice and peace?" Britain, Australia and anti-Muslim racism since 11th September 2001', *Journal of Intercultural Studies*, 27(4): 365–91.

Press Association (2007) 'Veil should not be worn, says Muslim peer', *The Guardian Unlimited*, 20 February, www.guardian.co.uk/religion/Story/0,,2017301,00. html.

Press Association (2015) 'Immigrant spouses "must speak English before entering the UK"', *The Guardian*, 8 November, www.theguardian.com/law/2015/nov/18/immigrants-spouses-must-speak-english-before-entering-uk.

Preston-Shoot, M. (2000) 'Stumbling towards oblivion or discovering new horizons? Observations on the relationship between social work education and practice', *Journal of Social Work Practice*, 14(2): 87–98.

Price, P. L. (2009) 'At the crossroads: Critical race theory and critical geographies of race', *Progress in Human Geography*, 34(2): 147–74.

Pritchard, C. and Amanullah, S. (2006) 'An analysis of suicide and undetermined deaths in 17 predominantly Islamic countries contrasted with the UK', *Psychological Medicine*, 37: 421–30.

Proschaska, F., 2006. *Christianity and Social Services*. Oxford: Oxford University Press.

Pryke, J. and Thomas, M. (1998) *Domestic Violence and Social Work*, Aldershot: Ashgate.

Quraishi, M. (2005) *Muslims and Crime: A Comparative Study*, Aldershot: Ashgate.

Raad, S.A. (1998) 'Grief: A Muslim perspective', in K.J. Doka and J.D. Davidson (eds) *Living with Grief: Who We Are, How We Grieve*, Philadelphia, PA: Brunner and Mazel, pp 47–56.

Rack, P. (1982) *Race, Culture and Mental Disorder*, London and New York: Tavistock.

Raqab, I.A. (2016) 'The Islamic perspective on social work: A conceptual framework', *International Social Work*, 59(3): 325–42.

Raqib, M. and Barreto, A.A. (2014) 'The Taliban, religious revival and minorities in Afghan nationalism', *National Identities*, 16(1): 15–30.

Rasanayagam, J. (2006) 'Healing with spirits and the formation of Muslim selfhood in post-Soviet Uzbekistan', *Journal of the Royal Anthropological Institute*, 12(2): 377–93.

Rasheed, S.A. and Padela, A.I. (2013) 'The interplay between religious leaders and organ donation among Muslims', *Zygon*, 48(3): 635–54.

Rashid, S., Copello, A. and Birchwood, M. (2012) 'Muslim faith healers' views on substance misuse and psychosis', *Mental Health, Religion and Culture*, 15(56): 653–73.

Rassool, H. (2000) 'The crescent and Islam: Healing, nursing and the spiritual dimension. Some considerations towards an understanding of the Islamic perspectives on caring', *Journal of Advanced Nursing*, 32(6): 1479–89.

Ras-Work, B. (1997) 'Female genital mutilation', in G.C. Denniston and M. Fayre Milos (eds) *Sexual Mutilations: A Human Tragedy*, New York: Plenum Press, pp 1137–52.

Raz, A. (2004) '"Important to test, important to support": Attitudes toward disability rights and prenatal diagnosis among leaders of support groups for genetic disorders in Israel', *Social Science and Medicine*, 59: 1857–66.

Razack, N. (2001) 'Diversity and difference in the field education encounter: Racial minority students in the practicum', *Social Work Education*, 20(2): 219–32.

Razack, N. (2009) 'Decolonizing the pedagogy and practice of international social work', *International Social Work*, 52: 9–21.

Read, J. (2003) *Disability, the Family and Society*, Maidenhead: Open University Press.

Reamer, F.G. (1995) *Social Work Values and Ethics*, New York: Columbia University Press.

Reavey, P., Ahmed, B. and Majumdar, A. (2006) '"How can we help when she won't tell us what's wrong?" Professionals working with South Asian women who have experienced sexual abuse', *Journal of Community and Applied Social Psychology*, 16(3): 171–88.

Rehman, T.F. and Dziegielewski, S.F. (2003) 'Women who choose Islam', *International Journal of Mental Health*, 32(3): 31–49.

Reitmanova, S. and Gustafson, ÆD.L. (2008) '"They can't understand it": Maternity health and care needs of immigrant Muslim women in St John's, Newfoundland', *Maternal Child Health Journal*, 12: 101–11.

Richardson, R. (2004) 'Curriculum, ethos and leadership: Confronting Islamophobia in UK education', in B. van Driel (ed) *Confronting Islamophobia in Educational Practice*, Stoke-on-Trent: Trentham Books, pp 19–33.

Rousseau, J. (1991) 'Gender and class in Central Borneo', in V.H. Sutlive (ed) *Female and Male in Borneo: Contributions and Challenges to Gender Studies*, Borneo Research Council Monograph series, Vol one, Williamsburg, VA: Borneo Research Council Inc., pp 403–14.

Runnymede Trust (1997) *Islamophobia: A Challenge for Us All*, London: Runnymede Trust.

Saadat, M. (2014) 'Association between consanguinity and survival of marriages', *The Egyptian Journal of Medical Human Genetics*, 16: 67–70.

Saeed, A., Blain, N. and Forbes, D. (1999) 'New ethnic and national questions in Scotland: Post-British identities among Glasgow Pakistani teenagers', *Ethnic and Racial Studies*, 22(5): 821–44.

Salih, F.A. and Al-Kandari, H.Y. (2007) 'Effect of a disability course on prospective educators' attitudes toward individuals with mental retardation', *Digest of Middle East Studies* 16(1): 2–29.

Sapp, S. (2008) 'Mortality and respect: Ageing in the Abrahamic traditions', *Generations*, XXXII(2): 20–4.

Sarfraz, A. and Castle, D. (2002) 'A Muslim suicide', *Australasian Psychiatry*, 10(1): 48–50.

Sarhill, N., LeGrand, S., Islambouli, R., Davis, M.P. and Walsh, D. (2001) 'The terminally ill Muslim: Death and dying from the Muslim perspective', *American Journal of Hospice and Palliative Medicine*, 18(4): 251–5.

Schott, J. and Henley, A. (1996) *Culture, Religion and Childbearing in a Multicultural Society*, Oxford: Butterworth Heinemann.

Schuster-Craig, J. (2015) '"Well-integrated Muslims" and adolescent anti-violence activism in Berlin', *German Life and Letters*, 68(1): 125–44.

Scourfield, J., Warden, R., Gilliat-Ray, S., Khan, A. and Otri, S. (2013) 'Religious nurture in British Muslim families: Implications for Social Work', *International Social Work*, 56(3): 326–42.

Shalhoub-Kervokian, N. and Khsheiboun, S. (2009) 'Palestinian women's voices challenges human rights activities', *Women's Studies International Forum*, 32(5): 354–62.

Sharifzadeh, V.-S. (1998) 'Families with Middle Eastern roots', in E.W. Lynch and M.J. Hanson (eds) *Developing Cross-Cultural Competence*, 2nd edn, Baltimore, MD: Paul H. Brookes Publishing Co., pp 441–78.

Sheikh, A. (1998) 'Death and dying – a Muslim perspective', *Journal of the Royal Society of Medicine*, 91: 138–40.

Sheikh, A. and Gatrad, A.R. (2000) 'Death and bereavement: an exploration and a meditation', in A. Sheikh and A.R. Gatrad (eds) *Caring for Muslim Patients*, Oxford: Radcliffe Medical Press Ltd, pp 97–110.

Shenk, G. (2006) 'What went right: Two best cases of Islam in Europe – Cordoba, Spain and Sarajevo, Bosnia', *Religion in Eastern Europe*, XXVI(4): 1–14.

Sheridan, L., Gillett, R., Blaauw, E. and Winkel, F. (2003) *Effects of the Events of September 11th on Discrimination and Implicit Racism in Five Religious and Seven Ethnic Groups*, Leicester: University of Leicester School of Psychology.

Sherwood, H. (2013) 'Israel's West Bank control "costing Palestinian economy billions"', *The Guardian*, 8 October.

Shimmel, A. (1992) *Islam: An Introduction*, New York: State University of New York.

Shorter-Gooden, K. (2004) 'Multiple resistance strategies: How African American women cope with racism and sexism', *Journal of Black Psychology*, 30(3): 406–25.

Shute, S., Hood, R. and Seemungal, F. (2005) *A Fair Hearing? Ethnic Minorities in the Criminal Courts*, Cullompton: Willan Publishing.

Sidell, M. (1995) *Health in Old Age: Myth, Mystery and Management*, Buckingham: Open University Press.

Simon, J. (1988) 'The ideological effects of actuarial practices', *Law and Society Review*, 22(4): 771–800.

Siraj, A. (2010) '"Because I'm the man! I'm the head": British married Muslims and the patriarchal family structure', *Contemporary Islam*, 4: 195–214.

Skalla, K. and McCoy, J.P. (2006) 'Spiritual assessment of patients with cancer: The moral authority, vocational, aesthetic, social and transcendent model', *Oncology Nursing Forum* 33(4): 745–51.

Soliman, A.M. (1991) 'The role of counselling in developing countries', *International Journal for the Advancement of Counselling*, 14(1): 3–14.

Solomos, J. (2003) *Race and Racism in Britain*, Basingstoke: Palgrave Macmillan.

Sonuga-Barke, E.J.S. and Mistry, M. (2000) 'The effect of extended family living on the mental health of three generations within two Asian communities', *British Journal of Clinical Psychology*, 39(2): 129–41.

Southwick, K. (2015) 'Preventing mass atrocities against the stateless Rohingya: A call for solutions', *Journal of International Affairs*, 68(2): 136–56.

Spalek, B. (2002) 'Muslim women's safety talk and their experiences of victimisation', in B. Spalek (ed) *Islam, Crime and Criminal Justice*, Cullompton: Willan Publishing, pp 50–71.

Spalek, B. (2005) 'Muslims and the criminal justice system', in T. Choudhury (ed) *Muslims in the UK: Policies for Engaged Citizens*, Budapest: Open Society Institute, pp 253–340.

Spalek, B. (2006) *Crime Victims: Theory, Policy and Practice*, Basingstoke: Palgrave Macmillan.

Spalek, B. (2007) 'Disconnection and exclusion: pathways to radicalisation?', in T. Abbas (ed) *Islamic Political Radicalism: A European Perspective*, Edinburgh: Edinburgh University Press, pp 192–206.

Spalek, B. and El-Hassan, S. (2007) 'Muslim converts in prison', *Howard Journal of Criminal Justice*, 46(2): 99–114.

Spalek, B. and Imtoual, A. (2007) '"Hard" approaches to community engagement in the UK and Australia: Muslim communities and counter-terror responses', *Journal of Muslim Minority Affairs*, 27(2): 185–202.

Spalek, B., Lambert, B. and Haqq-Baker, A. (2008) 'Muslims and crime', in H. Bui (ed) *Race and the Criminal Justice System*, London: Sage Publications.

Sparrow, A. (2016) 'Cameron: Migrants spousal visa may have to leave if English doesn't improve – Politics live', *The Guardian*, 18 January, www.theguardian.com/politics/blog/live/2016/jan/18/david-camerons-today-interview-politics-live.

Spruyt, B.J. (2007) '"Can't we discuss this?" Liberalism and the challenge of Islam in the Netherlands', *Orbis*, 51(2): 313–29.

Spruyt, O. (1999) 'Community-based palliative care for Bangladeshi patients in east London: accounts of bereaved carers', *Palliative Medicine*, 13(2): 119–29.

Stang Dahl, T. (1997) *The Muslim family: A study of women's rights in Islam*, Oxford and Oslo: Scandinavian University Press.

Stennis, K.B., Fischie, H, Bent-Goodley, T., Purnell, K. and Williams, H. (2015) 'The development of a culturally-competent intimate partner intervention – S.T.A.R.T.©: Implications for competency-based social work practice', *Social Work and Christianity*, 4(1): 96–106.

Steptoe, A., Breeze, E., Banks, J. and Nazroo, J. (2012) 'Cohort profile: The English longitudinal study of ageing', *International Journal of Epidemiology*, 1–9, doi: 10.1093/ije/dys168.

Stern, J. and Berger, J.M. (2015) *ISIS: The State of Terror*, London: William Collins.

Stoesz, D. (2002) 'From social work to human services', *Journal of Sociology and Social Welfare*, December, XXIX(4): 19–37.

Stuart, J., Ward, C. and Robinson, L. (2016) 'The influence of family climate on stress and adaption for Muslim immigrant young adults in two Western countries', *International Perspectives in Psychology: Research, Practice, Consultation*, 5(1): 1–17.

Suárez-Orozco, M.M. (2005) 'Rethinking education in the global era', *Phi Delta Kappan*, November, 85(3): 209–12.

Svoboda, S.J. (1997) 'Routine infant male circumcision: Examining human rights and constitutional issues', in G.C. Denniston and M. Fayre Milos (eds) *Sexual Mutilations: A Human Tragedy*, New York: Plenum Press, pp 205–15.

Swerdlow, A.J., Laing, S.P., dos Santos Silva, I., Slater, S.D., Burden, A.C., Botha, J.L. et al (2004) 'Mortality of South Asian patients with insulin-treated diabetes mellitus in the United Kingdom: A cohort study', *Diabetic Medicine*, 21: 845–51.

Swinford, S. (2015) *The Telegraph*, 7 July, http://news.bbc.co.uk/1/hi/programmes/newsnight/4442010.stm.

Taras, R. (2013) '"Islamophobia never stands still": Race, religion and culture', *Ethnic and Racial Studies*, 36(3): 417–33.

Taseer, A. (2005) 'Made in Britain', *The Sunday Times News Review*, 31 July, p 3.

Taylor, I. (1997) *Developing Learning in Professional Education*, Buckingham: Society for Research into Higher Education and Open University Press.

TCSW (The College of Social Work) and BASW (British Association of Social Work) (2014, 2016) *Professional Capabilities Framework*, www.basw.co.uk/resource/?id=1137.

The Express Tribune (2016) 'CII rules women's protection law "un-Islamic", 3 March, http://tribune.com.pk/story/1058773/top-pakistani-religious-body-rules-womens-protection-law-un-islamic/.

The Local (2015) 'Burqa ban five years on – "we created a monster"', www.thelocal.fr/20151012/france-burqa-ban-five-years-on-we-create-a-monster.

Thompson, N. (1993) *Anti-Discriminatory Practice*, Basingstoke: Macmillan and British Association of Social Work (BASW).

Thompson, N. (2005) *Understanding Social Work*, Basingstoke: Palgrave Macmillan.

Thornton, S. and Garrett, K.J. (1995) 'Ethnography as a bridge to multicultural practice', *Journal of Social Work Education*, 31(1): 67–74.

Tickle, L. (2006) 'Do not contact the parents', *The Guardian*, 10 October.

Trani, J.F., Bakhshi, P., Noor, A.A., Mashkoor, A., Helseth, S., Lopez, D., Schwarz, S. and Lavasani, L. (undated) *Disability in Afghanistan: Taking a Capabilities Approach to Look at Research Challenges and Policy Implications*, Research Report, The National Disability Survey in Afghanistan, www.ucl.ac.uk/lc-ccr/lccstaff/jean-francois-trani/HDCAconf0905.pdf.

Travis, A. (2016) 'Official data on forced marriages may hide true scale of abuse', *The Guardian*, 8 March, www.theguardian.com/society/2016/mar/08/number-of-forced-marriages-in-uk-continues-to-fall.

Treviño, A.J., Harris, M.H. and Wallace, D. (2008) 'What's so critical about critical race theory?', *Contemporary Justice Review*, 11(1): 7–10.

Tripathi, A. and Yadav, S. (2004) 'For the sake of honour: But whose honour? "Honour crimes" against women', *Asia-Pacific Journal on Human Rights and the Law*, 5(2): 63–78.

Tsang, A.K.T. (2001) 'Representation of ethnic identity in North American social work literature: A dossier of the Chinese people', *Social Work*, 46(3): 229–43.

TUC (Trades Union Congress) (2005) 'End UK Pakistani and Bangladeshi poverty and deprivation', press release, www.tuc.org.uk/equality/tuc–10401-f0.cfm.

Tufail, W. (2015) 'Rotherham, Rochdale and the racialised threat of the "Muslim grooming gang"', *International Journal for Crime, Justice and Social Democracy*, 4(3): 30–43.

Udwadia, F.E. (2001) *Man and Medicine: A History*, New Delhi and Oxford: Oxford University Press.

UN (United Nations) (1991) *United Nations Principles for Older Persons Adopted by General Assembly resolution 46/91 of 16 December 1991*, www.ohchr.org/Documents/ProfessionalInterest/olderpersons.pdf.

UN (2016) *'Staggering' Number of Civilian Deaths in Iraq*, UN Report, www.un.org/apps/news/story.asp?NewsID=53037#.Vp5MLTYwjlI.

UN News Centre (2014) 'UN rights chief urges action after pregnant Pakistani woman stoned to death by family', www.un.org/apps/news/story.asp?NewsID=47907#.V1PqNVc7cdU.

UNESCO (2015) *Education for All 2000-2015: Only a Third of Countries Reached Global Education Goals*, www.unesco.org/new/en/media-services/single-view/news/only_a_third_of_countries_reached_global_education_goals/#.V5kEdWU7e8U.

UNESCO-IBE (International Bureau of Education) (2007) *Preparatory Report for the 48th ICE on Inclusive Education: Regional Preparatory Work on Inclusive Education – the Gulf Arab States, Dubai, United Arab Emirates*, 27–29 August, Geneva: UNESCO-IBE.

Van Dam, J. and Anastasi, M.-C. (2000) *Male Circumcision and HIV Prevention: Directions for Future Research*, Washington, DC: Horizons at Population Council, www.popcouncil.org/pdfs/circumcision.pdf.

Vertovec, S. (2007) 'Super-diversity and its implications', *Ethnic and Racial Studies*, 30(6): 1024–54.

Waines, D. (2003) *An Introduction to Islam*, 2nd edn, Cambridge: Cambridge University Press.

Waldman, H.B., Perlman, S.P. and Chaudhry, R.A. (2010) 'Islamic views on disability', *American Academy of Developmental Medicine and Dentistry*, 40(6): 60–1.

Waldman, T. (2014) 'Reconciliation and research in Afghanistan: An analytical narrative', *International Affairs*, 90(5): 1049–68.

Wardak, A. (2000) *Social Control and Deviance*, Aldershot: Ashgate.

Warden, R., Scourfield, J. and Huxley, P. (2016) 'Islamic social work in the UK: The service user experience', *British Journal of Social Work*, http://bjsw.oxfordjournals.org/content/early/2016/04/14/bjsw.bcw006.abstract.

Wardere, H. (2016) *Cut*, London: Simon and Schuster.

Warnock Fernea, E. (1995) 'Childhood in the Muslim Middle East', in E. Warnock Fernea (ed) *Children in the Muslim Middle East*, Austin, TX: University of Texas Press, pp 3–16.

Webb, E., Maddocks, A. and Bongili, J. (2002) 'Effectively protecting black and minority ethnic children from harm: overcoming barriers to the child protection process', *Child Abuse Review*, 11(6): 394–410.

Webb, S. (2009) 'Against difference and diversity in social work: The case of human rights', *International Journal of Social Welfare*, 18: 307–36.

Weiss, M. (2002) *The Chosen Body: The Politics of the Body in Israeli Society*, Stanford, CA: Stanford University Press.

Weiss, M. and Hassan, H. (2015) *ISIS: Inside the Army of Terror*, New York: Regan Art.

Weller, P. (2011) *Religious Discrimination in Britain: A Review of Research Evidence, 2000-10, England and Wales*, Equality and Human Rights Commission, www.equalityhumanrights.com/sites/default/files/research_report_73_religious_discrimination.pdf.

Weller, P., Feldman, A. and Purdam, K. (2001) *Religious Discrimination in England and Wales*, Home Office Research Study 220, London: The Stationery Office.

Werbner, P. (1994) 'Diaspora and millennium: British Pakistani global–local fabulations of the Gulf War', in A.S. Ahmed and H. Donnan (eds) *Islam, Globalization and Postmodernity*, London/New York: Routledge, pp 213–36.

Werth, J.L., Blevins, D., Toussaint, K.L. and Durham, M.K. (2002) 'The influence of cultural diversity on end-of-life care and decisions', *American Behavioral Scientist*, 46(2): 204–19.

WHO (World Health Organization) (2002) *Active Ageing: A Policy Framework*, http://apps.who.int/iris/bitstream/10665/67215/1/WHO_NMH_NPH_02.8.pdf.

WHO (2003) *The Social Determinants of Health: The Solid Facts*, 2nd edn, Denmark: WHO, www.euro.who.int/__data/assets/pdf_file/0005/98438/e81384.pdf.

WHO (2016) *Female Genital Multilation*, http://www.who.int/mediacentre/factsheets/fs241/en/.

Wihtol de Wenden, C. (1996) 'Muslims in France', in W.A.R. Shadid and P.S. van Koningsveld (eds) *Muslims in the Margin*, Kampen: Kok Pharos Publishing House, pp 52–65.

Wikan, U. (1991) *Behind the Veil in Arabia: Women in Oman*, Chicago, IL and London: University of Chicago Press.

Williams, C. (1998) 'Towards an emancipatory pedagogy? Social work education for a multicultural, multi-ethnic Europe', in C. Williams, H. Soydan and M.R.D. Johnson (eds) *Social Work and Minorities*, London: Routledge, pp 211–30.

Williams, R. (2007) '21,000 girls at risk of genital mutilation, say campaigners', *The Guardian*, 10 October, www.guardian.co.uk/uk/2007/oct/10/gender.ukcrime.

Williamson, M. and Harrison, L. (2010) 'Providing culturally appropriate care: A literature review', *International Journal of Nursing Studies*, 47(6): 761–9, doi: 10.1016/j.ijnurstu.2009.12.012.

Williamson, I.R. and Sacranie, M. (2012) 'Nourishing body and spirit: Exploring British Muslim mothers' constructions and experiences of breastfeeding', *Diversity and Equality in Health and Care*, 9: 113–23.

Winlock, P. (1963) 'Death and the spirituality of ageing', in A. Jewell (ed) *Spirituality and Ageing*, London: Jessica Kingsley Publishers, pp 75–85.

Wintour, P. (2007) 'Minister gives schools right to ban Muslim veil', *Guardian Unlimited*, 20 March, http://education.guardian.co.uk/schools/story/0,,2038239,00.html.

Wiper, C. (2012) 'Responding to violence against South Asian women in the British violence movement', *Graduate Journal of Social Science*, 9(3): 38–46.

Wirz, C., van der Pilgt, J. and Doosje, B. (2015) 'Negative attitudes towards Muslims in the Netherlands: The role of symbolic threat, stereotypes and moral emotions', *Peace and Conflict: Journal of Peace Psychology*, http://dx.doi.org/10.1037/pac0000126.

Women's Aid (2015) 'Domestic abuse is a gendered crime', www.womensaid.org.uk/information-support/what-is-domestic-abuse/domestic-abuse-is-a-gendered-crime/.

Wood Wetzel, J. (2000) 'Women and mental health: A global perspective', *International Social Work*, 43(2): 205–16.

WRC (Women's Resource Centre) and WGN (Women and Girls Network) (2011) *Honour Based Violence: To Love and Cherish?*, London Council, Good Practice Briefing, http://thewomensresourcecentre.org.uk/wp-content/uploads/HBV_GPB.pdf.

Yasien-Esmael, H. and Rubin, S.S. (2005) 'The meaning structures of Muslim bereavements in Israel: Religious traditions, mourning practices and human experience', *Death Studies*, 29(2): 495–518.

Yeprem, S. (2007) 'Current assisted reproduction treatment practices from an Islamic perspective', *Reproductive BioMedicine Online*, 14(1): 44–7, www.rbmonline.com/Article/2445.

Yip, A.K.T. (2004) 'Negotiating space with family and kin in identity construction: The narratives of British non-heterosexual Muslims', *The Sociological Review*, 52(3): 336–50.

Yoshioka, M.R., Gilbert, L., El-Bassel, N. and Baig-Amin, M. (2003) 'Social support and disclosure of abuse: comparing South Asian, African American and Hispanic battered women', *Journal of Family Violence*, 18(3): 171–9.

Young, J. (1999) *The Exclusive Society*, London: Sage Publications.

Zarni, M. and Cowley, A. (2014) 'The slow-burning genocide of Myanmar's Rohingya', *Pacific Rim Law and Policy Journal Associates*, 23(3): 683–754.

Zlotogora, J., Habiballa, H., Odatalla, A. and Barges, S. (2002) 'Changing family structure in a modernizing society: A study of marriage patterns in a single Muslim village in Israel', *American Journal of Human Biology*, 14: 680–2.

Useful websites and resources

An-Nisa Society: www.an-nisa.org

Foundation for Women's Health, Research and Development (FORWARD): www.forwarduk.org.uk

Muslim Council of Britain: www.mcb.org.uk

Muslim Women's Council: www.muslimwomenscouncil.org.uk

Muslim Women's Network Helpline: www.mwnhelpline.co.uk

Muslim Youth Helpline: www.myh.org.uk

Muslim Youth Net: www.muslimyouth.net

NAZ Project London: www.naz.org.uk

Palestinian–UK Social Work Network: www.basw.co.uk/group/?id=27

Refuge: www.refuge.org.uk/what-we-do/our-services/asian-services/

Roshni: www.roshni.org.uk

Safra Project: https://en-gb.facebook.com/Safra-Project-116664066494/

Sisters in Islam: www.sistersinislam.org.my

Social Work First No Borders – social work solidarity with refugees in Calais and Dunkirk: https://twitter.com/hashtag/socialworkfirstnoborders?src=hash

Southall Black Sisters: www.southallblacksisters.org.uk

The Interfaith Network for the UK: www.interfaith.org.uk

Index

References to notes are followed by n

purdah 70–1
victimisation 174
Banks, S. 56, 57
Barise, A. 56, 62, 63–4, 66–8
Barn, Ravinder 70
Basharat, T. 83
Bedouins 89–90, 108, 143
Belgium 82
Bhatti-Sinclair, K. 100
bi'da 95
bin Laden, Osama 27, 29, 30
Blair, Tony 24
blood vengeance 89–90
Booth, Jane 118
Bosnia 32, 35–6
boys
circumcision 131, 132–3, 135
in foster care 121
mothers of 73–4
Bradford 104, 112, 124n
Bradley, G. 49
breastfeeding 131
Britain First 4, 26
Brunei 162
Brussels bombing 26
burqa 81, 82

C

Cairo 125
Cameron, David 37, 75–6
Campinha-Bacote, J. 66
Canada 18, 75, 149
care
disability 138, 140–2, 147
elderly 152, 155–61
end-of-life care 168–9
health and social care systems 157–8
Care Act 2014 157, 161
Chand, A. 111–12, 114–15
Charlie Hebdo 19, 26
Chilcot Report 30
Child Protection and Online Exploitation Centre (CEOP) 116
childbirth 130–1, 134
children
abuse of 110–21
adoption 123–4
in care 121–2
disabled 139, 140–4
parenthood and child-rearing 2, 77–9
refugees 112
religious education 24
reproduction 127–31
see also boys; girls
China 82
Christianity 4, 17
charitable donation 57
death 167

individual freedom and social conformity 58
prayer 62
sexuality 79–80
suicide 150
Christians
economic and social deprivation 3
victimisation 177
Cinnirella, M. 92
circumcision 131, 132–3, 135
Clinton, George 119
clitoridectomy 134
clothing 81–5
coerced marriages 75, 104–6
Coffey, Ann 117
Cohen, S. 139
Colombia 133
conflict resolution 89–90
consanguineous marriages 76–7, 143–4
CONTEST 91
contraception 128
converts 32, 80, 81, 84
in prison 183–5, 186
Corbyn, Jeremy 40
Cordoba 125
Cowburn, M. 106
crime 181–3
criminal justice 9, 173
crime 181–3
and ethnicity 173–4
prisons and rehabilitation 183–7
victimisation 174–81
criminology 14–15
critical incident analysis 47
critical race theory (CRT) 50
culturagrams 48–9
cultural competence 8, 47–9
child protection 115, 116
elderly care 161
cultural deficits 7
cultural humility 50
cultural literacy model 8

D

Daesh 2, 26, 29, 190
British members 3, 91
and homosexuality 92
Palmyra 28
women 86–7
Danso, R. 49
Darwin, Charles 143
Darwin, George 143
Dauood, Mohammed 117
Davanna, Tracey 15–16
Davies, Shelley 117
Dean, Hartley 57, 58
death 166–72
Denmark
cartoons of Mohammed 19, 26